READING DESIRE

READING DESIRE

In Pursuit of
Ernest Hemingway

Debra A. Moddelmog

CORNELL UNIVERSITY PRESS

ITHACA AND LONDON

First published 1999 by Cornell University Press

Printed in the United States of America

Library of Congress Cataloging-in-Publication Data

Moddelmog, Debra.
  Reading desire : in pursuit of Ernest Hemingway / Debra A.
Moddelmog.
    p.   cm.
  Includes bibliographical references (p.   ) and index.
  ISBN 0-8014-3604-4 (cloth : alk. paper). — ISBN 0-8014-8635-1
(pbk. : alk. paper)
    1. Hemingway, Ernest, 1899–1961—Criticism and interpretation.
  2. Psychoanalysis and literature—United States—History—20th
century.   3. Desire in literature.   I. Title.
PS3515.E37Z7424   1999
813'.52—dc21   99-30772

Cornell University Press strives to use environmentally responsible suppliers and materials to the fullest extent possible in the publishing of its books. Such materials include vegetable-based, low-VOC inks and acid-free papers that are recycled, totally chlorine-free, or partly composed of nonwood fibers. Books that bear the logo of the FSC (Forest Stewardship Council) use paper taken from forests that have been inspected and certified as meeting the highest standards for environmental and social responsibility. For further information, visit our website at www.cornellpress.cornell.edu.

Cloth printing   10 9 8 7 6 5 4 3 2 1
Paperback printing   10 9 8 7 6 5 4 3 2 1

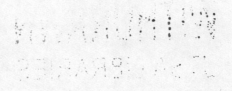

FOR DEBIAN

CONTENTS

LIST OF ILLUSTRATIONS

ACKNOWLEDGMENTS

In the course of writing this book, I have received considerable insight, input, and support (of all kinds) from a number of individuals and organizations. Among the friends and colleagues who read parts of this book and gave helpful and encouraging feedback are Jamie Barlowe, Ian Barnard, Marilyn Brownstein, Brenda Brueggemann, Maureen Burgess, Sari Champagne, Mac Davis, Leigh Gilmore, John Hellmann, Ruth Ann Hendrickson, Valerie Lee, Debian Marty, Todd McGowan, Linda Mizejewski, Jim Phelan, Matt Ramsey, Paul Smith, Susan Yadlon, the students in my Twentieth-Century American Literature seminar in the winter of 1994, and the students in my Theories of Bodies and Desires seminar in the spring of 1996. Along the way, I also received excellent advice from Susan Beegel and Rose Marie Burwell. Thanks to all. Thanks, too, to Melanie Rae Thon for supportive words and a celebratory walk.

I owe special gratitude to Ruth Ann Hendrickson for providing much-needed support, advice, and encouragement during the early stages of this project. Her faith in this project inspired me to keep writing. I also owe a huge round of thanks to Ian Barnard and Todd McGowan, each of whom read several versions of various chapters and provided detailed, kind, and intelligent feedback. Their deep engagement with my work always pushed me to see things in new ways without losing sight of the way I had already chosen.

The friendship, perceptive comments, creative flair, wit, and culinary skills of Linda Mizejewski sustained me throughout the writing of this book. In particular, our "working dinners" and our energetic multimedia presentation gave me all sorts of nourishment and motivation. I feel incredibly lucky to have such a generous colleague, confidante, reader, and friend.

The late Paul Smith counseled me well on all sorts of matters. He had a way of giving no-nonsense advice—and of pointing out errors of fact and style—that made me very glad he was on my side. He also convinced me to write on Hemingway's "The Snows of Kilimanjaro," an essay that developed into an important section of this book. I miss him deeply.

Kathryn Bernish served me well as a research assistant, digging up all sorts of obscure historical and critical information. I also appreciate the expert help of Stephen Plotkin and Allan Goodrich of the Hemingway Collection at the John F. Kennedy Library in Boston.

Parts of this book were published previously. A small portion of Chapters 1 and 2, and a section of Chapter 4 appeared in different form in my essay "Reconstructing Hemingway's Identity: Sexual Politics, the Author, and the Multicultural Classroom," reprinted here by permission from *Narrative*, Vol. 1, No. 3 (October 1993). Copyright 1993 by Ohio State University Press. All rights reserved. Much of Chapter 3 appeared previously in *Prospects*, copyright 1996 Cambridge University Press. All rights reserved. A section of Chapter 4 appeared in *New Essays on Hemingway's Short Fiction*, ed. Paul Smith. Copyright 1998 Cambridge University Press. All rights reserved. I thank both Ohio State University Press and Cambridge University Press for permission to reprint these essays here. Portions of this book were presented as talks sponsored by various groups, and I am grateful to them for inviting me to speak about my work: The Hemingway-Fitzgerald International Conference, July 1994, held in Paris, France (I especially thank Robert Scholes for asking me to be part of his session on Hemingway and gender, and for his enthusiastic response to my work); the International Narrative Conference of 1997, held in Columbus, Ohio; the Ohio State Gay, Lesbian, and Bisexual Students Services; the Ohio State Women's Services; and the Ohio State Department of English.

I also received financial support from the Ohio State Department of English and the College of Humanities, which granted me several

Scholarly Research Assignments that gave me time to write; and from the John F. Kennedy Library Foundation, which awarded me a much-appreciated Hemingway Research Grant for doing archival research in the Hemingway Collection.

I thank Bernhard Kendler and Candace Akins of Cornell University Press for their professional handling of my book, from the moment it arrived on their desks to the moment of publication. I also am indebted to Cornell's readers, who gave excellent advice for revisions along with their encouraging words. And I am extremely grateful to Herman Rapaport for his thoughtful, meticulous, and engaged copyediting.

To my family by birth, I owe endless gratitude for their love, patience, faith, and good humor. My parents never lost their belief in me, even when they reminded me that Sue Grafton had written three books in the time it took me to write this one. Knowing that I can always count on them for love, understanding, a sense of belonging, and house-repair help has been a big reminder of what's important in this world. Steve and Hala Moddelmog, and Susan and Jim Miller have also given me unconditional love and support, and have listened eagerly (or faked it pretty well) whenever I've explained what I'm working on. Ty and Kierstin Moddelmog have been some of my biggest fans and publicists; I thank them for their enthusiasm and love.

Finally, in writing this book, I owe the most to my family by choice. I am particularly grateful to Sabaka, who taught me to be ever-hopeful. Rocky, Cora, and Roshi have been steadfast allies and excellent teachers of how to live in the present moment. Debian Marty improved my work through her engaged listening and reading, and through the example of her own work. Our conversations over the past three years have covered every topic in this book—desire, race, the author, Hemingway, multiculturalism, ethics, pedagogy, identity, the body, and history—and I know that this is a different and much better book as a result. I count myself extremely fortunate to have shared my life and work with such a thoughtful, compassionate, and generous person.

READING DESIRE

INTRODUCTION

One writes with one's desire, and I am not through desiring.
—Roland Barthes (*Roland Barthes By Roland Barthes*)

The poststructuralist challenge to the unified subject and the so-called death of the author need not mean that literary critics abandon the historical author as an interpretive reference, since there are strong epistemological, psychological, political, and ethical reasons for maintaining an author concept. In an age of mass communications and multimedia, we are inundated with images of authors—from portraits that grace the covers of literature anthologies, to headnotes that precede an author's writings, to descriptive blurbs on book jackets, to entries on computer encyclopedia software, to full-length films and biographies that reconstruct authors' lives, to the recent and very public "culture wars" debating which authors should be taught and therefore valued. Those of us who teach literature at the college level often underestimate the influence these images have on how we and our students approach an author's work. More importantly, because these authorial images emerge from the representational practices of the media, literary critics, booksellers, editors, teachers, publishers, biographers, and authors themselves, they are tied to systems of knowledge, desire, and power. They thus convey more than simple information about an author's life and writing practices. They also transmit value-laden notions about subjectivity and identity, notions that affect how we live in the world. To comprehend and become accountable for these effects, those of us who teach literature and write literary criticism must also theorize the politics and ethics of authorial construction. The "our" and the "we" in the following pages thus refer to this professional group of critics and teachers.

As this emphasis on construction suggests, the practice of reading advanced here attempts not to tell *the* "truth" or the "facts" about the author's life nor to use that life as a template for understanding his or her work. Along with many critics influenced by poststructuralist insights about language and subjectivity, I no longer believe in the possibility of recovering the "real" author or the "true" story of his or her life. Still, I am not so ready as some to see this situation as grounds for excluding the author from the interpretive act. I am interested in exploring how this exclusion can become a kind of denial that, together with other denials, restricts how we talk about interpretation. The denials I link together, question, and resist are these: (1) that representations of an author's history and identity do not significantly affect our reading and teaching of his or her work, (2) that our erotic desires are irrelevant to authorial constructions and textual interpretations, and (3) that writing criticism or biography and teaching literature are practical, intellectual, and sometimes political, but not ethical, endeavors. Like those critics working in fields such as cultural studies, queer theory, ethical criticism, feminism, multicultural pedagogy, and autobiographical criticism, I want to examine these denials and expose the critical territory they protect.

This territory is especially guarded in the case of Ernest Hemingway who serves as the extended example for substantiating my argument. In fact, I have selected Hemingway as my subject because the attention he has received is so clearly overdetermined and thus makes visible what is often hard to see: that critics' desires play an integral role in the construction of authors and the interpretation of their works. Talking to literary critics across the country (and even across the world), one quickly discovers that people have high stakes in circulating a particular image of Hemingway and in reading and teaching his work in a specific way. Some still revere him as a positive masculine icon, agreeing with the Barnes and Noble catalogue that advertises him as the "He-Man of American Literature." Others view his masculinity as negative machismo. They consider him the worst example of a sexist, racist, homophobic man, and often refuse to read or teach Hemingway, or make apologies when they do. More recently, another group of scholars has critiqued both of these views, recasting Hemingway's identity along less conventional lines. This intense, sometimes heated discussion about the meaning of Hemingway's identity can be connected to shifting views of gender roles and sexual categorizations; it also suggests that the critic's own desires and anxieties about such shifts are entangled in a process of authorial construction.

As I recount in Chapter 2, those scholars who reconstruct Hemingway's masculine/macho identity do so in light of supposedly new information about his life and posthumously published materials. As I understand it, this activity has taken two paths. Critics following the first path seek to reconceive Hemingway's psyche—and the psyches of some of his male and female protagonists—as androgynous. Led by Mark Spilka, critics and biographers who engage in this reconstructive work replace Hemingway's intransigent macho image with a gentler, more sensitive, and also (supposedly) more complex identity, one that combines traits traditionally figured as feminine and masculine. The other group of critics is represented most persuasively by Nancy Comley and Robert Scholes and attempts to complicate Hemingway by insisting that he was interested in and sympathetic to subjects he has been perceived as being hostile toward: male homosexuals, lesbians, and women. Emphasis falls on reconceiving Hemingway's intellect, his capacity for experimenting aesthetically, and for imagining the feelings of people unlike himself. Hemingway risks writing about sexually taboo subjects such as homosexuality and miscegenation because this risk carries the possibility of breaking into new aesthetic territory and reaching a deeper level of truth.[1]

Because I engage these approaches in Chapter 2, I won't rehearse that full discussion here. I refer to them in order to sketch out briefly what is at stake for me in reading an author's desires, specifically Hemingway's desires. My involvement in this project began with being (only slightly) puzzled about why so many Hemingway critics skirt the question of whether their work on gender might urge a reconsideration of Hemingway's sexual identity or his desires. While I don't want to set up inevitable correlations between gender identification and sexual orientation, I am fascinated by the refusal of most Hemingway critics to entertain this possibility in any extended way. I suspect that gender can be a smoke screen that blocks the more incendiary topic of sexuality. "Have we been trying to show that Hemingway was gay?," Nancy Comley and Robert Scholes ask. "No," they immediately answer. "If anything, we have been trying to show that such a question is too simple. . . . What we have been trying to show is that Hemingway was much more interested in these matters than has usually been supposed—and much more sensitive and complex in his consideration of them" (143–44).

But where do interest and identification leave off and desire take over?[2] Can we so readily accept a mind/body split that presumes the partitioning of Hemingway's *thought* desires from his *felt* ones? Further, where do Comley's and Scholes's own desires start and end in their formulation of an "imagined Hemingway" that is "as realistic or 'true'" as they can make him (xi) yet still a fiction (141)? By raising the question whether they are trying to show that Hemingway was gay, Comley and Scholes evoke the very possibility they then renounce without further comment. But why do they feel compelled to deny that possibility? How might *their* imagined-but-realistic-as-possible Hemingway emerge from their own fantasies and investment in a heterosexist system of sexuality?

These questions, and others like them, provide my entry into Hemingway scholarship. I seek, first, to eliminate the hesitation that prevents most critics from asking questions about Hemingway's heterosexuality—and about the heterosexuality of his male protagonists—or from exploring those questions with the seriousness they deserve. Significantly, this effort has evoked various misconceptions about my work. In the several years that I have been working on this book, some people have assumed that I am simply reversing Comley and Scholes's negative answer to the question of whether Hemingway was gay. I have heard colleagues describe my research as both an "outing" and a "queering" of Hemingway. Usually these are individuals who don't know my work but presume that because I identify myself as lesbian and am writing on Hemingway, I must be doing something perverse to him. If nothing else, this assumption illustrates one of the points I make in this book: that constructions of the author's identity (mine in this case) enter into how we read a work. Even though identity is constructed and unstable, we often act and read as if it is not.

Leaving aside the mistaken perception that outing and queering are identical processes, I might agree that from one vantage point my study of Hemingway seems to fulfill Eve Sedgwick's declaration that "no one *can* know *in advance* where the limits of a gay-centered inquiry are to be drawn, or where a gay theorizing of and through even the hegemonic high culture of the Euro-American tradition may need or be able to lead."[3] Sedgwick encourages critics to inquire into the structure, function, and "historical surround" of same-sex love in and for various authors, and then names many writers—a list of "almost infinite elasticity"—for whom these questions might prove illuminating: "Homer or Plato or Sappho? What, then, about Euripides or Virgil? If a gay Marlowe, what about Spenser or Milton? Shakespeare? Byron? But what about Shelley? Montaigne, Leopardi . . . ? Leonardo, Michelangelo, but . . . ? Beethoven? Whitman, Thoreau, Dickinson (Dickinson?), Tennyson, Wilde, Woolf, Hopkins, but Brontë? Wittgenstein, but . . . Nietzsche? Proust, Musil, Kafka, Cather, but . . . Mann? James, but . . . Lawrence? Eliot but . . . Joyce?" (*Epistemology*, 53).

While my particular construction of Hemingway's identity might seem to prove the infinite elasticity of Sedgwick's list, I hope it will become clear that I am not positing a gay Hemingway. Nor would I say, at least without defining the term beforehand, that I am constructing a "queer" Hemingway, although surely my Hemingway is both gayer and queerer than most Hemingways.[4] This does not mean that my project isn't political and perverse, for the primary implication of my work is that the effects of a *desire*-centered inquiry are always political and when the inquiry refuses to limit its scope or its evidence, the results can seem perverse, especially to those who are used to reading desire in discrete and exclusive categories. In fact, one reason for choosing the word "desire" over related terms such as "sexuality" and "sexual behavior" is that I want to explore ways in which desire is formed within all sorts of identity structurings—including those of race, nationality, and able-bodiedness—and their intersections, and not simply within the category of sexual orientation. Even though I might privilege the structuring of desire around gendered object choice, following such privileging in twentieth-century American society, I nevertheless attempt to explain how that structuring is inflected by desires connected to other identity structures.

This focus on interconnected structurings of desire is one way my book differs from others that have considered how desire functions in the reading encounter. Such an explanation should also make clear that my approach to desire is socially determined, which separates it from studies that are more explicitly psychoanalytical, such as Peter Brooks's *Reading for the Plot*. Without discounting the role of the psyche in regulating, transferring, and instating desire, I concentrate on the way desire takes shape within the social. I am interested, ultimately, in what most books fail to state explicitly: how our relation to our own desires—that is, the frame of intelligibility through which we understand desire to come into existence, to be assigned value, and to circulate among bodies—affects our construction of the author and our reading of desire in an author's texts. I put my focus here because these frames exert political power in society, having the power to name and assign meaning, for instance, by pronouncing one desire normal and another abnormal.

Most critics who have attempted to chart the circulation of desire in the reading encounter have done so in a post death-of-the-author climate. Such a climate, as Emma Wilson observes, presumably liberates the reader to construct his or her "own interpretation of a text radically divorced from its author's orbit."[5] Wilson speculates that without the historical author hovering over every read word, there is more possibility that the text will engage its reader in fantasy construction and voyeuristic participation as it literally arouses the imagination: "The text may thus offer the reader new images of him/herself as desiring subject with which to identify, and new scenarios for the performance of an identity category" (5). Although Wilson allows for the continued presence of the author in some form, she is more interested in arguing that the author's death has been a preliminary step to liberating the reader's libidinal energies.[6] As I hope to show in this book, readers need not lose the author to find their libidinal energies. The desire that the reader infers in a text has implications for how the reader constructs an author's desire, and simultaneously, how a reader constructs an author's desire will influence the way he or she reads desire in the text. This is so because the historical author is a construction that the reader derives from and projects into the text and extratextual material.

Wilson's work provides one final reference point for distinguishing my own, since Wilson chooses texts by Marcel Proust, Marguerite Duras, Hélène Cixous, and Michel Tournier that "question and represent reading practices which may work to undo the fiction of a unified identity" and that may thus "be seen to challenge the regulatory matrix of heterosexuality and its required reading positions" (56). In contrast, Hemingway's texts have usually been read as upholding this very matrix and its reading positions. My point is not that my framework and my selection of Hemingway create a conflictual reading encounter between, as Wilson puts it, a reader who identifies in some way as queer and a text that upholds and reinscribes the social patterns of heterosexuality (52). Rather, I argue that a reader's relation to desire—be that relation foundational (desire as innate and unalterable), or antifoundational (desire as socially constructed), or some variation of these two views—will affect how he or she reads desire into a text and into the constructed author. A gay reader who reads and relates to desire foundationally might chart the flow of his desire through Hemingway's Major in "A Simple Enquiry." A lesbian reading the same way might see her desire reflected in Catherine Bourne, Marita, or Mrs. Elliot. This is a unilateral transfer of erotic energy, shaped by a gender-based and narrow definition of identification, that stabilizes current social formations of sexuality. If, however, we read desire antifoundationally—regardless of whether we identify as gay, lesbian, heterosexual, bisexual, or are attracted to people we think of as belonging to our own race or to another race, etc.—then we begin to see cracks in apparently airtight spaces, in our explanations of desire, and even in a writer who appears to be the model of seamless heterosexuality. This approach to reading desire opens up many possibilities for questioning the power relations, ethics, and "truth" of our sexual systems and of our own desires.

My argument proceeds in the following way. In Chapter 1, I juxtapose the tendency of scholars to read Hemingway's works biographically with poststructuralist theory that dispenses with the idea of authorial biography. In setting up this juxtaposition, I align myself with various feminist, queer, and multicultural critics who have attempted to find middle ground between author-centered and author-effaced criticism. To begin staking out the specifications of my own middle ground, I return to the famous anti-authorial essays of Roland Barthes and Michel Foucault. With this return, I demonstrate how the historical author evades both men's attempts to remove his presence. This demonstration serves as a starting point for rethinking the place of the historical author in the act of interpretation.

In the next chapter, I present an argument for approaching authors from a poststructuralist perspective in which we locate their subjectivity in history, textuality, and the critic's own desire or, more accurately, what I rework as the "desire to desire." To support this presentation, I look first at recent critical and biographical activity regarding Hemingway's identity, proposing that this activity constitutes an overdetermined effort to maintain a conventionally masculine and heterosexual Hemingway. Locating my own "desire to desire" as based upon an antifoundational perspective, I then situate Hemingway's sexual identity in the tension between the homosexual and the heterosexual. I also consider what is at stake, both ethically and politically, in circulating this particular construction of Hemingway.

Chapters 3 and 4 read Hemingway's texts in light of my construction of Hemingway and read my construction of Hemingway in light of his texts. In Chapter 3, I look extensively at the original manuscript of the posthumously edited and published *The Garden of Eden*. My argument is that Hemingway's publisher developed a version of the novel that would promote the popular image of Hemingway as unquestionably masculine and heterosexual in order to retain Hemingway's commodity value in the marketplace. However, pages cut from the published version of *The Garden of Eden* suggest an alternative view: that desire flows between binaries—such as homosexual/heterosexual and male/female—and never find a resting place on either side. Chapter 4 consists of a series of readings of desire in Hemingway's work and life, from an exploration of gender-bending and sexual crossings in *The Sun Also Rises*, to a postcolonial reading of "The Snows of Kilimanjaro" and Hemingway's "Africanization" during his second safari to Africa in 1953–54, to an investigation of the homoerotic function of the wound in Hemingway's novels. In all these readings, I emphasize how desire flows through various identity structures—sex, gender, race, sexuality, able-bodiedness, nationality—and how this flow of desires has ethical and political consequences for both the subject who desires and the subject who is desired.

Such an emphasis also motivates my final chapter, which turns to pedagogical matters and explores the link between the circulation of criticism and biography and the teaching of literature. In this chapter, I consider how my work on Hemingway might inform a critical multicultural approach to American literary studies and the literature classroom. I begin by asking if, where, and how so-called canonized writers fit in the project of critical multiculturalism. Arguing that we should view the identities of these authors as both stable and unstable, I then propose that literature instructors might help students comprehend how identities, including authorial identities, are formed and to measure the social and political effects of constructing an identity in a particular way. In other words, I recommend that we teach students to analyze authorial constructions, the ones we and our students bring to a text as well as the ones we and they take away from it. We can encourage this analysis by helping students to ask questions such as the following: What evidence has been used to generate a particular construction? Why is the author being constructed in this way and not another? How does this construction affect our reading of an author's texts? Where does this construction fail to cohere? How is this construction motivated by desire? Such questions will enable students to recognize, first, that authors *are* constructions and, second, that these constructions contribute to the regulation and meaning of identity and desire in our society.

1

READING HEMINGWAY AFTER
THE AUTHOR'S DEATH AND RETURN

> The concept of the author is never more alive than when pronounced
> dead.
>
> —Seán Burke (*The Death and the Return of the Author*)

In 1979, in a book titled *On Men and Manhood*, Leonard Kriegel felt safe
in saying about Hemingway,

> His life does not serve our needs today. In the current drift toward a
> unisex culture, Hemingway has been demoted to being one of the en-
> emy. But in the future, after our gender battles have quieted down, we
> may again be able to put him to use. He may, after all, be able to help us
> approach one of the problems we are probably never going to be rid
> of—exactly what it is we mean by manhood. For the idea of manhood
> will not disappear into an androgynous ether. We are still going to have
> to face that male adolescent as he asks how he can get beyond narcis-
> sism and yet accept the challenges the world has in store for him.[1]

Much has happened since Kriegel advanced this analysis and this prediction. I doubt that many people would claim that "our gender battles
have quieted down," nor, as we'll see, has androgyny disappeared from
our vocabulary. Nonetheless, the relentless deluge of Hemingway biographies written since 1979 suggests that Kriegel was wrong to presume that Hemingway's life had become outdated. In fact, his life remains at the updated crux of gender and sexuality debates.

Hemingway has always inspired the biographical. Since his death in 1961, he has been the subject of no fewer than twenty biographies, although the exact number is difficult to establish and depends upon what one means by "biography." In 1983, Jackson Benson eliminated "bogus biographies, picture books, and scrapbooks" and still came up with "fourteen, more-or-less legitimate books of memoir or reporting" on Hemingway.[2] Even acknowledging that Hemingway readers have always trafficked in the biographical, I would still say that the biographical output on Hemingway during the last fifteen years has been remarkable. In those years, five full-length biographies of Hemingway have been published. If one counts pages (which I have: more than 3,000 of them), these five biographies multiply in density since two of them are multivolume works and still in progress. If one adds to this calculation recent biographical work covering part of Hemingway's life—such as Henry Villard and James Nagel's *Hemingway in Love and War* (1989), Charles Whiting's *Papa Goes to War* (1990), William Burrill's *Hemingway: The Toronto Years* (1994), Rose Marie Burwell's *Hemingway: The Postwar Years and the Posthumous Novels* (1996), and Leonard Leff's *Hemingway and His Conspirators: Hollywood, Scribners, and the Making of American Celebrity Culture* (1997)—the number of pages devoted to Hemingway's life mounts to incredible proportions.

This outpouring of work on Hemingway's life gives rise to a number of questions, beginning with the possibility that Kriegel predicted. Are we now "putting him to use," in the service of helping us to comprehend the meaning of white American manhood? Does that comprehension require that we retell his life again and again—and yet again? How many times does Hemingway's story have to be told before the biographers can rest? How many times do we have to *read* that story before we can rest? How many times, if any, do we *want* to read it?

To be more cynical, are we simply witnessing a number of people attempting to cash in on the continuing fame of Hemingway's celebrity? Aren't these people, cashing in or not, thereby ensuring that this celebrity continues? After all, Hemingway's name and figure still sell products.[3] "Hemingway wore khakis," a recent Gap ad proclaims across a photograph of Hemingway descending the steps of the Finca Vigía, his Cuban home, gingerly carrying a cat, one of thirty or so that lived there, many of them six-toed, his favorite kind. (See how many details about Hemingway's life one has at her fingertips if she reads all those biographies?) Are these biographies keeping alive Hemingway's endorsement potential by ensuring that his status as a cultural figure continues, a status that

A photograph of Hemingway and his cat, Boise, recently used by Gap to advertise khaki pants in national magazines (John F. Kennedy Library, courtesy Hans Malmberg, Stockholm-Vällingby).

is inseparable from the popular association of Hemingway with manliness and heroism—bringing us back to our first series of questions around gender? Are they also sustaining his reputation as a premier writer of American literature during a time when that reputation is being pressured by the redirections of multiculturalism? Finally, do we need these biographies in order to read or appreciate Hemingway's fiction?

My book is concerned with all these questions, but it is framed by the last one. When moved from the particular case of Hemingway to the general subject of the author, this question engages us in a controversy that has been central to literary studies for many years. What role should the author's life play in the interpretation of his or her texts? As Valerie Ross points out, American literary studies have always had a troubled relationship to literary biography, a trouble she traces all the way back to the formation of literature departments in the United States late in the nineteenth century. According to her, literary studies in the U.S. has defined and fortified its "territory and mastery" by repressing biography, which has been seen as "the unruly 'inside' that must be kept 'outside' of institutional discourse."[4] This attitude toward biography is both "generic and gendered," embodying institutional anxieties about "women, class, popular culture, affect, social and domestic existence, and other 'outside' challenges to institutional literary authority" (Ross, 137). From this vantage point, signs of the periodic resurfacing of the repressed (feminized) biographical presence can be found in axioms such as the intentional fallacy and the biographical fallacy, which "drown out any notes of domesticity and writer—or reader—particularity" (Ross, 157). It can also be found in the more developed form of these axioms: the methodology of the New Criticism which subordinated authorial particularity in order to focus on formal features and the organic unity of literary works.

As Ross's account suggests, the stakes over authorial biography have been raised again and again in this century. However, at no time have those stakes seemed higher than since the late 1960s and early 70s when critics such as Roland Barthes, Michel Foucault, and Jacques Derrida supposedly struck the final blow to the empirical, historical author. When this new wave of anti-authorialism began to permeate U.S. literary studies, it met with strong resistance, primarily because of the strength of its attack on the author's identity. Whereas the New Critics had disregarded this identity for methodological and pragmatic reasons, the anti-authorialism of Barthes, Foucault, and Derrida was grounded in linguistic and ontological principles that unsettled the very concept of the historical author. For some American feminist and African American critics, such as Adrienne Rich, Henry Louis Gates, and Barbara Christian, the pronouncement of the author's death seemed if not a deliberate conspiracy, then an unfortunate irony. At the very moment that the literary works of white women and people of color had started to gain critical attention, the author was declared obsolete. As Ross puts it, structuralists and poststructuralists (at least some of them) reacted to the "noisy challenges of feminists, African-Americans, gays and lesbians, the working class, and other 'outsiders'" by littering the discursive field with "fragmented, functionalized, and dead authors," and once again condemning biography as "the domain of the naive, essential, humanist unsophisticate, which, in the 1990s, certainly must be worse than being 'feminine'" (157). When the marginalized come calling, the dominant clear the playing field and change the rules. Or so it seemed to some.

The dedication of some literary critics to celebrating the historical author and the insistence of others that it was time to write this author's obituary created one of several chasms within literary studies in the 1970s and 80s, a chasm that can still be discerned today. On the one side were those who practiced various kinds of structuralist and poststructuralist criticism in which the author was apparently absent and the reader, or the text, was the starring performer; on the other side was the canon debate and critics who advocated various kinds of feminist, ethnic, multicultural, and gay and lesbian studies in which the author was very much alive or in the process of being recovered. Of course, the division has never been as pure as this description implies, and a number of critics have labored to build theories of authorship in the space supposedly dividing the two sides. For instance, many feminist, queer, and cultural critics influenced by poststructuralist insights have sought to complicate notions of the author without reducing the impact of gender, race, sexual orientation, and other identity structures on the writing process and product. Nancy Miller, for example, proposes that feminist readers work "with and through the fragmentation" of the female writing subject.[5] Starting from a similar poststructuralist feminist position, Cheryl Walker has outlined the principles for a "persona criticism" in which the critic finds an author-persona in the text but relates this functionary to "psychological, historical, and literary intersections quite beyond the scope of any scriptor's intentions."[6]

Of equal importance is that a number of scholars have argued that most American critics have misunderstood or exaggerated the author's death. Writers such as Barthes, Foucault, and Derrida might have resisted the author—and, it is important to note, resisted him to different degrees and on different grounds—but they never totally dismissed him (the pronoun is deliberate, as I explain below). Critics who adduce this misconception often do so by looking at the body of work written by Barthes, Foucault, and Derrida, showing how they later revised, clarified, or contradicted their early anti-authorial positions. However, many also point to the ways in which the famous anti-authorial essays—Barthes's "The Death of the Author," Foucault's "What Is an Author?," and Derrida's "Signature, Event, Context"—have been misread. For instance, David Saunders and Ian Hunter note that "What Is an Author?" can be seen as favoring both anti-authorialism and a recognition of the author as an historical entity.[7] They point to a sentence near the end of Foucault's essay as indicating his acceptance of the author's continued presence in literary interpretation: "It would be pure romanticism," Foucault writes, ". . . to imagine a culture in which the fictive would operate in an absolutely free state, in which fiction would be put at the disposal of everyone and would develop without passing through something like a necessary or constraining figure."[8] Although Foucault predicts that in the future this constraining figure will no longer be the author, he believes that some form of constraint will modulate our literary interpretations for some time to come.

In light of a growing body of work that envisions intersections between the poststructural and the historical, it is interesting to note that Hemingway critics have almost always leaned toward the latter. Hemingway criticism exhibits few signs of the controversy over the author's death, even though one might have expected Hemingway, as a "Master Author" of American literature, to be one of the first to threaten to slip out of sight. Rarely, however, have critics approached Hemingway's identity as "the negative where all identity is lost, starting with the very identity of the body writing."[9] As Benson states, "Recent theorists pooh-poohing the relevance of biography to literary study have proposed that the 'author is dead,' but certainly in Hemingway's case the author has been too much with us early and late."[10]

It would be a wonderful twist to the history of literary criticism were I able to propose that Hemingway critics have been at the vanguard of contemporary criticism, exposing the inadequacies of anti-authorial theory and leading the way toward reconfiguring the author within a poststructuralist perspective. This would hardly be accurate, though. By and large, Hemingway scholars have been a conservative lot, ignoring or rejecting poststructuralist approaches in favor of formalism and traditional biographical criticism. A great deal of Hemingway criticism from the 1960s to today resembles the kind of criticism that Barthes objected to in "The Death of the Author": "The *explanation* of a work is always sought in the man or woman who produced it, as if it were always in the end, through the more or less transparent allegory of the fiction, the voice of a single person, the *author* 'confiding' in us" (143). But even though Hemingway critics cannot be credited with systematically challenging the concept of the author's death, both their reluctance if not their inability to let go of Hemingway have much to tell us about the personally invested dynamics of the interpretive process.

The source of this inability exists in all those biographies, since their very existence testifies to Hemingway's status as cultural figure. After all, his life and work are everywhere for us to read: on film ("The Moderns," "Wrestling Ernest Hemingway," "In Love and War," "City of Angels"), on television (a mini-series starring Stacy Keach, an episode of "The Adventures of the Young Indiana Jones," an A & E film based on *A Moveable Feast*), in novels (*Hemingway's Notebook, The Hemingway Hoax, Hemingway's Suitcase, I Killed Hemingway, Hemingway's Chair, The Hemingway Sabbatical*), in newspapers, in magazines, in comic strips, in the Hemingway Days Festival held every summer in Key West, in advertisements, and even as a category on "Jeopardy."[11] With some narrative of his life, or parts of it, coursing through our collective national unconscious, how can we hope to remove Hemingway from our individual interpretations? He is there whether we consciously bring him there or not. The reluctance to let go of Hemingway is even more telling. It is the reason why he has become a cultural figure, why so many biographies have been written about him, why his name is now shorthand for various representations of masculinity that have importance in our society: the man's man, the sporting expert, the sexist bully, the wise Papa. It is, as I hope to show, a reluctance driven by desire.

As I will argue, both the inability and the reluctance to make the author disappear are not unique to Hemingway studies but are endemic to the act of interpretation, especially for those of us who read and teach literature for a living. Although Hemingway critics have often been reductive and naive in their uses of the biographical, the urge to interrelate the author's life and work can be justified on epistemological, psychological, political, and ethical grounds. By complicating this interrelationship I will lay the foundation for a biographical approach informed by certain poststructuralist precepts as well as by theories about how meaning is personally, culturally, historically, and socially produced.

In conducting this investigation, I necessarily enter an area of contested definitions over terms such as the subject, identity, the individual, subjectivity, and social positioning. Rather than explaining the histories and debates surrounding these terms, I will set forth a tentative framework of understanding. I am particularly concerned to distinguish among the subject, subjectivity, and identity, which I view as connected but discrete terms. As opposed to the individual, which has been associated with the self-determining and self-contained human being of liberal humanism, the subject is produced in and by language, its stability being an effect not of biology or psychology but of ideology. Within this perspective, subjectivity is an encompassing term, referring both to the condition of subject formation and its activities. As Wendy Brown describes it, subjectivity "is local, particular, psychoanalytic, concerned with the problem of consciousness and unconscious, body and psyche, and desire and culture."[12]

Within literary and cultural studies, the terms "subject" and "identity" are often used interchangeably, an understandable slippage since the assumption of identity is a primary way in which the subject comes into being. By identity assumption, I mean the process whereby the subject is "taken up" by identity categories, such as white, heterosexual, and disabled.[13] Whether a subject can resist or alter this process is a matter of contention. William Connolly notes that an identity is established "in relation to a series of differences that have become socially recognized," but he adds that this indispensable relation contains "a second set of tendencies, *themselves in need of exploration*, to congeal established identities into fixed forms, thought and lived as if their structure expressed the true order of things."[14] Connolly's definition points to a naturalizing imperative that comes with an identity, convincing us that this identity is self-evident and inherent when it is socially derived. That subjects can acknowledge and theorize this imperative and, to some extent, resist certain identities or take up others, suggests that subjects have a degree of agency. They are able to alter the imposed process of identity assumption into the self-conscious one of identity construction.[15] As Judith Butler contends, for an identity to be an effect of signification means "that it is neither fatally determined nor fully artificial and arbitrary."[16] Agency emerges in the negotiation between the inevitability and the arbitrariness of identity. The important point is that identity assumption is a moment (or a series of moments) in subject formation, not its sum total. Still, we can learn a great deal about subjectivity, resistance, and social positioning by exploring the processes of identity assumption as well as the processes of a more self-conscious identity construction. When identity is constructed by others—as in the case of authors whose identities are constructed by literary critics, historians, and biographers—we can also learn a great deal about the politics and ethics of representation.

The Body of the Subject Writing:
The Trace of the Historical Author

To investigate the status of the author's identity and history in literary interpretation, it seems appropriate to return to two essays that inaugurated the contemporary mode of anti-authorialism: Roland Barthes's "The Death of the Author" and Michel Foucault's "What Is an Author?" After 30 years of critical response to these essays, such a beginning might seem anticlimactic, especially since critics such as Seán Burke have convincingly demonstrated that Barthes and Foucault retained an active concept of the author even as they articulated the author's disappearance.[17] Nevertheless, to establish the ways in which an author's identity and history permeate literary interpretation, it seems logical to start with two critics who, at least initially, tried to do away with such material. In showing how Barthes and Foucault fail to erase the author's body, I am particularly interested in explaining why and how that body remains. For it is in this trace of the historical author that I locate my own labor of joining a poststructuralist theory of the social construction of identity with a multicultural concern for the political and ethical reality of living a specific identity.

Barthes opens "The Death of the Author" by asserting that "Writing is that neutral, composite, oblique space where our subject slips away, the negative where all identity is lost, starting with the very identity of the body writing" (142). Thus he sets forth the terms by which he will clear authors from the interpretive scene, transferring their previous hold over textual meaning to the properties of language and to the reader who, as he later insists, also lacks history, biography, and psychology (148). Yet this description of Barthes's beginning is slightly inaccurate since he doesn't actually open by declaring the writing subject's disappearance. Instead, Barthes's first words name Balzac as the author of the example he uses to show the impossibility of determining "Who is speaking thus" (142). Are the sentiments in the Balzac passage spoken by the hero of the story, Balzac the individual, universal wisdom, Romantic psychology? We shall never know, Barthes contends, because "writing is the destruction of every voice, of every point of origin" (142).

Citing Balzac's name and quoting from his work (*Sarrasine*) might seem a minor transgression, even no transgression at all, of Barthes's representation of writing as a space where all identity is lost, but it does undermine that representation in important ways. Barthes might invoke Balzac's name only to show how it is then subsumed by the ceaseless deferral of language and the infinite intertextuality of texts, but the name still serves to mark the words as initially *his:* "In his story *Sarrasine*," Barthes writes, "Balzac, describing a castrato disguised as a woman, writes the following sentence . . . " (142). Attaching Balzac's name to *his* work, to the act of writing, does more than introduce the privileged term, *author*, that Barthes will then dissipate into the structure of language.[18] It also illustrates how difficult it will be for Barthes, and by extension for all contemporary literary critics, to remove the author's identity and history from the process of reading. As much as Barthes wants to eliminate the biographical from the theater of interpretation, that element slips through the back door in the guise of identity structures such as gender, sex, race, sexuality, nationality that play a major role in subject formation.

Balzac's white, male, French identity surfaces in his name, and although this might seem like the bare bones of a biography, it has been enough since at least the eighteenth century, when the notion of the artist as professional writer emerged, to guarantee him access to the title of author and the privileges that come with it. Because of literacy opportunities, patriarchal and racist social structures, class arrangements in capitalist economies, and the institutional practices of publishers, literary critics, and educators, the category of author in the Western world has been historically reserved for enfranchised white men. As Maurice Biriotti observes, "Traditionally, Western thinking has constructed the subject as white, male and bourgeois. Subjectivity, and indeed authorship itself, have been denied for huge portions of the population: those oppressed on grounds of race, gender and sexuality [and, I would add, class]."[19] Barthes's effort to abandon the author category in favor of a disembodied scriptor and a performative *écriture* cannot transcend this thinking. His selection of examples to support his theory—not only Balzac but also Mallarmé, Valéry, Proust, Brecht, de Quincey, and the whole host of authors assembled under the rubric of Surrealism—reveals how difficult it is to erase the patriarchal culture and history of authorship. The classic author and his white male identity are ghosted over the impersonal postmodern scriptor and *écriture*.[20]

Soon after Barthes's essay was published, Michel Foucault explicitly addressed the matter of the author's name as it served to coalesce what he termed the author-function. In taking up the question "What does it matter who is speaking?" Foucault seems ready to account for practical, historical, and ethical concerns that Barthes overlooked. However, he too ultimately misses the full political dimensions of the author category and the extent to which constructions of the author's identity and history affect the functioning of his name.

Foucault argues that certain notions promoted as replacements for the author, such as "work" and "writing," have prevented us from taking full measure of the author's disappearance. He then sets out to locate this unmarked space. To engage this pursuit, Foucault argues that he will first have to clarify the problems posed by the use of the author's name: what is it? how does it function? Rather than answering these questions, he proposes to examine some of the difficulties that the author's name presents (105). Like any proper name, the author's name is "more than an indication, a gesture, a finger pointed at someone, it is the equivalent of a description" (105). Aristotle's name calls forth a series of significations: "the author of the *Analytics*," "the founder of ontology," and so on (106). But the author's name functions differently from the proper name of non-authors. It performs a classificatory function, permitting us "to group together various texts, define them, differentiate them from and contrast them to others. In addition, it establishes a relationship among the texts" (107). In short, the author's name grants a specific authority to the discourse to which it is attached. It tells us this is a kind of speech "that must be received in a certain mode and that, in a given culture, must receive a certain status" (107). The author's name identifies discourse as literary, or as literature.

However, consider the inverse. Certain discourse achieves status as literature and thereby grants the name of author to the writing subject, who until this consignment has possessed only a personal name. To put this another way, discourse identified as literature has the power to lift the personal name out of its non-special category into the special one of author. As a result of this interaction, the author's name becomes indelibly linked to his text: "the author's name, unlike other proper names, does not pass from the interior of a discourse to the real and exterior individual who produced it; instead, the name seems always to be present, marking off the edges of the text, revealing, or at least characterizing, its mode of being" (107). Which comes first, then, the designation of literature or the designation of author? It would seem that the naming of literature precedes the authorial naming, although once the author has been named, other discourse discovered to have been written by him is practically guaranteed the title of literature. Still the question of origins could be answered another way. What comes first is neither the naming of the author nor the naming of literature but the subject who names. In other words, the designation of author is not transcendent and timeless but originates with literary critics, historians, and biographers. Foucault spells this out when he writes, "these aspects of an individual which we designate as making him an author are only a projection, in more or less psychologizing terms, of the operations that we force texts to undergo, the connections we make, the traits that we establish as pertinent, the continuities that we recognize, or the exclusions that we practice" (110).

Foucault thus draws attention to the critic's role in making authors. The author function, he suggests, "does not develop spontaneously as the attribution of a discourse to an individual. It is, rather, the result of a complex operation which *constructs* a certain rational being that we call 'author'" (110; emphasis added). In addition, Foucault emphasizes that we pay attention to the history of this practice. The present usage of "author" developed during a "privileged moment of *individualization* in the history of ideas, knowledge, literature, philosophy, and the sciences" (101); and Foucault insists that "it would be worth examining how the author became individualized in a culture like ours, what status he has been given, at what moment studies of authenticity and attribution began, in what kind of system of valorization the author was involved, at what point we began to recount the lives of authors rather than of heroes, and how this fundamental category of 'the man-and-his-work criticism' began" (101). Such observations about the social conditions behind the emergence of the author category open the way for a full acknowledgment of the sexual, racial, and class politics that have conditioned the naming of authors. Yet, like Barthes, Foucault does not address this side of history. From our present vantage point—informed by the work of feminist, multicultural, and postcolonial critics—such an omission looms large. For instance, in identifying the grounds for the "author function," Foucault recognizes that certain discourses are "endowed with the 'author function,' while others are deprived of it" (107). He refers here to types of discourses—contracts, posters, letters—that lack the necessary aesthetic power for convincing literary critics to assign the author function to their writing subject. But such a statement cries out for another kind of recognition: that the endowments and deprivations of discourses might be connected to the gender, racial, class, and/or national biases of publishers, editors, booksellers, and critics.[21]

Equally problematic is Foucault's stance on authorial biography. Even though he doesn't explicitly dismiss the possibility that revisions in an author's biography might alter the functioning of the authorial name, he doesn't give that possibility much of a chance. For Foucault, changes in the function of an author's name are tied to changes in the discourses attributed to that name. For instance, if we were to learn that Shakespeare did not write those sonnets that pass for his, this new knowledge would significantly change how Shakespeare's name functions. In contrast, finding out that Shakespeare was not born in the house we visit today would "not alter the functioning of the author's name" (106). But what if we were to discover that Shakespeare had a loving, sexual relationship with the male friend to whom he addresses a number of sonnets? Would this not constitute personal information that would change the way Shakespeare's name functions for contemporary readers? Not that readers would construct Shakespeare as gay—which would be ahistorical (although some critics have made this move)—but that they could no longer read Shakespeare's works with their heterosexual presumption—also ahistorical—in tact. In choosing such a seemingly innocuous example as Shakespeare's home, Foucault stacks the cards against biography as having the power to affect the author function. But surely biographical material does influence the way an author's name functions, and changes in this material can modify the ideological work that the author's name performs (would William Bennett still urge the teaching of Shakespeare in U.S. high schools if these biographical findings came to light?).

Although Foucault ends his essay with the proposal that one day it will no longer be important to determine who is speaking, that day has not yet come, nor do the gaps in his reasoning suggest that it will.[22] Not only does it matter who is speaking but it also matters how literary critics construct that author's identity. This point has been recently highlighted through the controversy surrounding the publication of Salman Rushdie's *The Satanic Verses*. In examining the variety of responses to Rushdie's perceived sacrilege against Islamic belief, Máire Ní Fhlathúin asserts that "a major concern for many participants in this affair has been the construction of an author to fit a particular reading of the book" (276). Among the many constructions which Ní Fhlathúin reviews are Rushdie as a representative of Western society, as a man of "dedication and commitment," as someone who sees himself as part of two worlds, and as someone familiar with Islam and determined to do injury to "the very core of the Indian subcontinental culture" (278). Rushdie's life literally depends on these constructions and upon those his readers select as most accurate. The removal of the historical author from the interpretive process is thus not only epistemologically and psychologically impossible, it is potentially unethical. To quote Ní Fhlathúin: "In a profession which deals with the power and manipulation of images, it may be unwise to speak too glibly of the death of the author—particularly since it is in practice impossible to separate the author as literary force from the author as legal entity or human being" (277).

Such a situation urges us to think more deeply about the power of authorial constructions, the interconnectedness of such constructions with an author's texts, and our own accountability, as teachers and critics, for the authorial constructions we promote. In the following chapter, I will develop this line of reasoning by presenting an argument for approaching authors from a poststructuralist perspective in which we locate their subjectivity in history, textuality, and desire. To make this argument as concrete as possible, I will support it by examining recent critical and biographical activity that seeks to maintain Hemingway's heterosexuality. In addition, I will propose an alternative construction of Hemingway's identity, and attempt to indicate what is ethically and politically at stake.

2

THE DESIRE FOR AND OF THE AUTHOR:
RECONSTRUCTING HEMINGWAY

But what a story [would be] that of the real Hem, and one he should
tell himself but alas he never will. After all, as he himself once mur-
mured, there is the career, the career.
—Gertrude Stein (*The Autobiography of Alice B. Toklas*)

It is dangerous to make authors into cultural icons.
—Cheryl Walker ("Persona Criticism and the Death of the Author")

Although it would be rash to offer only one reason for the recent out-
burst of biographical activity surrounding Hemingway, a principal impetus has been the opening of Hemingway's papers in 1975 and the subsequent housing of this collection at the Kennedy Library in Boston in
1980.[1] Because this collection contains thousands of Hemingway's "private" papers, its opening encouraged many readers to predict that the
"true" Hemingway might finally be known. As early as 1977, Aaron
Latham announced that the unpublished manuscripts "reveal quite another human being from the one we have known."[2] One of the first to
sift through the collection, Latham asserted that now "we can see not
only how distressed he was, but his attempt to come to grips with the
problem of his masculinity" (52).

The feeling that the real Hemingway might lie among his papers was
fueled by the recognition that the public Hemingway was a creation that
masked as much as it revealed. Writing extensively about the emergence
of Hemingway as a public writer, John Raeburn notes that early in his

career, "Hemingway began to shape a public personality which quickly became one of his most famous creations, during his lifetime perhaps the most famous one. For the rest of his career he advertised his public personality in his considerable body of nonfiction, for whatever his nominal subject, his real subject was himself."[3] The treasure trove of material in the Hemingway Collection promised to aid the search for the private man behind the public mask.

As promised, the Hemingway Collection *has* yielded various revelations, with scholars announcing the discovery of everything from Hemingway's aesthetic principles to his editorial decisions to his personal grudges and fantasies. However, as Latham surmised in his early examination of the collection, the disclosures rousing the most interest have had to do with Hemingway's masculinity. This masculinity has, of course, been under scrutiny for years. In 1926, Zelda Fitzgerald reportedly said of Hemingway that no one could be that masculine;[4] a year later, Virginia Woolf called him "self-consciously virile."[5] But despite this lengthy history of a masculinity in crisis—or, perhaps, because of it—the holdings in the Hemingway Collection intensified the study of Hemingway's gender identity. Exerting the strongest pressure have been the archival manuscripts of an unfinished novel, "The Garden of Eden," and the radically edited, published version of these manuscripts, *The Garden of Eden* (1986). With its extended depiction of sexual reversals, sodomy, twinning, a ménage à trois, and lesbianism, *Garden* is the work that, in manuscript, inspired Latham to make his prediction (I discuss the editing of *Garden* in Chapter 3).[6]

Even in its reduced, published form, *Garden* has been responsible for a sea change in Hemingway criticism. Susan Beegel speculates that the publication of *Garden* "has forced critics to confront for the first time themes of homosexuality, perversion, and androgyny present throughout Hemingway's career in short stories like 'Mr. and Mrs. Elliot,' 'A Simply Enquiry,' 'The Sea Change,' and 'The Mother of a Queen,' widely available for at least 50 years."[7] While it is not true that before 1986 critics completely overlooked homosexuality, "perversion," and androgyny in Hemingway's fiction, those writing since then have found it harder to ignore such "themes."[8] Further, given that Hemingway's work has always been read as autobiographical, *Garden* has also encouraged critics and biographers to acknowledge experiences in Hemingway's life that had previously been minimized or evaded.

Take, for instance, Hemingway's childhood twinning experience. In 1962, Hemingway's older sister, Marcelline, revealed that Grace Hemingway had raised Marcelline and Ernest as twins "even into [their] school life," giving them dolls and air rifles alike. Grace even delayed Marcelline's schooling for a year so that she and Ernest could enter the first grade together.[9] A 1902 photo included in Marcelline's book about her family life showed her and Ernest dressed in fancy dresses and flowered hats. Seven years later, in the first scholarly biography of Hemingway, Carlos Baker carefully downplayed this childhood twinning. He referred to Grace's "fancy for dressing Ernest and Marcelline alike," and noted that at nine months Hemingway had been photographed in "a pink gingham dress and a wide hat ornamented with flowers."[10] This is the extent of Baker's interest in the twinning. In the very next sentence he assures readers that Hemingway "began to assert his boyhood" during the summer of 1900 by walking alone for the first time, "roaring in a lion's voice," "riding a cane for a hobbyhorse," and storming with rage when his wishes were denied (4–5). This is a one year old whom we can easily imagine will become the most famous Papa of his generation.

In 1975, one of Hemingway's younger sisters, Sunny, denied that the twinning ever happened. In her chapter, "Setting the Record Straight," she maintained that "the many family pictures that Mother kept for each of the children in the baby books refute the idea that got started about Mother dressing Ernest as a girl, and that he and Marcelline were dressed as twins."[11] Sunny's denial did not prevail as history, although her need to "straighten" out the record hinted at the anxiety that would surround future interpretations of this time in Hemingway's life and of transgendered characters in his work.[12]

In the early 1980s, a few critics began to discuss the twinning experience in more detail. The most prominent was Mark Spilka who, in a series of articles, maintained that Hemingway's strenuous defense of his maleness was part of a "larger struggle with his own androgynous impulses rather than a sustained form of homosexual panic."[13] Spilka drew generously upon Grace Hemingway's memory book of Ernest, from the Hemingway Collection, to show that Grace attempted to raise her son according to an androgynous model of genteel manhood portrayed in novels such as Dinah Mulock Craik's *John Halifax, Gentleman* (1856) and Frances Hodgson Burnett's *Little Lord Fauntleroy* (1886). Like Fauntleroy, whom Burnett likened to a "fairy prince," the young Hemingway was "a sturdy little fairy," "an affectionate, tender-hearted, considerate child who wore Dutch locks and infant dresses and called his mother 'Fweetie.'"[14] However, he soon rebelled against that identity, a rebellion that, according to Spilka, lasted a lifetime.

As strong as Spilka's argument seemed to be, at least to some critics, the published version of *Garden* increased its credibility. Here was a vivid picture of a young married couple attempting to look and be the same by dyeing their hair blond, tanning their bodies, and cross-sexing themselves in bed. Although the merger of male and female had presented itself in other Hemingway fiction, *Garden* gave it an emphasis found in no other work. Spilka himself recognized the importance of *Garden*—especially in its original unfinished version which became part of the Hemingway Collection after 1986—to his psychobiographical theory. When Spilka eventually assembled a book around his essays, he reserved the final chapter for Hemingway's novel and claimed that with *Garden* Hemingway created for us, "as for himself, a retrospective key to his own lifelong quarrel with androgyny" (3).

After 1986, then, scholars began to pay more attention to the twinning experience and to link that examination to *Garden*. In his 1987 biography, Kenneth Lynn declared that *Garden* compels critics to reluctantly recognize that Hemingway was not the writer or man he was thought to be, and he explained that difference by connecting Hemingway's anxiety and insecurity to his twinned childhood.[15] Five years later, James Mellow suggested that Hemingway "seems not to have suffered any dire psychological effect from the early cross-dressing"; however, "some aspect of the sexual transference of brother into sister, and vice versa, kept its fascination for a lifetime, served him as a theme in later stories and quite probably inspired the ambiguous combinations of sexual play between heroes and heroines in his novels, particularly the posthumously published *The Garden of Eden*."[16]

The changing status of the twinning experience, promoted if not prompted by the publication of *Garden*, reminds us that the facts of history (with which biography is affiliated) never speak for themselves but are always the product of narration and interpretation. We often speak of discovering evidence, yet even if we learn something that was previously unknown—for example, that the FBI kept a file on Hemingway, something that he claimed for years—that discovery occurs only when someone perceives it as biographically relevant and relates that perception through narrative and analysis, as Jeffrey Meyers does when he states, "The FBI file proves that even paranoids have real enemies."[17] The constructed and interpretive nature of history and biography is also why "the private Hemingway behind the public mask" will never be found; he is always being invented. As Joan Scott states, "the appearance of a new identity is not inevitable or determined, not something that was always there simply waiting to be expressed," but is rather "a discursive event."[18] The identity of Hemingway—or of any biographical subject —is a process of becoming or, more accurately, a process of being articulated into being.

This act of articulation is related to what Hayden White describes as emplotment, a process by which the historian encodes "facts" into a specific plot structure. By arranging facts into a recognizable form, the historian constructs a history that can serve as a possible "object of thought." But, White notes, the historian "does not bring with him a notion of the 'story' that lies embedded within the 'facts' given by the record," since there are "an infinite number of such stories contained therein." What the historian brings to a consideration of the record are "general notions of the *kinds of stories* that might be found there."[19] Because the historian is always faced with a number of stories from which to choose—a formula that applies equally to the biographer—every history tells two stories. The first story is that of the text itself, a story of inclusion. This means that the text includes not only the plot that the historian selects out of many but also those experiences that allow this plot to cohere. The other story exists only in the negative, the absent, for it is a story of exclusion: the numerous plots that the historian rejects and those experiences that must be suppressed or found irrelevant for the sake of narrative unity and ideological consistency.[20]

In regard to biography, William H. Epstein notes that this process of inclusion and exclusion is "a closely monitored cultural process . . . in which the Western world's dominant structures of political, social, economic, and cultural authority are deeply implicated."[21] The stories available to the biographer are, typically, stories that are meaningful and acceptable within dominant power structures such as the nation, white racial hegemony, capitalism, and compulsory heterosexuality. The experiences and facts that the biographer identifies as legitimate and relevant—or illegitimate and irrelevant—to emplotting those stories are also culturally inscribed and socially approved. For instance, the refusal until recently to consider Hemingway's twinning experience suggests that it has carried a threat of difference that could unsettle the mainstream belief in a heteromasculine Hemingway. As Joan Scott notes, in its traditional application in history and biography, experience "reproduces rather than contests given ideological systems" (778). The inscription of experience is never simply descriptive or empirical but is also ideological and political.

Biographical inscription involves, then, a complex negotiation of the visible and the invisible, the conscious and the repressed, the extant and the absent, the coded and the uncoded, the dominant and the marginalized. I have traced this practice because it has much to tell us about the critical and cultural construction of authors. In the case of Hemingway, one way to account for the recent biographical activity is to view it as an overdetermined wish that certain possibilities remain repressed: inaccessible, subordinated, excluded. To put this another way, the overt project of "recovering" Hemingway's private identity has behind it the covert project of preventing this identity from being articulated through one of the most famous public-private tropes, that having to do with homosexuality: out/closeted, manifest/latent, conscious/repressed. Granted, a few critics (such as Cathy and Arnold Davidson, and Nancy Comley and Robert Scholes, whose work I will discuss later) address homosexual or other so-called "deviant" possibilities in their constructions of Hemingway. However, the majority of scholars writing in the wake of *Garden* promote approaches which ensure that the Hemingway "hidden away" in his manuscripts does not differ too greatly from the Hemingway we have always known.

This promotion is most noticeable in the response of critics who regret that *The Garden of Eden* was posthumously published. Ostensibly, these critics argue that publication controverts Hemingway's wishes, contradicts his reputation as a consummate artist who carefully controlled the publishing of his fiction, and confuses beyond usefulness the idea of intentionality. Yet given their attitudes toward some of the subjects treated in *Garden*, these critics seem motivated by more than just the concern to protect Hemingway's professional reputation. Consider, for example, Earl Rovit's reasoning: "It's unfortunate [*Garden*] was commercially published because it's a rotten book. There are lovely things in it and the business of this unorthodox ménage à trois, and the haircuts, and what not. All struck me as personal material that a writer is getting rid of for his own therapy and is unable to universalize or make representative of anything other than his own peculiar warts and whims." [22] In this objection, Rovit presumes that Hemingway's portrayal of a ménage à trois and his characters' eroticization of hair *must* be the act of an author projecting and expelling his neuroses, a private attempt to cure his own peculiar "tendencies." Even if one were to accept Rovit's assessment of Hemingway's subject matter as peculiarly personal to Hemingway this is an odd charge to bring against a writer celebrated for his talent of turning the autobiographical into the fictional. Certainly Rovit would not wish to remove from critical scrutiny the many stories in which

Hemingway draws upon his injury in World War I, his efforts to hunt big game, or his experience with his father's suicide.

In fact, Rovit and Gerry Brenner, who co-authored the revised edition of the Twayne Series book on Hemingway, often approve of his use of experience, stating for instance that, "it was probably a fortuitous accident that Hemingway's personal wound and relationship of estrangement from the Booth Tarkington mores of Oak Park should result in the compelling symbolism of *The Sun Also Rises*, but such are the graces of literary history."[23] Further, Rovit and Brenner welcome the posthumous publication of other Hemingway material assembled by editors, such as *Islands in the Stream* and *A Moveable Feast*, for such work "richly supplements—albeit problematically—the Hemingway canon" (153). Because *The Garden of Eden* was published the same year as their book, Rovit and Brenner could not be expected to discuss it, yet one wonders why, recognizing the difficulties imposed by their editing, Rovit would not later recommend that *Garden* be read according to the guidelines he and Brenner advance for other posthumously published Hemingway manuscripts (156).

Clearly the problem is not that Hemingway may have written *Garden* for therapeutic reasons, a purpose he often attributed to his writing, but the kind of experience he was seeking to understand. Rovit's back-to-the-closet attitude discloses the fear of many readers that *Garden* might compromise Hemingway's identity as a "normal," red-blooded, all-American heterosexual. As Mark Spilka puts it, there is a growing anxiety among many Hemingway admirers that the Hemingway "who gave us male definitions of manhood to ponder, cherish, even perhaps to grow by" is about to be lost (327–28).

But the anxiety that Spilka refers to surfaces not only in the desire to exclude certain works or information from the textual and biographical record; it also makes itself known in scholarly acts of inclusion. A closer look at the work of critics, like Spilka, who have eagerly employed materials from the Hemingway Collection to reshape our understanding of Hemingway and his fiction reveals that these critics share many of the attitudes expressed by those scholars who want to return these materials to Hemingway's—or the Kennedy Library's—closet. Simply put, although these revisionist critics claim to be doing feminist service to Hemingway's history and fiction, their efforts actually reinstate both within a sexist, heterosexist, and homophobic matrix.

Occasionally, a critic's language reveals that he is positioned within this matrix, as in Spilka's references to the Hemingway "who gave *us* male definitions of manhood . . . to grow by," to "that one-eyed myth of mystical [male] camaraderie *we* have *all* more or less embraced" (328), and to Hemingway's ability to overcome "his own and *everyone else's* fear of female dominance" (213; emphasis added). More frequently, the sexism and heterosexism are inherent in the paradigm of androgyny that these critics use to explain the gender complexities in Hemingway's life and work. One might say, then, that the attitudes are institutional more than personal, although one could also argue that critics have chosen this paradigm because such attitudes are ingrained within it.

Spilka's *Hemingway's Quarrel with Androgyny*, the most well-known example of the critical application of androgyny to Hemingway's life and work, is simply the most sustained representative of a widespread trend. For instance, Gerald Kennedy identifies androgyny as Hemingway's "secret and potentially scandalous desire," which he struggled to exorcise in writing *The Garden of Eden* and which was on his mind when he wrote *A Moveable Feast*.[24] Adopting a similar perspective, Robert Gajdusek examines "androgeneity" by investigating thematic connections between *The Garden of Eden* and other Hemingway works.[25] Finally, in *Hemingway and Nineteenth-Century Aestheticism*, John Gaggin looks at androgyny as one of many "decadent issues" that Hemingway explores.[26]

Some current biographers have also adopted the paradigm of androgyny in order to analyze Hemingway. Michael Reynolds, for example, proposes that Hemingway learned in Paris that, "to write, a man must cultivate the feminine side of himself, become both male and female." Reynolds then suggests that Hemingway began growing his hair to reach the bobbed length of Hadley's (Hemingway's first wife) so that they could be the same person: "man and woman blending to oneness in sexual union, the whole person at last: Plato's egg reunited."[27] The androgynous approach has thus been pervasive, and its influence remains strong. Androgyny was the topic for the Hemingway Society's meeting at the 1988 Modern Language Association convention; its predominance was further certified at the 1993 South Atlantic Modern Language Association convention when this Society centered its session on "Androgyny: The New Key to Reading Hemingway."

At first glance, androgyny might seem the ideal way to conceptualize the self and the romantic union of a man and a woman in Hemingway's life and work. As a matter of fact, it's the word Mary Hemingway chose to describe her relationship with her husband: "[W]e were," she wrote, "smoothly interlocking parts of a single entity, the big cogwheel and the smaller cogwheel. . . . Maybe we were androgynous."[28] In addition, for some feminists in the early 1970s, androgyny was the byway to liberation and equality as represented in works such as Carolyn Heilbrun's *Toward a Recognition of Androgyny* and some of Adrienne Rich's poems ("The Stranger," "Diving into the Wreck").

Yet at the same time that some feminists were touting androgyny as a solution to sexism and gender roles, others were insisting that it reinstated the stereotypes it sought to uproot. In the mid-1970s Rich reversed her position, reasoning that because critics rarely critique the sexual politics behind androgyny, it had become a "good" word, meaning many things to many people and thereby lacking political bite.[29] In "Androgyny: The Sexist Myth in Disguise," Daniel Harris wrote that "[f]or feminist men as well as for feminist women, the myth of androgyny has no positive value." According to him, "We cannot discuss the myth, in psychological terms, without resorting to sexist polarizations for the definition of identity. . . . [T]he myth, because it is a microcosm of heterosexual power relations within the dominant culture, can only perpetuate the habits of oppression we seek to reject."[30] In 1980, even Heilbrun had decided she was willing to give up androgyny, seeing it as a step along the way to gender equality but not the end itself.[31]

So although androgyny seems to promise a way out of masculine-feminine binarism, it simply moves that binarism from the social realm to the individual psyche. This move prevents—even prohibits—a political reading in which the critic exposes the binarisms that readers hold in place while they read.[32] Instead the critic becomes trapped into unwittingly embracing sexist polarizations. Consider, for example, the assumptions that make possible a description of Frederic Henry lying wounded in a hospital bed as having "finally arrived at something like a woman's passive power" (Spilka, 212) or those behind Robert Crozier's suggestion that Robert Jordan learns from Maria of *For Whom the Bell Tolls* the essentially feminine value of mystical knowledge.[33] Or consider the way that stereotypes about masculinity and femininity are reproduced in Sukrita Paul Kumar's conclusion that Maria is "a perfect blend of feminine gentleness and masculine firmness and the sense of hardness of life."[34]

Androgyny can, admittedly, express a utopian vision of transcending current gender roles completely, which is how many modernist women writers seemed to articulate its possibility. But most Hemingway critics who have used this model remain oblivious to its pitfalls. Indeed, none of them seems aware that feminists have critiqued androgyny since its popularization in the 1970s.[35] This lack of awareness creates the problems in their work that I have outlined above; it also supports my suspicion that androgyny has been chosen not just for what it includes but for what it excludes. A term related to gender roles, androgyny neutralizes any sexual component of Hemingway's upbringing and role-playing, and of his characters' impulses. The concept of androgyny gives critics permission to avoid looking at Hemingway's explorations of sexual identity. This license to ignore seems to explain, in part, why androgyny has become so popular with Hemingway critics: it permits them to turn away from the recurring rumor that Hemingway—or his male heroes— had homosexual "tendencies." The caveats that critics provide whenever their discussion comes close to confusing the androgyne for the homosexual support such a possibility, as in Spilka's assertion that he is not implying that Jake Barnes "would also like to make it with bullfighters and other males" (204). The homosexual, as Catharine Stimpson observes, is "a far more threatening figure than the androgyne," in part simply because the homosexual exists: "The androgyne is nothing more, or less, than an idea."[36]

Interestingly, if critics were to study Hemingway's own use of "androgyny," they would have a more difficult time avoiding a conversation about homosexuality. Hemingway's understanding of this concept was ambiguous but included homosexual attraction, a usage that can also be found in some writings on sexual inversion in the late nineteenth and early part of the twentieth century.[37] For example, Hemingway's son, Patrick Hemingway, recalled in 1982 that Hemingway had forbidden him to visit Grandmother Grace because she was "androgynous." This restriction seems to have come about because of Grace Hemingway's relationship with Ruth Arnold, her live-in voice student, a relationship that was so close it caused Hemingway's father to "rant" about Ruth and ban her from their house.[38] The association of androgyny with homosexuality appears also in *Death in the Afternoon*, where Hemingway refers to the "saints, apostles, Christs and Virgins with the androgynous faces and forms that filled [El Greco's] imagination."[39] He then recounts a time when he wondered whether El Greco was a "maricón" (defined in the glossary of *Death* as "a sodomite, nance, queen, fairy, fag, etc." [417]) since the figures in his paintings were classic examples of maricones. As Nancy Comley and Robert Scholes note, "Hemingway reasoned from the androgynous images produced by a painter to the painter's sexuality" (119).

Lest I overstate the situation, let me acknowledge that Hemingway critics of the past fifteen years, even those working primarily with the androgyny model, have not completely ignored homosexuality. Yet their approaches to homosexuality often reflect uneasiness, ignorance, and a determination to shield Hemingway from suspicion.[40] For instance, many critics who deal with homosexual desire in Hemingway's work and life deal only with lesbian desire. Moreover, their conception of lesbian desire leaves much to be desired, delineated as it is along heterosexual lines. Both Kenneth Lynn and Spilka suggest that Jake Barnes's war injury puts him in the position of a woman, more significantly that of a lesbian, whose dilemma is that she cannot penetrate her lover's body with her own (Lynn, 323; Spilka, 203). But this is a peculiarly phallic definition of lesbian lovemaking, assuming, as it does, that lesbian sex must involve penetration and that penetration must involve a penis. This definition of Jake's situation also ignores or refuses the additional possibility that his love for the "mannish" Brett—and hers for him—contains a dimension of male homosexuality. Such a refusal reconfirms my point that many critics are attempting to defend Hemingway's identity as monolithically heterosexual; under this ideology, it is safer to make Jake a lesbian because he can never really be one. Once we take seriously the idea that Jake has homosexual desires, it is a short step to taking seriously the idea that Hemingway's "attraction" to lesbians is one instance of the displacement of his own homosexual desires.[41]

A few critical works provide exceptions to the claim that Hemingway critics avoid male homosexuality because noticing it might compromise Hemingway's heterosexual identity. These works deserve closer attention because they have the potential to reconstruct Hemingway without being bound by either homophobia or heterosexism. For example, Gerry Brenner, writing three years before the publication of *Garden*, maintains that "Hemingway's fixation on, and ambivalence toward, father figures obliges me to draw the necessary inference, that Hemingway was latently homoerotic" (19). Despite the promise of Brenner's argument to challenge the purity of Hemingway's heterosexuality, his verb choice here suggests that this diagnosis is being squeezed out of him. To make sure we understand his position on both Hemingway and homoeroticism—a word Brenner prefers over homosexuality because "it denotes a wider range of erotic displacements and sublimations" (241)—Brenner assures us that Hemingway's "latent homoeroticism does not prove him to be abnormal. Without a doubt he led a relatively normal heterosexual life" (20). Brenner's attitude toward male homosexuality limits his ability to revise our understanding of Hemingway; the homoeroticized Hemingway he gives us is hypernormal, harboring "a deeply rooted wish" for his father's "approval and affection" (20), not unnatural desires for other men.

More auspicious is Comley and Scholes's *Hemingway's Genders* (1994). This book is composed of four interrelated essays which attempt to "read Hemingway by putting questions of gender ahead of all others" (ix). To a great degree this aim as well as their title is misleading since sex and sexuality are as much Comley and Scholes's subject as gender. Their choice of gender as a controlling term leads one to wonder whether Comley and Scholes selected it because gender is less controversial than sexuality or sexual orientation, or simply because a title like *Hemingway's Genders* was catchier and more marketable than one like *Hemingway's Genders, Sexes, and Sexualities*. In Comley and Scholes's focus on gender, one senses a residue of androgyny.

But this may be nit-picking at a book that does more than any so far to investigate Hemingway's portrayal of the "complexity of human sexuality" (144). Like other critics who are reassessing Hemingway's identity and work, Comely and Scholes see *Garden* as central to their argument and devote parts of two chapters to it. But they also fill in this analysis with reference to other Hemingway texts, published and unpublished. In addition, in their final chapter, they examine narratives by Hemingway that specifically deal with male homosexuality, an examination that promises to generate a more radical reconstruction of Hemingway than any other recent critical work. Yet two major omissions, or retreats, frustrate the fulfillment of this promise.

The first is a refusal to consider whether their extensive analysis of Hemingway's homosexuals (in *Death in the Afternoon*, "There's One in Every Town," "A Simple Enquiry," "A Lack of Passion," "The Mother of a Queen," "The Undefeated," and "A Real Man") might call for a rereading of Hemingway's other male characters, especially his "male heroes." At one point, Comley and Scholes come close to recognizing that such a rereading is merited. They suggest that "The Light of the World" is about the sexual orientation of the narrator and his male friend. But many critics, they conclude, "believing that the narrator is Nick [Adams] who is Ernest Hemingway who is not a maricón simply cannot see sexual orientation as an issue in the story" (142). As Comley and Scholes imply here, reading a (supposed) Nick Adams story as a story about homosexuality is risky since Nick has been closely aligned with Hemingway. Yet surely Comley and Scholes's delineation of Hemingway's extended work on homosexuality, lesbianism, and bisexuality demands a more global reconsideration of what they call "The Hemingway Text," especially that part of the "Text" containing male protagonists whose names now denote masculinity in our cultural imagination: Jake Barnes, Frederic Henry, Nick Adams, and Robert Jordan, to name just a few. And surely Comley and Scholes's exploration also calls for a more detailed response (their second omission) to their question, "Have we been trying to show that Hemingway was gay?" (143). Declaring that Hemingway's sexual orientation has *not* been their point but that they have instead been "trying to show that such a question is too simple . . . . [that] Hemingway was much more interested in [matters of sexuality] than has usually been supposed" (144) is a cop out which splits mind and body, allowing the heterosexual Hemingway to *think* of homosexual desire without having to *feel* it. This move seems to contradict Comley and Scholes's own critical approach that puts Hemingway at the center of their study and seeks to make "[their] imagined Hemingway as realistic or 'true'" as possible (xi).

Comley and Scholes readily admit that "there is more to be done" with all the matters they address (146). As I will show in later chapters, some of this work has been done by critics such as Arnold and Cathy Davidson—although their scope is limited to *The Sun Also Rises*—and by Carl Eby—who examines the function of the fetish for Hemingway. But for the most part, Hemingway critics and biographers have been unable, or unwilling, to break from conventional societal codes in their efforts to reconstruct Hemingway. This constraint has enabled them to dress the old Hemingway in new clothes without leading anyone to utter the words "transgendered" or "queer."

Critical Desires and Authorial Constructions

In the preceding section I argued that "the real Hemingway" can never be recovered even though many critics and biographers proceed as if he can and are especially interested in retaining Hemingway's "real" identity as purely heterosexual.[42] In this proceeding, Western humanism meets American individualism and reasserts the autonomy of the essentialized self. Yet, one might object, don't my criticisms of these critics imply that the real story of Hemingway could be written if only we would gather the right evidence and read it through the correct paradigm? The problem is one encountered by anyone working within a poststructuralist framework, but it is especially acute for politically concerned critics who want to challenge prevailing regimes of truth. Once we accept that full presence cannot be located anywhere—whether "in the psyche, in history, in culture, or in the text"[43]—how do we talk about such foundational concepts as identity, history, desire, social justice, literature, and the author?

In this section I will advance a three-part argument for retaining a concept of the author without lapsing into essentialism but also without giving up a sense of "the real," that is, the author's existence in history. In brief, I will propose (1) that the historical author is a necessity, but (2) that this author is accessible only in the *process* of his or her history and in textuality, and (3) that the critic's own desire plays a major role in conceptualizing this historical-textual author as a desiring subject. In identifying an interpretive role for desire, I am not suggesting that the critic completely makes the author over into his or her own erotic image or object of desire. Rather, I am proposing that critics develop authorial constructions partly out of their relation to their own sexual desire, a relation that is invested in a particular sexual system, be that system a dominant one or one that endeavors to resist or reform the dominant order.[44] My position is grounded upon the premise that desire is socially, historically, and politically situated, and therefore insists that a person's investment in a particular way of desiring and the critical work that ensues from such an investment have political, material, and ethical consequences.[45] To illustrate this latter part of my argument I will maintain that critics have built recent constructions of Hemingway out of a foundational relation to desire and their commitment to heteronormativity. These constructions, in turn, have bolstered dominant regimes of thought, desire, and identity. However, I will also lay out my own desire for constructing Hemingway differently.

Recent work on the author has devised various approaches for avoiding the trap of essentialism (which perceives the author as a recoverable entity) without recommending boundless pluralism. One of the most intriguing views is that of Jacqueline Rose who, in *The Haunting of Sylvia Plath*, pushes aside Plath's "actual biography," which she claims is unknowable, in order to concentrate on a "textual biography." For Rose, the fiction or, to use her term, the "fantasy" of the author derives not only from the author's work but also from a history of critical and cultural discourses responding to that work. She argues that when we write about Plath, we are dealing not with Plath herself but with "her representations, her own writing, together with all the other utterances which have come to crowd it—joining in the conversation, as one might say."[46] The effect of all these utterances is that readers finally cannot separate

Plath from the frame of "the surrounding discourses through which her writing is presented" (69). This frame works as a repressed memory for the society that constructs it, "carrying the question of what we can bear to think about ourselves" (6). In short, the fetishization of Sylvia Plath—by critics, her family, her fans, her publishers, and the media—compels Rose to abandon the search for Plath's identity and history, and to focus instead on the psychic processes of Plath's readers.

Rose's approach has the advantage of retaining a notion of the author that does not collapse into biographical essentialism. But although it might be consistent with much poststructuralist theory to claim that the textual author is all we can know, such a position deserves closer scrutiny before we take it up as a model of authorship. First, even though the move to "the textual" can be seen as an antifoundational move, we should not deceive ourselves into believing that a textual author is automatically less foundational or more recoverable than a biographical one. Interpretation and narration play as much a part in our constructions of the textual author as they do in our constructions of the biographical. In the same way that literary biographers select the evidence and the plot that will give meaning to the life-history of the author, literary critics select and interpret those authorial representations, those "other utterances," those texts of the author that will comprise the (story of the) textual author. Because we are selecting and interpreting, our vision of the textual author will be partial and subject to further revision. To cast this critique concretely, I am arguing (as Rose would surely concede) that Rose's Plath is also a construction, inflected by Rose's engagements with psychoanalysis and feminist theory.

Next, we must question whether a textual author can function independently of some notion of the historical author. Surely our selections of the critical and cultural discourses that comprise the textual author are based on preconceived ideas, however ambiguous or contradictory, of the author as an historical subject. This seems to be the case even for someone like Rose who acknowledges that "facts" are simultaneously provisional and capable of being manipulated, for she builds a number of arguments around specific biographical moments and, more generally, on the tension and troubles between Plath and her husband, Ted Hughes. Rose even expresses her gratitude to Hughes and his sister for providing her with corrective commentary "where the previously known details of an incident were incomplete" (x).[47]

I am arguing for retention of the historical author, first of all, from a practical standpoint, proposing that readers cannot resist the psychological effects that biographical data and scholarship have on their perception of an author and his or her work, even when they claim to be ignoring the author's personal history. Although biographical information about an author is available to most readers (through book-jacket blurbs, formal biographies, headnotes in literary anthologies, newspaper and magazine articles, even made-for-tv and educational films), the more we are entrenched in the profession of teaching and writing criticism, the greater our chances of being exposed to this information. It is thus ironic that proclamations about the author's death should have been taken literally by those working inside the academy, the environment where information about an author's life circulates most freely.

Hemingway's birthdate, his wounding in World War I, his relationship with Agnes von Kurowsky, Hadley's loss of Hemingway's manuscripts on a train, the promise to stay away from Pauline for 100 days while he was still married to Hadley, his "liberation" of the Ritz, his suicide—these are all signs of the historical Hemingway. If nothing else, such signs remind us that the author lived (or is living) and, as a condition of that existence, *has* a history. We might agree with William Epstein that, like all facts, these signs of the historical Hemingway are "enmeshed in a network of cultural signification constituted by the documentation of church, state, family, commerce, history, tradition, and other cultural institutions."[48] We might also recognize that these facts can alter over time as we acquire new information or interpret them differently. Nonetheless, it seems disingenuous to claim that our knowledge of them, however temporary or contested that knowledge might be, plays no part in our formulation of the textual Hemingway. In fact, quite the opposite is true, since such knowledge has been a primary impetus behind the cultural fascination with and the fantasizing about Hemingway in the first place. Without the historical Hemingway, there would be no textual Hemingway.

Even if readers were able to set aside their encounters with the historical author, I still find compelling reasons to pay attention to the historical dimension of the author. Most immediately, attending to this dimension enables us to account for the shaping effects on the author of power differentials associated with "difference" and to trace those effects to the political, economic, and social structures (such as the nation-state, patriarchy, capitalism, and white racism) that they sustain. In explaining the importance of noticing such matters, Cheryl Walker states, "As long as gender, class, race, sexual orientation, and other forms of difference are constituted hierarchically by power politics, they will remain important features of both writing and reading. The choice to ignore such issues, in the end, serves the status quo."[49] In addition, Walker argues, as have a number of other critics, for expanding the space which the historical author inhabits from the "purely" personal to the social. Janet Wolff, for instance, reminds us that the author has been "constructed by social and ideological factors—and moreover, constantly *re*-constructed in this way—rather than as an entity above these factors, developing by some internal logic of its own."[50] This emphasis on the historical-social conditions in which an author lived and by which he or she was formed as a subject has the distinct benefit of establishing a field of meaning for reading an author's work. It delineates, as Richard Dyer notes, those discourses that an author might have access to on account of who he or she is, discourses that can make their way into an author's work with or without his/her conscious knowledge.[51] By taking notice of the historical moment in which an author lived (a perspective revived by New Historicists), critics can thereby sketch a horizon of meaning for reading beyond an author's individual experiences or intentions, the customary starting and ending point of author-based criticism.

Yet we must be careful not to assume that enlarging the space of the historical author from the personal to the socio-political instantly moves us to firm ground. First of all, Wolff's reminder that the author is constantly reconstructed by social and ideological factors encourages us to see the historical author as a subject moving through history, a shifting, fragmented figure rather than a stable, arrested absolute. Second, as I discussed earlier, a historical narrative emerges out of a complex negotiation of the visible and the invisible, the conscious and the repressed, the dominant and the marginalized. As Hans Robert Jauss states, fictionalization "is always at work in historical experience. The *what* of the event is always conditioned by the perspectival *when* of its being perceived or reconstructed. It is further conditioned by the *how* of its representation and interpretation. Thus, its meaning is continually adjusted by additional determining factors."[52] Our renderings of social and ideological factors that produced the author as subject, and of the author's relationship to those factors, will be approximations rather than absolutes. Our understanding of the author as a subject in history and as a subject moving through history must therefore be conditional. In sum, mapping the historical field of meaning and the shape-shifting of an author engages us in unending textual activity.

This does not mean that we throw up our hands and decide that because an author's history cannot be definitively known, we should abandon the author as a subject in history. Fredric Jameson has repeatedly noted that "history is *not* a text, not a narrative, master or otherwise," but is "an absent cause." As such, "it is inaccessible to us except in textual form, and . . . our approach to it and to the Real itself necessarily passes through its prior textualization, its narrativization in the political unconscious."[53] To approach history at all, we must immerse ourselves in the textual. Further, when conditions change so as to allow the marginalized, the repressed, and the absent to be coded as history, we must not halt that activity because we know from past experience that it, too, will marginalize, repress, and omit.[54] To do so would be to promote current forms of oppression. In a postmodern world, our awareness that absolutes are only approximations should not keep us from acting, at some point, as if those approximations were absolutes. By not acting so, we run the risk of removing subjectivity from the material realm, a dangerous and potentially apolitical move because it implies that social, political, and economic conditions have no effect on subjectivity and therefore need not be changed.

As this discussion suggests, textual and historical authors cannot be divorced. Just as the textual author bears the imprint of the historical, so the historical author exhibits a textual nature that is simultaneously stable and unstable, tentative and determined, illusory and graspable. Far from being an essentialist entity, the historical author exists in a dialectic between the real and the representational, the existential and the textual. Our critical discourse about an author and his/her work draws upon historical narratives, and biographical writings about an author build upon previous critical discourse about the author and his/her work. To put this another way, the textual author (the author as subject *of* history) is filled with traces of the historical author (the author as subject *in* history); and the historical author comes to us as a (series of) textual production(s) presented at different moments in history. The textual author is always also historical; and the historical author is always also textual.

The paradox, as Lacan reminds us, is that there is no subject except in representation, even if no representation captures the subject completely.[55] There is no subject without interpretation, without theory and history, but no theory or history can account for the whole of the subject. Because any theory or history is ultimately inadequate to the task of delineating an author's subjectivity, we are left with, or return to, the question of how we decide which history and which theory to employ when constructing the author. To quote Jauss again, what are those "additional determining factors" that condition how we render history, how we construct the author as a subject *in* and *of* history?

Susan Lanser has recently proposed an answer to this question (although without directly addressing it) in her claim that what critics "choose to support, to write about, to imagine" is "as much a function of [their] own desire as of any incontrovertible evidence" that a particular aspect of narrative, history, or biography is proper or improper, relevant or irrelevant.[56] Lanser's proposal seems particularly applicable to literary critics' and biographers' constructions of the author. In constructing the author as a desiring subject, the critic will inevitably reveal his or her own desire. As a starting point for exploring the nuances of this assertion, we might return to Rose's conceptualization of Plath as a "fantasy." Rose observes that the act of interpretation involves the psychoanalytic processes of transference and projection. "In relation to literature," Rose writes,

> transference refers to the way critics read their unconscious into the text, repeating in their critical analysis the structures of meaning called up by the writing. Thus transference suggests a process of mutual implication (the critic repeats and enters into the text). In the case of projection, on the other hand, that same repetition works by exclusion—a structural incapacity, that of psychosis, to recognise your relation to something which seems to assail you from outside. The subject expels what he or she cannot bear to acknowledge as his or her own reality, only to have it return even larger, and more grotesquely, than reality itself . . . . (14)

By applying this psychoanalytic model to the relation of the critic to the textual author (who, as I've shown, is inextricably tied to the historical author), Rose is able to explain how the subject in analysis can turn into the analyst of those who analyze her. Through the psychoanalytic processes of transference and projection, and here I would add disavowal as well, critics impose and expose their desires. As Marlon Riggs, director of the film *Tongues Untied*, once said to his critics, "Do you honestly think you can so closely, critically examine me without studying or revealing yourself?"[57]

Like the critics who are the target of Riggs's reproach and the Plath critics whom Rose includes in her study (including Rose herself), all critics reveal themselves in the act of interpretation, be it the interpretation of a text or an author. Such revelations are especially pertinent when the critic speaks about the author as a desiring subject and about the desires circulating through an author's texts. Hemingway scholars reconstructing Hemingway's identity and rereading his fiction in light of that reconstruction provide a forceful illustration of this premise. By making Hemingway androgynous, latently homoerotic, or simply "interested" in all kinds of sexuality but nonetheless certifiably heterosexual, these scholars express their anxieties about the possible presence of homosexual desire in their own makeup. Their strategies disclose a concern that the loss of a heterosexual Hemingway might put their own sexual identity under suspicion or might test the truths of white American heteromasculinity in general.

Indeed, as I have already hinted, one reason for the biographical explosion surrounding Hemingway might have to do with the threat that recent gay and lesbian activism and queer studies have posed, simply by their existence and their increasing prevalence, to Hemingway's heterosexuality. For this reason, the identification and retheorization of desires that have been historically suppressed, pathologized, or demonized threaten to rewrite Hemingway's intense homosociality as homosexuality. To deflect this possible rewriting, those critics whose desire is invested in compulsory heterosexuality introduce identity paradigms, such as androgyny, that suppress any implications of Hemingway's non-heterosexual desires. Mine is the book these scholars have been responding to, despite the fact that I am writing after them.

To say that Hemingway critics are responding to my work *a priori* is not to dismiss the ways in which mine is responding to theirs. But while the response is recriprocal, the psychological dynamics are not. One way to explain the difference is to say that their desire, invested as it is in heteronormativity, is dependent on repressing mine, but my desire is intent on rupturing theirs. What I mean by this is not that I want to eliminate heterosexual desire from constructions of the historical-textual Hemingway, but that I want to disrupt the homophobic and heterosexist strategies that critics and biographers (not to mention general readers, booksellers, publishers, teachers, editors, and the media) use to portray Hemingway's desire if not to maintain the integrity of their own desire. In addition, I want to ask what kind of Hemingway might be constructed if we approached him and his texts from a perspective that was not homophobic but quite the opposite: one that was willing, even eager, to explore the possible existence of "queer" desires and their potential significance in Hemingway's erotic makeup. In other words, what if we approached Hemingway and his work with a *desire to desire* differently?

Although the idea of a desire to desire has been introduced by a number of critics, what I mean by it here is the relation we have to desire.[58] This relation consists, in part, of the frame of intelligibility through which we read and assign meaning to desire. In general, Hemingway's critics have viewed desire as an innate sexual disposition. From this perspective, Hemingway can be constructed only as heterosexual or as a closeted homosexual. But if we read desire antifoundationally, seeing it as a tension toward the other produced, or at least conditioned, by the social, then we might construct Hemingway's desire, and his identity as a desiring subject, differently.

The word "desire" has a complicated history and many meanings, but in our present academic climate, it is usually associated with the theories of human sexuality developed by Freud and those theories as reinterpreted by Lacan, especially in his formulation that desire is instantiated in the subject as "the desire of the Other." In his return to Freud, Lacan argues that because our desire is the "desire of the Other," it is indeterminate and unattainable. One's desire is "eternally stretching forth toward the *desire for something else.*"[59] Desire is not an appetite for satisfaction nor the demand for love but something that emerges in the margin between need and demand, a desire for recognition by the Other (287, 311). Lacan thus coordinates desire "not with the object that would seem to satisfy it, but with the object [the Other] that causes it."[60] Because desire is indeterminate and unconscious, it is also inherently radical—one never knows where it might evade or resist current power structures—which is why power must institute proper homes for desire, like heterosexual marriage.

The intersection of power with desire is the intersection of the social with the psychic, of the conscious with the unconscious. This is not to say that desire originates exclusively in the psyche or in the social—or in some innate sexual instinct.[61] But if not the place where desire originates, the social is certainly the place where desire is externalized, where it takes a particular shape, where it is assigned meaning and value, where one kind of desiring is deemed acceptable and another deemed perverse, where it is reoriented from the object that causes it to the object that can satisfy it. To put this another way, although the functioning of the unconscious ensures that desire can never be completely regulated by the social, we are constantly being told what and how to desire through discourses on desire and fantasies developed and promoted in the social. As Jonathan Dollimore observes, "Desire is of its 'nature' saturated by the social."[62]

To the extent that the social assigns meaning, value, and form to desire, it produces it. From this perspective, the discourse of psychoanalysis itself—insofar as it attempts to explain the workings of desire—participates in the social production of desire. Saturated by the social, desire also finds form and meaning in eroticizations based in race, class, ableness, and other differentials of identity. For example, a white person's desire for a person of color never traverses neutral social territory. Such desire is intertwined with discourses about race, such as racist fantasies about the exotic other or imperialist fantasies about the superiority of one body type over another.[63] I am not suggesting that interracial desire originates or resolves itself in these fantasies. Rather, the production of desire in the social realm necessarily means that desire passes through these social discourses and fantasies about the other, however the other might be defined. Acknowledging the racial dimension of desire also makes us aware that our desire for someone of our own race has political, material, and psychological ramifications as well, although those ramifications will map out differently for people of different races and for bi- or multi-raced individuals. As Sagri Dhairyam states, reflecting on racial identity through sexuality highlights "the color of the body as both all-too-material difference and fantasy."[64] In fact, many people of color who acknowledge the pull of same-sex desire have wanted not simply to challenge the typical associations of "gay" and "lesbian" with whiteness but also to assert different experiences of desire, and thus different desires. According to Phillip Brian Harper, some groups of black men who might have identified as gay "have chosen instead to designate themselves by terms they feel reflect a specifically Afrocentric experience." Harper refers to some black men in both Philadelphia and Boston who have used the word "Adodi" to name themselves.[65]

In attempting to explain the interaction of the social and the psychic on sexual identity, Teresa de Lauretis proposes that desire exists through fantasy and is "a tension toward the other(s), a drive toward something or someone outside the self."[66] But as de Lauretis is aware, the fantasy that compels desire to take a particular shape and the tension that characterizes it are a form and effect of power. However, the power that attends a particular fantasy or discourse on desire is not unilateral and monolithic, nor is it universal and timeless. For example, most of us are raised in an environment that promotes heterosexual desire not simply by celebrating it but also by disparaging same-sex desire. We often internalize this disparagement to the point of expressing disgust toward any same-sex desire we might feel. Creating this relation to same-sex desire is one way that compulsory heterosexuality wields its power. Yet most people who come to identify as gay or lesbian are able to do so because they resist this intolerable internalization.

This resistance typically occurs because we take up what Foucault describes as a reverse discourse which approves of and therefore sustains that desire. As Foucault argues, a dominant discourse on sex also gives rise to a reverse discourse so that a desire, such as homosexual desire, that is prohibited or deemed unnatural can begin "to speak in its own behalf, to demand that its legitimacy or 'naturality' be acknowledged, often in the same vocabulary, using the same categories by which it was medically disqualified."[67] Although Foucault's personification here is typical within his work, and in line with his view that discourses are "tactical elements or blocks operating in the field of force relations," he also understands that to evaluate the tactical function of a discourse, we must ask "who is speaking, his [or her] position of power, the institutional context in which he [or she] happens to be situated" (*History of Sexuality*, 100–102). An abstraction such as homosexuality speaks because individuals take up the reverse discourse in an attempt to understand, account for, or justify this desire. In the case of homosexuality, it is more appropriate to refer to reverse discourses rather than a solitary reverse discourse, for a number of positions have been proposed for countering the religious, medical, scientific, political, and legal discourses that construct homosexuality as a sin, illness, aberration, vice, and/or crime. This proliferation of reverse discourse has made it possible for contemporary gays and lesbians to explain same-sex desire differently, to offer new material to psychic fantasy structures, and to position this desire within a perspective that not only permits it but multiplies its possible forms.[68]

The reversal of a dominant discourse on desire need not end simply in the inversion of meaning, whereby the abject desire is given positive value. David Halperin has suggested that the homosexual reverse discourse not only revalues homosexual desire but also presents new ways of desiring. I agree with Halperin, but not for the reasons he gives. According to him, this opening of meaning makes available to lesbians and gay men "a new kind of sexual identity, one characterized by its lack of a clear definitional content."[69] The homosexual now embraces the position of negativity that the dominant discourse on sexuality assigns to him or her, and happily claims "an identity without essence" (61). From this open space, the homosexual can create new possibilities for desire, new ways of desiring, and can become "queer."

But Halperin's celebration of the homosexual as an identity without an essence seems to ignore other differentials, such as race, class, or gender, that also mark homosexual identity and desire. Only a desiring subject unmarked by those differentials—in other words, a white, middle-class man—can embrace such a positioning. Thus, I argue that if the reversal of the homosexual from object to subject opens up a desiring space, it is because denaturalizing a desire (such as heterosexual or intraracial desire) urges a reconception of desire itself. This denaturalizing move highlights the contingency of all desire as well as of the binary system that structures sexual identity. It makes us aware that this binary system *is* a system, an effect of the historical organization of knowledge and a means by which the nation-state exercises power on the bodies of its citizens. Ultimately, this denaturalizing move gives us a new social discourse—a discourse of antifoundationalism—for understanding and thus relating to desire.

We should be careful not to imagine that relating to desire from this antifoundationalist position will enable us to escape the complex political technology of sexuality that oppresses us as desiring subjects. Given that this technology has produced or at least disciplined our desire, to escape it (even if that were possible) would not necessarily mean the emancipation of our desires. As Judith Butler notes in her critique of Foucault's embrace of "pleasure" as a liberatory concept, "pleasures are always already embedded in the pervasive but inarticulate law and, indeed, generated by the law they are said to defy" (*Gender Trouble*, 98). The same can be said of desires.

Nor does an antifoundationalist relation to desire necessarily mean that we take up a position of oppositionality advocated by many sectors of queer activism and theory, resisting any form of desire that is configured as normal, legitimate, or dominant. As some critics of queer theory and politics have argued, by advocating the unrestricted expression of all desires, one ultimately promotes the harm of people who cannot defend themselves. Consider, for example, the unequal power dynamics of a parent who urges a child to engage in incest. Equally crucial, oppositional resistance can end up replicating the pattern of binary thinking that attaches positive value to one side of a duality (in this case, anything or anyone "queer") and negative value to the other side (the "non-queer"). This kind of thinking breeds oppression not simply because it organizes desires into dualistic hierarchies but also because it tends to insist that desire belongs only to the individual who expresses it (the pervert, the normed heterosexual) and is not also socially formed and motivated. This is not to say that we shouldn't acknowledge the desires we have and take responsibility for the ways in which we choose to express them. It is to emphasize, to the contrary, that our desiring always has social and political effects. Even though we are taught to think of desire as a personal and private experience, it is a thoroughly social enterprise.

In short, desiring to desire from an antifoundationalist position need not lead to oppositionality or to a conviction that one can elude the dominant desiring system. Instead, taking up this relation to our desire might point in a different direction, moving us into the very heart of the system that shapes us as desiring subjects. From here we can recognize the ways in which our desire depends on the discourses that speak it into existence but also inevitably exceeds the identities provided for it. For instance, as Butler has argued, if heterosexual identity is made possible through not only the production of heterosexual desire but also the repression of homosexual desire, then that identity always contains both kinds of desires and its coherence is an impossibility. The same is true for homosexual identity. As Dollimore observes, "absence or exclusion simultaneously becomes a presence" (229). Add to these identities the presence of other kinds of desires out of which the desiring subject is produced, such as incestuous/nonincestuous, intraracial/interracial, intragenerational/intergenerational, and one can understand why Dollimore argues, "The inversion of a binary produces not merely reversal but proximities where there was difference" (229).

Consequently, we can begin to identify ways in which desires that seem mutually exclusive (such as homosexual/heterosexual, incestuous/non-incestuous, interracial/intraracial) are, in fact, interconnected and intersecting. Such recognition is not adequately represented by the trite saying that homosexuals and heterosexuals are identical because desire is universal, for the kind of recognition I am talking about pushes against the tendency to align desire and identity in a one-to-one correspondence. It asks us to acknowledge not only that homosexual and heterosexual, interracial and intraracial, incestuous and exogamous, able-bodied and disabled, and so on, depend upon each other for their very existence, but also that the lines between them are flexible and porous rather than solid and impermeable. As desiring subjects, we are formed out of a radical interconnectedness of many kinds of desires, and these desires are never simply private, somatic, and psychic, but are also caught up within a web of social discourses and power arrangements.

The consequences of an antifoundational approach to desire are myriad, and I doubt that I could trace them all here even if it were relevant to do so. A few points must be delineated since they have crucial relevance to the work of this book. First, this approach implies that contemporary sexual identities—gay, lesbian, bisexual, heterosexual, queer—are not truths about our desire but strategies of power and, potentially, strategies of resistance. While this statement may be obvious, it is worth emphasizing because it helps to explain why someone who relates to desire from an antifoundationalist perspective might still choose to identify as gay or lesbian or Adodi or transgendered. Because most of our laws and policies regarding desire are based on the sexual identities discursively provided for us, it will be still expedient to take them up for political purposes. As Davina Cooper (building on the ideas of Abdul Jan Mohamad) states, when focusing on the productive nature of power, it is important "not to marginalize rules, orders and violence (physical and psychological). Doing so underestimates the extent to which the experiences of oppressed communities are shaped by violence, prohibitions, and mandates" (16).

Second, so as not to underestimate the extent of oppression when thinking about the interconnections of desires, it is absolutely necessary to think also about the uneven power relations among those desires and the social arrangements that they maintain or resist. For example, even though the expression of both incestuous desire and homosexual desire is disparaged (to different degrees and for different reasons) today, the parts those expressions play in the maintenance of heterosexist power relations are very different. But in saying this, I also want to emphasize the importance of not viewing desires as monolithic in their effects or in the ways that they can be expressed. Neither desires nor behaviors are inherently subversive of or complicit with oppression. It is necessary to consider how the expression of these desires functions in relations of power at any given moment and place.

Finally, understanding desire and power as integrally linked means that we cannot view authorial constructions and interpretations of texts as matters of opinion: they are not only the effects of power but also its purveyors. The case of Hemingway illustrates this premise brilliantly, for it reveals that the cultural construction of Hemingway as an exemplar of white American heteromasculinity has simultaneously derived from and contributed to the maintenance of dominant notions of selfhood and sexuality. This construction has influenced how millions of people think about American individuality, masculinity, and heterosexuality. In examining the ways that critics have dealt with evidence of a transgendered or sexually ambiguous Hemingway, we have already seen the powerful pull of the status quo; subsequent chapters will extend this examination. Here, however, it's worth citing one more example, this one from the popular media, to illustrate how a reconstituted Hemingway is performing the same public relations function for heteromasculinity as did the representation of Hemingway featured most prominently in *Life* and *Look* magazines during the 1950s.

In a letter written to Ann Landers in the fall of 1990, a father and husband ("Mr. T. B.") related the story of his six-year-old son ("Jack") being raised as a girl by his mother, the writer's wife ("Susan"). When Jack was born, Susan was disappointed because she had wanted a girl. As a result, Susan had raised Jack as a girl. When the boy started kindergarten the year before, he was enrolled as a girl, and no one at the school knows differently. The writer believes that Susan is ruining their son for life, but Susan thinks otherwise, noting the example of famous men who were raised as girls, including Hemingway. She insists that when Jackie reaches puberty, she's going to turn him into a male, and "he will be as manly as Hemingway." The writer is not convinced.

Landers's reply is brief and to the point. She confirms that Hemingway's mother dressed him in girls' clothes, attempting to create the impression that he and his older sister were twins. With this confirmation, Landers shifts to her diagnosis. Even though Hemingway was a successful artist, "his personal life was a mess." His mother was a "bizarre woman," and his father was "an angry, bitter man, trapped in a nightmarish marriage." Landers lists the suicides in the family: Hemingway's father, his sister Ursula, and his brother Leicester. With this context to aid her, she then determines that the writer's wife needs counseling and the son requires help too. Landers urges the writer to "enlist the cooperation of the child's pediatrician, his teachers—anyone who will help [him] to rescue the unfortunate boy from this sick situation."[70]

In this letter and Landers's response, Hemingway's identity and history are invoked as strategy: their example of both what a man can and shouldn't be reinforces the morality of our binary system of gender and sexuality. Deviate from that system, either in child-rearing practices or in behavior/desire, and you are unfortunate, in need of help, or fostering a sick situation. Medical personnel, the educational system, the family, and a particular construction of the historical-textual Hemingway all collaborate to ensure that no other conclusion can be reached. The possibility that it is the sex-gender system that is unfortunate, in need of help, or an abettor of a sick situation is never considered. Nor could it be given that the logic of that system subtends the construction of Hemingway that is used to prove its logic.

The Conjunction of History, Theory, and Desire

In acknowledging that desire permeates our interpretive energy (a not-so-original premise given the work of such critics as Roland Barthes), the question arises as to whether we are thereby allowed to read authors and their work in any way we desire. In fact, I have already answered this question. Our desire is guided by history and theory. We cannot go beyond our perspective of desire, our understanding of how the desiring subject is formed, be it through biological instincts, psychological processes, identity structures, social conditions, or a combination of these. Nor can we go beyond the limits set by our understanding of history and of the author as a historical subject.

Yet, as I have also said, theory and history shape and enable our desire as well. For the past twenty years—with the advent of such fields as gay and lesbian studies, African American studies, and postcolonial studies—historians have retold the history of desire so that desires that were once avoided, neglected, or denied by mainstream history are being inscribed into narrative. In the case of gay and lesbian studies, some of this historical work has been the kind that recovers gays and lesbians from the heterosexualization of history. While such history-writing has been crucial for contesting the heterosexist presumption of most histories, it sometimes fails to examine its own presumptions about the origins of sexual desire (within such narratives, individuals from the past who showed evidence of loving members of their own sex become proto-lesbians or gays). In other cases, however, the history draws upon the antifoundationalist work of writers such as Foucault to explore the ways in which the production and distribution of desires in a particular place and time were connected to technologies of self, sex, and power.[71]

As should be clear by now, my own desire to desire has been influenced by and is caught up in this latter project. Given this connection, one of my strongest urges is to unravel the invisible seams of the construction of Hemingway that depicts him as purely heterosexual, be that heterosexuality linked to the homosocial misogynist that many feminists have detested or to the androgynous gender explorer envisioned by recent Hemingway critics. Instead, I would construct Hemingway's sexual identity on the border between the heterosexual and the homosexual, in the tension of negotiating these supposedly incompatible identities. Such a construction begins with the recognition that Hemingway came to sexual awareness in the early twentieth century in the United States and Paris, a time when the dichotomization of sexual identity into homosexual and heterosexual was taking shape in both places. But it also contends that while he became bound by this system, he continued to feel the effects of its instabilities and to question its validity as a grid for understanding human desire. Consider the following:

———

Writing about working class culture in turn-of-the-century New York City, George Chauncey argues that the lines between "normal" and "abnormal" were differently drawn than they are today. Because sexual desire was regarded as "fundamentally gendered," men were permitted to engage in sexual relations with other men, "often on a regular basis, without requiring them to regard themselves—or to regard each other—as gay." The distinguishing identity was that of the "fairy," who announced his sexual desire for other men through his "womanlike character."[72]

In an early draft of *The Sun Also Rises*, Bill Gorton tells Jake that New York circles have marked him (Bill) as "crazy": "Also I'm supposed to be crazy to get married. Would marry anybody at any time. . . . Since Charley Gordon and I had an apartment together last winter, I suppose I'm a fairy. That probably explains everything." Bill then lashes out at New York society: "My God," he says, "it would make you sick. They don't talk about complexes anymore. It's bad form. But they all believe it. And every literary bastard never goes to bed at night not knowing but that he'll wake up in the morning and find himself a fairy. There are plenty of real ones too."[73]

George Seldes, a writer who knew Hemingway in the 1920s and 1930s: "At Gertrude Stein's weekly literary parties I'm sure there were lesbians and male homosexuals. Hemingway saw them all the time. I always thought his masculine prowess was a cover-up for a feeling that he was exhibiting slightly feminine traits simply because he was an artist and one of the literary set."[74]

A "dark young man" in a blue suit waits for the coiffure and presumes that the man in the next chair is some kind of pimp. But the dark young man corrects this presumption when he sees the man walk. The man isn't a pimp, he decides, but a homosexual. He wonders why he should think the man wasn't a homosexual: "Because I'm in here myself. Just like an 'upsidaisy.'"[75]

———

Books that Hemingway owned: Havelock Ellis, *Studies in the Psychology of Sex* (1936, 4 vols.); George William Henry, *All the Sexes: A Study of Masculinity and Femininity* (1955); Alfred Charles Kinsey, Wardell B. Pomeroy and Clyde E. Martin, *Sexual Behavior in the Human Male* (1948); Anton Kristen Nyström, *The Natural Laws of Sexual Life: Medical-sociological Researches* (1919); Theodor Reik, *Of Love and Lust: On the Psychoanalysis of Romantic and Sexual Emotions* (1957); Eugen Steinach, *Sex and Life: Forty Years of Biological and Medical Experiments* (1940); Michael George Schofield [Gordon Westwood], *Society and the Homosexual* (1953).[76]

"In January [of 1921], Ernest started reading Havelock Ellis's *Psychology of Sex*. Hadley told Ernest she'd tried to read the serialized version in the *Literary Digest*, 'but scanning the heads of chapters told me frankly I didn't want it—probably should have pushed on; don't know enough about the facts of life but calculate neither did Adam & Eve.' Ernest became obsessed with the seven-volume work and referred to it in all his letters."[77]

Havelock Ellis: "Not only a large proportion of persons who may fairly be considered normally heterosexual have at some time in their lives experienced a feeling which may be termed sexual toward individuals of their own sex, but a very large proportion of persons who are definitely and markedly homosexual are found to have experienced sexual attraction toward, and have had relationships with, persons of the opposite sex. . . . While therefore the division into heterosexual, bisexual, and homosexual is a useful superficial division, it is scarcely a scientific classification."[78]

"Late in life, [Bill] Bird recalled that on one of their train trips together . . . they had discussed homosexuality. Perhaps as a joke or as an at-

Hemingway, fourth from left, with bullfighter friends on a swimming and paella party near Madrid (John F. Kennedy Library, photographer unknown).

tempt to shock his friend, Hemingway suggested that it might be worth experimenting. It was an uneasy occasion—at least Bird remembered it as such—and it left a decidedly unsettling impression on his mind."[79]

When Brett Ashley and her homosexual companions enter the bal musette where Jake Barnes is waiting, he thinks, "I was angry. Somehow they always made me angry. I know they are supposed to be amusing, and you should be tolerant, but I wanted to swing on one, any one, anything to shatter their superior, simpering composure."[80]

◢━◣

The narrator of *Death in the Afternoon:* "If [El Greco] was [a fairy] he should redeem, for the tribe, the prissy exhibitionistic, aunt-like withered old maid moral arrogance of a Gide; the lazy, conceited debauchery of a Wilde who betrayed a generation; the nasty, sentimental pawing of humanity of a Whitman and all the mincing gentry."[81]

In examining this passage, Nancy Comley and Robert Scholes comment: "(it is interesting that [Hemingway] takes Whitman's [homosexuality] for granted at a time when many would have denied it fiercely)," but the "most intriguing of the condemnations is that of Wilde. One would like to know what Hemingway had in mind as Wilde's betrayal of a generation. Did he mean that by provoking his own legal difficulties Wilde made it harder for other homosexuals? Or that by writing the saccharine prose and verse of *De Profundis* and *The Ballad of Reading Gaol* he betrayed the wit and irony of his earlier work? These are real questions, but we have no easy answers for them. In the manuscript he had written 'betrayed a generation and himself'—which might tilt the interpretive balance toward reading this as a condemnation of Wilde's coming out of the closet so disastrously (K50, 7)."[82]

So how did Wilde betray a generation? Alan Sinfield writes, "Oscar Wilde's celebrated speech about the love that dare not speak its name—when you come to look at it—is justifying non-sexual love. 'My image of Oscar in the dock loses its halo,' Neil Bartlett observes; 'He lied, and he lied at a crucial moment in our history, just when we were about to appear. If he had told the truth, everything might have been different.'"[83]

From *A Moveable Feast* after Hemingway claims to have overheard Gertrude Stein speaking intimately with Alice B. Toklas: ". . . I could never make friends again truly [with Stein], neither in my heart nor in my head. When you cannot make friends any more in your head is the worst. But it was more complicated than that."[84]

———◆———

"A lesbian and gay population, moreover, is defined by multiple boundaries that make the question who is and is not 'one of them' not merely ambiguous but rather a perpetually and necessarily contested issue."[85]

Marita to David Bourne: "It's not perversion. It's variety."
"Is that what variety is? . . . I like our variety," David said. "Our infinite variety."[86]

From the Kinsey report on male sexuality: "Males do not represent two discrete populations, heterosexual and homosexual. The world is not to be divided into sheep and goats. Not all things are black nor all things white. It is a fundamental taxonomy that nature rarely deals with discrete categories. Only the human mind invents categories and tries to force facts into separated pigeon-holes. The living world is a continuum in each and every one of its aspects. The sooner we learn this concerning human sexual behavior the sooner we shall reach a sound understanding of the realities of sex."[87]

David Bourne to himself: "Maybe it's how people always were and never admitted and they made rules <against it> as stupid <as many of the others are. Who knows how anything really was? They lie enough about how things are that we know about>."[88]

In Hemingway's "The Sea Change," the woman who is leaving her male lover for another woman tells him:
"We're made up of all sorts of things. You've known that. You've used it well enough."
"You don't have to say that again."
"Because that explains it to you."
"All right," he said. "All right."
"You mean all wrong. I know. It's all wrong. But I'll come back. I told you I'd come back. I'll come back right away."
"No you won't."
"I'll come back."
"No, you won't. Not to me."[89]

"Did it happen that way?" A. E. Hotchner asked Hemingway in 1954. "Did Charley [the man Hemingway claimed was the source for the male protagonist in 'The Sea Change'] take her back?"

"I don't know," Hemingway supposedly replied. "But one afternoon I saw Charley's girl walking along the beach with the girl she had gone to. Had expected other girl to be a typical bull-dyke: pompadour hair, tweed suit, low oxfords. But she was as pretty as Charley's girl. Those two beauties walking hand in hand on the beach."[90]

As the preceding mosaic implies, I construct Hemingway's desire not only through reading his life history but also through reading his fictional texts, including his fictional women. In this, I am in accord with a critic such as Barthes: "The text is a fetish object, and *this fetish desires me*. The text chooses me, by a whole disposition of invisible screens, selective baffles: vocabulary, references, readability, etc.; and lost in the midst of a text (not *behind* it, like a *deus ex machina*) there is always the other, the author" (*Pleasure*, 27). The text, as a product not simply of the desiring subject who writes and of the one who reads but also of the social out of which those subjects are formed, is a primary place where the author's desire is everywhere to be read and is everywhere being read.

Of course, locating Hemingway's desire in the tension between heterosexuality and homosexuality gives rise to the obvious question: how many people living in the twentieth-century Western world haven't had their desires situated in the same way and space? Including me. In fact, my sexual experiences have made me acutely aware of the way in which desire is constituted through social discourses and of the tensions that arise in negotiating supposedly antithetical desires. Although I now identify as lesbian, I have a lengthy history of identifying as heterosexual. I've become aware of how desire lies in the gaps, in the overlaps, in the contradictions, in the ambiguities of our sex/gender system, an experiential awareness that has been shaped and supported by my antifoundationalist understanding of desire. But to argue that Hemingway's desire (like mine) can be located in the tension between heterosexuality and homosexuality is, in fact, part of my point. I am theorizing the faultlines of our sexual system, especially as that system claims the existence of permanent and coherent sexual identities, by looking at a man who has become one of the most consistent and persistent icons of heteromasculinity in our age. Obviously, I have only begun this exploration, which besides requiring further support also needs to consider the part that other desires—particularly those connected to race and the able-body, two key components of Hemingway's image—play in constructions of the desiring Hemingway and interpretations of his fiction. The next two chapters will render many of these details as I reread key Hemingway works and representations of Hemingway's identity within new contexts for understanding desire.

Finally, what I hope will emerge from this book is a recognition of the way in which biographical reading in a postmodern age is inescapable, complicated, and political. Hayden White suggests that when we recognize that history-writing is "not a matter of choosing between objectivity and distortion, but between different strategies for constituting 'reality' in thought so as to deal with it in different ways," we must then make choices "with a full understanding of the kind of human nature to the constitution of which they will contribute if they are taken as valid" (22–23). White thus addresses the limits of discursive representation and of the historian's bias by proposing that the historian accept responsibility for the models of human consciousness that he or she circulates. Such accountability is paramount, White implies, because history-writing is not an academic exercise but has effects in the material world. As Rosemary Hennessy argues, when historical narratives are "no longer taken to be transparent vehicles of an empirical archive," the reasons for reading and writing histories "can be taken to lie in the ideological force which they—or their narration—(continue to) exert on the present" (118). I am arguing that, like history-writing, the enterprises of constructing authors and of interpreting their texts are thoroughly political, for they have consequences for how people think, act, and desire.

3

CASTING OUT FORBIDDEN DESIRES FROM *THE GARDEN OF EDEN:* CAPITALISM AND THE PRODUCTION OF HEMINGWAY

> It would be a pity if the criticism of [Hemingway's] literature contin-
> ued to shellac those texts, immobilizing their complexities and power
> and luminations just below its tight, reflecting surface.
> —Toni Morrison (*Playing in the Dark*)

> "I didn't know I'd ever be like this."
> —Hemingway's Catherine Bourne in *The Garden of Eden*

The Hemingway text that has done the most to encourage critics to reconsider Hemingway's identity is the posthumously published *The Garden of Eden*. This encouragement has intensified as scholars have begun
to study Hemingway's original manuscripts and to measure them against
the published novel. What these scholars have shown is that the editor of
The Garden of Eden, Tom Jenks, had a heavy hand in the book's composition, despite his comments to the contrary. In terms of Hemingway's
identity and reputation, what Jenks—acting on behalf of Hemingway's
publisher, Scribner's—left out of *The Garden of Eden* turns out to be as
tantalizing as the apple that the serpent offered to Eve.

The publisher's note prefacing *The Garden of Eden* states that "some
cuts" have been made to Hemingway's manuscript but nothing added.
This note concludes, "In every significant respect the work is all the au-

thor's." Such statements reassure us that the novel we are about to read is the one Hemingway wrote, that the task of editing has consisted of eliminating a few words or passages that were perhaps repetitious or infelicitous, something Hemingway would have done had he lived long enough to see the project through to publication. Ever since scholars have gained access to the manuscripts of *The Garden of Eden*, this publisher's note has seemed more and more suspicious. E. L. Doctorow was among the first to suggest that this disclaimer of editorial interference is more fictional than the novel itself. Given that the published novel is one-third the length of the longest manuscript—a cut of approximately 130,000 words—the phrase "some cuts" is, as Doctorow suggests, disingenuous at best.[1] Having studied the manuscripts at the Kennedy Library, I can confirm, however, that there is a kind of truth behind Jenks's statement that the publisher's note is generally accurate and that "beyond a small number of minor interpolations nothing has been added to *The Garden of Eden*."[2] Paradoxically, it is also accurate to say, as Barbara Solomon does, that Jenks has so significantly changed this published version that the publisher's note can be reversed to read: "In almost no significant respect is this book the author's."[3] How is it possible that *The Garden of Eden* is and is not Hemingway's work?

The answer is that Jenks's *Garden* is a reading of Hemingway's *Garden* based on the popular, commodified Hemingway and his work. As I will argue shortly, Jenks organized his version of Hemingway's story in accord with the popular image of Hemingway, thus creating a book that the public could imagine Hemingway would write and that critics could defend as Hemingway's even if it isn't the book he did write. More accurately, Jenks's version isn't the book we can claim Hemingway wrote when we have access to the full manuscript. Jenks has actually done what many Hemingway critics have been doing for years: he has filtered Hemingway's work through the lens of the cultural construction of Hemingway.

Even those critics who have examined the manuscripts and provided insight into the meaning of the excised pages have failed to explore the most radical implications of Hemingway's work on this book, a failure that suggests the extent to which the Hemingway public image conditions what we are able to see—or say. The critics who have come closest to comprehending these implications are Nancy Comley, Robert Scholes, and Carl Eby. In *Hemingway's Genders*, Comley and Scholes argue that Hemingway's manuscript connects erotic fantasies about race change and sex change, a thesis that resembles that of Toni Morrison (*Playing in the Dark*), who arrived at her position without benefit of the full manu-script.[4] Comley and Scholes's thesis has since been taken up and pursued from a psychoanalytic perspective by Eby.

However far these critics have taken us into the heart of Hemingway's unfinished novel, they have not gone far enough in explaining the nature and significance of the changes and why Jenks felt he had to excise them from his version. Most important, Comley and Scholes fail to give ade-quate attention to lesbian desire and male homosexual desire, desires that are crucial to the drama and that, I maintain, precipitate the central con-flicts of the text. Eby has filled in some of this missing material, especially in regard to David's "homoeroticism" and the significance of "racial and sexual 'others'" for Hemingway.[5] Indeed, Eby's greatest contribution lies in his explication of the numerous references to Africa that Jenks cut from the Hemingway's manuscript and their implications for reconfig-uring Hemingway's identity. Still, like Comley and Scholes, he does not fully elaborate the important ways in which Catherine's efforts to change her race are different from her experiments with changing David's sex, as well as her own.[6]

By referring to scenes and characters that Jenks cut from Heming-way's manuscript and by reading the actions of Hemingway's characters within the context of discourses of sex, gender, race, and sexuality promi-nent early in the twentieth century and often functional today, I argue that Hemingway's manuscript is obsessed with desires that transgress societal laws. This obsession centers especially around the laws of sexual difference (the requirement of distinct gender identities for men and women), compulsory heterosexuality, and miscegenation. To put this another way, Hemingway's characters are preoccupied with attempting to step outside the social to discover "the natural" and "the way things really are." But to step out of society into a more "natural" state is im-possible because social discourses structure the subject and the concept of "the natural." Even resistance to these discourses can be part of them. As Foucault puts it, in the case of sexuality, prohibitive laws eroticize the very practices that come under their scrutiny so that prohibitions be-come imbued with power: "power asserting itself in the pleasure of showing off, scandalizing, or resisting" (*History of Sexuality*, 45). From this perspective, the transgressive act does not stand in opposition to the dominant order but is firmly rooted within it.

This does not mean that the prevailing system can never be challenged because, ironically, discourse also "undermines and exposes [power], ren-ders it fragile and makes it possible to thwart it." This reverse discourse can then begin to speak in its own behalf, to demand, as has homosexuality, "that its legitimacy or 'naturality' be acknowledged, often in the same vocabulary, using the same categories by which it was medically disqualified" (Foucault, *History of Sexuality*, 101). Hemingway's characters never take up this reverse discourse, despite their assumptions that their behavior is outrageous and "tribal," that is, against or outside societal imperatives. However, their repeated efforts to change their sex and to engage in an outlaw sexuality does finally serve as a kind of reverse discourse. This subversive element evokes many questions, which I will address later in this chapter, about how we might construct Hemingway's relation to his public image. It also contrasts sharply with Jenks's edited version which, endeavoring to protect that image, reinscribes the dominant regime page by page, and thereby enacts the desire of capitalism.

This chapter will thus extend my work on Hemingway by examining the role that patriarchal capitalism has played in controlling the representation of desire in his work and in constructing his identity as unconditionally heterosexual. Although my focus is Hemingway, the kinds of controls I explore—editorial, publishing, marketing—influence ("manage" might be a better word) how critics and readers construct all authors, and my argument might therefore be read as pointing toward this larger context. In addition, by expanding my scope to the structuring of desire promoted by capitalism, I will interrogate further the personal, cultural, and historical processes of meaning-making delineated in Chapter 2. To state this differently, I will attempt to situate those processes more fully by connecting them to the dominating socio-economic structure of the United States: a patriarchal capitalism that is also racist and heterosexist. Finally, this chapter begins the process of providing additional evidence for my argument that Hemingway's identity might be constructed at the border between the heterosexual and the homosexual, in the tension of negotiating these supposedly antithetical desires.

Jenks's Hemingway

One of Jenks's harshest critics, K. J. Peters, has called for Jenks to "explain his criteria, so that we may judge his interpretation and see past any biases he may possess."[7] Although Jenks does not state his criteria as explicitly as Peters wishes, he has revealed his editorial policy. In the few interviews and lectures given before he announced that he would not discuss *The Garden of Eden* again, Jenks frequently indicates that he was working in line with Hemingway's "vision." For example, in a 1986 interview, he states that he discarded the work of a previous editor who had attempted to prepare *The Garden of Eden* for publication because "The editor had made cuts without any true understanding of the author's vision" ("Interview," 83). In a case like this, Jenks insists, an editor must be careful "not to damage what the writer is doing" ("Interview," 85).

How did Jenks know what Hemingway was doing when he was writing *The Garden of Eden*? Jenks's immediate response is that he saw in the manuscript "Hemingway's desire to take on his own myth without, however, destroying or relinquishing it."[8] Yet Jenks's own attitude towards editing Hemingway actually runs counter to the intentions he presents in this answer. Jenks states that he became a sort of medium for the spirit of Hemingway: "The book, its author did pass through me in a powerful and intimate way" ("Editing Hemingway," 31). Moreover, he tells us that serving as Hemingway's conduit was no easy task: "It was like sitting under a mountain to work with him," Jenks discloses. "Make no mistake—he was very present and exacted a tribute from me. I had never imagined sacrificing myself to anyone the way I wound up having to sacrifice myself to him. The authority for a work must always rest with the writer" ("Interview," 86). Jenks's account of the editing of Hemingway's work begins to sound much like the writing of Genesis itself. "Literature," Jenks tells us, "is embodied in Hemingway. The man is immortal. There's no question" ("Interview," 86).

A portrait of the artist begins to emerge: this "Hemingway" who passed through Jenks and exacted sacrifice is the public Hemingway that Jenks claims Hemingway was attempting to "take on" in writing *The Garden of Eden*. In part, this image of Hemingway is related to the traditional notion of the author as an isolated genius who controls the meaning of his text. One thinks of the infamous stories about Hemingway's strict instructions regarding the publishing of his work and his anger at those, such as Philip Young and Charles Fenton, whom he thought had misread him. Never mind that Jenks's own involvement in the project of preparing Hemingway's manuscript contradicts the notion of the artist as the sole creator and source of meaning. To ensure that no one questions the "authority" of Scribner's *Garden*, Jenks must promote this notion—even though in doing so he ends up sounding like some sort of New Age channeler of Hemingway's spirit.

But Hemingway's public image is also connected to his reputation as a writer of stories about and for men, and Jenks is ultimately guided by this connection. When Jenks was trying to decide whether the manuscript he had assembled was worth publishing, he gave it to two contemporary writers—Raymond Carver and Tobias Wolff—to read, writers "who themselves *write in the language that men use*" ("Interview," 84; emphasis added). Jenks's Hemingway, a demigod among men and male writers, is the cultural myth created by critics, readers, biographers, journalists, editors (like Jenks), and, of course, Hemingway himself. This is the Hemingway who Leonard Kriegel says is "part precursor, part prophet, a man whose writing resonated with those specific kinds of experience which promised to separate me [and other men of his generation] from the fate that might conceivably be mine" (95).

Considering his view of Hemingway, it is hardly surprising to learn that Jenks was concerned with "honoring and protecting" Hemingway ("Editing Hemingway," 33). With these vows of commitment guiding his editorial decisions, Jenks gave us a novel written, in effect, by way of a cultural myth. Because Hemingway was often guided in his writing by that myth, one cannot totally fault Jenks for being controlled by it; in fact, one could argue that Jenks was following Hemingway's "vision" insofar as he let the myth influence the work. To that extent, Jenks has been true to Hemingway. Still, one expects an editor to have more distance than an author, and the fact that Jenks lacked such distance simply reconfirms my argument that many people are invested in the heterosexist discourse that underwrites the traditional identity of Hemingway.

One might also argue that Jenks's decisions were hardly personal ones, conjoined as he was by the profit-making interests of Scribner's. The exclusive publisher of Hemingway's work since the 1920s, Scribner's has always had the most to gain financially from the circulation of Hemingway's cultural identity, although Scribner's has not been the sole benefactor, as is indicated, for instance, by a recent Barnes and Noble catalogue that promotes Hemingway as the "He-Man of Twentieth-Century Literature." Given the conservative interests of the book publishing industry, it seems plausible that Charles Scribner, Jr. himself, chose Jenks—a former editor at *Esquire*—to assemble Hemingway's text because he knew he would produce a novel that would protect the Hemingway legend. Certainly Scribner could have refused, as he had on at least one occasion, to publish any version that did not meet with his approval.[9]

Speculating in this way brings the intersections among capitalism, the heterosexual hegemony, and Hemingway's cultural image to the fore. On the one hand, American capitalism has relied heavily on a continued heterosexual dominance, and this reliance has undoubtedly influenced the construction of Hemingway as an icon of heterosexual masculinity. Whether manifested in the control that Scribner's has held over material that is publicly linked to Hemingway's name or whether located, more generally, in the heterosexism that permeates work on Hemingway, the mark of capitalism is all over the historical-textual Hemingway. On the other hand, the critical and cultural configuration of Hemingway as a model of white heterosexual masculinity has been one of patriarchal capitalism's most successful agents for promoting white heteromasculinity. However we delineate the association between capitalism and the traditional construction of Hemingway, in Jenks's redaction of *The Garden of Eden*, consumer capitalism joined forces with the psychic, social, and sexual needs of a segment of the U.S. population.

Exploring The Garden: The Difference between Suntanning and Sodomy

One of the most notable differences between Hemingway's manuscript and the published novel is the amount of space each gives to Marita. The manuscript devotes many more pages to her, especially after Catherine's departure. Some of these pages are given over to continuing the fantasy that co-stars Marita in the published version in which David "converts" Marita to monogamous heterosexuality. In those pages we learn that Marita has never been sexually fulfilled, by either a man (even her ex-husband) or a woman, until she sleeps with David (422.1–16, p. 21).

Marita's unsatisfactory sexual experiences with both men and women combine to make her the most desirable woman in the world, at least within the context of a *Playboy* fantasy. She is the virgin whose first lover sends her singing orgasmic praise, the divorcée whose bad experience with men is erased by one night with Mr. Right, as well as the lesbian who is converted forever to heterosexuality by the sexual prowess and skill of her first male lover. Significantly, her history makes Marita a combination of all women who threaten patriarchy (virgin, divorcée, lesbian), but this threat is defused when it turns out that, as patriarchy suspected all along, she simply needed to meet the right (heterosexual) man. To reinforce both Marita's sexual conversion and her initiation into the joys of heterosexual sex, we hear a great deal about how Marita progresses from feeling pain to feeling pleasure (422.1–18, p. 11, 2nd p. 11). So stimulated is Marita by David that at one point she climaxes simply by kissing him (422.1–19, p. 18). As the ultimate sign of David's sexual vigor and

Marita's receptiveness, Marita thinks they have conceived a child (422.1–29, p. 27; 422.1–34, p. 15). Given all that David has done for her, it is no wonder, within the realm of the *Playboy* fantasy, that Marita makes him her mission in life: from strategically touching him while he sleeps to induce erotic dreams (422.1–27, pp. 31–35) to supporting his work. Marita calculates her every move; everything she does, she does for David.

But if the Marita of the manuscript is a pumped-up version of the happily heterosexual, happily monogamous, self-sacrificing, stand-by-her-man Marita of the published novel, she also provides crucial information about David that the novel refuses us, information that has to do with David's desires and needs. Comley and Scholes note that Jenks's editing of the novel gives the impression by means of its omissions that Marita restores David to a more "normal" erotic life, whereas the manuscript indicates that it is precisely the "abnormality" of their relationship that refreshes and renews his creative energies (102). Curiously, Comley and Scholes do not fully identify or explore this "abnormality," an oversight that must be emended if we are to understand what "abnormality" consists of and how it functions in Hemingway's manuscript.

The key is Catherine, as Marita acknowledges in the manuscript. As she makes her way into David's life, Marita repeatedly thinks about her debt to Catherine (422.1–27, p. 33; 422.1–36, p. 35). She admits that she was jealous of Catherine and David's nighttime activities, knowledge she gained by reading David's narrative of their adventures. Marita is determined to use this knowledge in her relations with David because she believes that David must have liked what he and Catherine did or he couldn't have written about it so well in the narrative (422.1–36, p. 14). In fact, Marita will not only replace Catherine, she will eclipse her: "We can do everything," she thinks, and then continues: "It will be all new and all we don't know will be new. We're darker than she was inside I know. . . . She was adventurous and compelled. . . . I'm compelled but not by me. By him and what he can do. I suppose it's a magic and it was so wonderful I could know about it" (422.1–36, pp. 14–15). What is it that Marita feels more qualified to do than Catherine? What is it that she thinks David must miss (422.1–36, p. 14)? What is it that David wants but doesn't want?

The answer to these questions lies in the nature and implications of the changes that Catherine introduces into their lives, one (skin darkening) which requires sunlight, and the other (sex/gender role reversals) which requires darkness. Part of Catherine's reason for initiating these changes is to challenge theories that operate as prescriptions within the "civilized" world: "Why do we have to go by everyone else's rules? We're us" (*Garden*, 15).[10] This is a mission that David also occasionally voices: "Maybe it's how people always were and never admitted and they made rules <against it> as stupid <as many of the others are. . . . Who knows how anything really was? They lie enough about how things are that we know about>" (422.1–8, 2nd part of chap. 13, p. 7). But in their attempt to discover how things really are (nature), David and Catherine reveal how impossible it is to extricate themselves from the social, "everyone else's rules." For example, Catherine's effort to alter her racial identity does not challenge the ideology of racism but instead reinstates that ideology with a vengeance.

Toni Morrison observes that "Catherine well understands the association of blackness with strangeness, with taboo—understands also that blackness is something one can 'have' or appropriate . . . . Whiteness here is a deficiency" (87). In fact, Catherine's longings to "become" a Somali and to visit Africa are driven by what bell hooks identifies as a white imperialist fantasy that imagines the African body as the site of extreme sexual pleasure and Africa as "a real primitive paradise."[11] "Is it true that Somali women have ways of holding a man so he can never leave them?" Catherine asks David (422.1–17, p. 25). Assuming that it is, and David confirms this assumption by recounting his personal experience with Somali women, Catherine decides that she is "going to be so dark" that David will be "helpless": "White women will always bore you" (quoted in Comley and Scholes, 92).

By darkening her skin, Catherine expects to increase both her pleasure and David's. She will become the transgressive desiring and desired subject, the sexual primitive who knows how to find and to give complete sexual pleasure. Catherine's wish to alter her race is thus drawn from the ideology of white racism that depends upon retaining strict boundaries between blacks (nature) and whites (culture). In coloring her skin, she is not demonstrating the artificiality of racial designations but is attempting to implement a white fantasy about the racialized Other. The success of Catherine's tanning will be realized when she and David are made to sit at a separate table on their way to Africa, that is, when the rules of racism are enforced (422.1–2, chap. 4, p. 3).

Catherine's immersion in the ideology of white racism is reflected in her continual lightening of her hair, an action that accentuates her identity as a white woman. With her blond hair and her other white features, Catherine might be the darkest white woman some people have ever seen, but she is unmistakably white. In this context, Catherine's "darkness" comes to signify not so much her changing racial identity as her shifting spiritual or moral state, a state that is gauged by the things she and David do in the dark. Indeed, Catherine's nighttime games tell a different story because they actually pose a threat to another dominant ideology, the ideology of compulsory heterosexuality. The seriousness of this threat can be measured by the changes Jenks made to Hemingway's manuscript, for although he removed many passages in which Catherine, David, and Marita discuss Africa and the African people, his deeper cuts involve scenes that render, or might be interpreted as rendering, homosexuality.

By excising most of the exchanges regarding Africa, Jenks reduced the impression that Hemingway and his characters were obsessed with the African Other, especially as that Other represents an opportunity for the civilized white to transgress cultural proscriptions and discover a more "natural" self. Jenks thus reduced the chance that critics might use *The Garden of Eden* as another piece of evidence verifying Hemingway's racism. But as Morrison's reading of the published novel reveals, one can still detect the obsession with Africa and race in the scenes that Jenks retained. Similarly, the published version contains substantial traces of the manuscript's obsession with homosexuality, although critics of both the novel and the manuscript have avoided exploring these vestiges, preferring to talk instead about "abnormal" or "transgressive" sexuality or androgyny.[12] But these ambiguous terms are deceptions preventing us from seeing what's really at hand.

Tracking the traces of homosexuality to the manuscript, we discover the extent to which Hemingway and his characters are fascinated with homosexual desire, especially as it appears to represent "natural" desires that society has tried to suppress through religious and scientific discourse. However, as I will describe in more detail in a moment, their fascination is complicated by early twentieth-century scientific-medical discourse that correlated erotic desire with either the homosexual or the heterosexual body. Because it is actually possible for someone who *acts* heterosexual to *be* homosexual under the dictates of this discourse, Catherine's and David's crossing of sexual boundaries becomes more complex, and more dangerous, than their crossing of racial ones.

Early in both the manuscript and the novel, Catherine and David seem to be the perfect heterosexual couple, newly in love, newly married, and insatiable in their honeymoon lovemaking. Their union could even serve as a model of the companionate marriage advocated for husbands and wives in the 1920s and 1930s, a marriage based on friendship and sexual

satisfaction for both partners.[13] But late one afternoon Catherine introduces trouble into this idyllic world by springing a "big surprise." She
has cut her long hair "as short as a boy's" and now declares, "I'm a girl.
But now I'm a boy too and I can do anything and anything and anything."[14] Catherine asks David if he sees why it's dangerous, and he says
he does. Word of her haircut spreads through the village. Soon many of
the villagers stop by the café where Catherine and David are sitting to
look at Catherine's hair "without being rude." As the narrator explains,
"No decent girls had ever had their hair cut short like that in this part of
the country and even in Paris it was rare and strange and could be beautiful or could be very bad. It could mean too much or it could only mean
showing the beautiful shape of a head that could never be shown as well"
(*Garden*, 16).

Whether Catherine's haircut will mean too much or nothing at all
seems to be answered that night when she and David are in bed and she
wants him to become her girl, "Catherine," while she becomes "Peter."
By selecting for herself a name that is a slang term for the penis,[15] Catherine signifies her desire to assume the power of the privileged male, to be
able to "do anything and anything and anything." She recognizes that
lacking the phallus defines her condition as woman, a condition of boredom and societal impotence. As we learn later, Catherine's feeling of impotence is amplified by the fact that she has not yet become pregnant
(*Garden*, 71)—she cannot even enjoy the only social role that gives
women power—and by the fact that her husband's power is increasing
daily as his authorial reputation spreads. By changing her sex, Catherine seeks a way to uncastrate herself, to possess the power of her writer-
husband.

But Catherine's nighttime plans imply more than her longing to experience male power; they also indicate her desire to experience male desire, specifically, David's desire. By giving her name to David, in effect
transforming him into herself, and by adopting a name that represents
the physical locus of David's desire, Catherine becomes David's desire
while he becomes hers. To enact this transfer, she replays their lovemaking, with the roles reversed. With Catherine on top of him, David feels
"something and then her hand holding him and searching lower and he
helped with his hands and then lay back in the dark and did not think at
all and only felt the weight and the strangeness inside and she said, 'Now
you can't tell who is who can you?'" (*Garden*, 17). "No," David replies,
and with this, Catherine asserts that he is changing and is now her girl

Catherine: "Will you change and be my girl and let me take you?" (*Garden*, 17). Although reviewers of the novel criticized Hemingway (or Jenks) for being elliptical in this passage, wanting specifics about the couple's actions, clearly Catherine has sodomized David. This is what is meant by "the strangeness inside" and by Catherine's request to "let me take you." Several crossed out words in the manuscript support this interpretation. Originally Hemingway wrote that David felt "something that yielded and entered" (422.1–1, p. 20). But with or without the phrase, there's no doubt that Catherine/Peter is penetrating David/Catherine. In this way, the marriage union is completed with each partner knowing how it feels to be the other, an exchange of desire and identities.

Of course, the exchange and change are not that simple. That Catherine's and David's transformations involve more than a simple reversal of the heterosexual union is configured in the directions Catherine gives David for making the change. Entreating him to love and understand her, Catherine asks David to change like the sculpture in the Rodin museum (422.1–1, pp. 20–21). Catherine's reference to the Rodin statue is another part of Hemingway's manuscript that Jenks omitted, and it is significant in that Rodin's sculpture, *The Metamorphoses of Ovid*, depicts two women embracing, one reclining in the arms of the other who is kneeling over her. Although Catherine's description of the statue seems to convey her impression that one of the figures has changed—or is in the process of changing—sex, the developed breasts of both figures clearly identify them as female.[16] Not incidentally, Rodin's models for this sculpture were "two inseparable lesbian dancers from the Paris Opera," and the embracing figures are found in the upper right corner of Rodin's *The Gates of Hell*, where they are also known as *The Damned Women*.[17]

By referring to Rodin's *Metamorphoses*, Catherine points to her hidden desire and suggests that same-sex attraction compels their sex/gender metamorphosis. This suggestion is reinforced by the exchange itself wherein David and Catherine are simultaneously male and female, belonging to one sex "in the imagination" and to the other "in reality." The instability and duality of their sexual identities means that when Catherine is a boy making love to a girl, she can also be a wife making love to her husband, a girl making love to another girl, or a boy making love to a boy. This potential for crossover grows when we consider that Catherine and David rarely make or reverse the change at the same time and that Catherine identifies herself as both boy and girl, a power she eventually assigns to David as well.[18] "But it's so nice just to feel and hold you and know you're my boy and know you're my girl too" (422.1– 12, chap. 18, insert after p. 10). Making "the change" becomes an opportunity to situate themselves as both male and female but also to explore both homosexual and heterosexual desires.

Thus, in Catherine's and David's sex changing, sexual desire is represented as multiple and gender identity as fluid. I will explore the significance of this representation later since to reach that point we must first view a larger picture that is characterized by anxiety, repression, rationalization, and remorse. This is all caused by the fact that Catherine and David are transgressing a socio-scientific discourse that insists upon relations of coherence and continuity among sex, gender, sexual practice, and desire. An understanding of what Catherine and David are up to and also up against requires that we consider them within this history.

At the time the novel takes place, medical practitioners were formulating and arguing over theories which insisted that gender inversion was inherently tied to homosexuality. Foucault observes that sexologists created the category of the homosexual in the late 1800s by transposing sexual practices such as sodomy "onto a kind of interior androgyny, a hermaphrodism of the soul" (*History of Sexuality*, 43).[19] Desire became located in a specific identity (heterosexual or homosexual), and this identity revealed itself through signs on and of the body, the most important sign being adherence to or departure from traditional gender roles.

George Chauncey points out that as the medical investigation of sexuality developed in the early twentieth century, many doctors began to distinguish between gender role reversal and erotic object-choice.[20] For example, in 1913 Havelock Ellis stated that sexual inversion refers "exclusively [to] such a change in a person's sexual impulses, . . . that the impulse is turned towards individuals of the same sex, while all the other impulses and tastes may remain those of the sex to which the person by anatomical configuration belongs" (quoted in Chauncey, "Sexual Inversion," 122).[21] Similarly, Freud maintained that one must separate physical sexual characteristics, mental sexual characteristics, and sexual object-choice. "The mystery of homosexuality is . . . by no means so simple as it is commonly depicted in popular expositions—'a feminine mind, bound therefore to love a man, but unhappily attached to a masculine body; a masculine mind, irresistibly attracted by women, but, alas! imprisoned in a feminine body.'"[22]

Still, sexologists and psychoanalysts did not consistently apply the notion that gender identity and sexual object-choice are unrelated. Both Ellis and Freud had more trouble applying their observation to lesbians than they did to homosexual men. As Chauncey surmises, "doctors were less willing—perhaps culturally less able—to distinguish a woman's behavior in sexual relations from other aspects of her gender role" ("Sexual Inversion," 124). For instance, even though Ellis argued that the actively inverted woman may not necessarily be what is called a "mannish woman," he reinforced this popular perception of the lesbian by insisting that inverted women exhibited a masculine element. "The commonest characteristic of the sexually inverted woman," Ellis wrote, "is a certain degree of masculinity or boyishness" ("Sexual Inversion," 244).[23] Freud's work contains similar contradictions. As Judith Roof points out, in his papers and psychoanalytic sessions, Freud "still tends to want to characterize the lesbian as masculine and must catch and correct himself when he does it." Roof proposes that Freud sees the lesbian as masculine in order to solve the mystery of lesbian sexuality by rendering it heterosexual, "a relation between a woman who thinks she's a man and another woman."[24]

Not surprisingly, given the inability of medical professionals to abandon equations linking sexual object-choice and gender orientation, the popular understanding of homosexual identities and categories continued to be connected to gender roles. In the early part of the century, men who assumed the cultural roles of women, especially in their sexual practices, were classified as inverts, fairies, faggots, or queens (Chauncey, *Gay New York*); and the "mannish woman" image of the lesbian was codified by Radclyffe Hall's *The Well of Loneliness* (1928) and the obscenity trial that followed its publication. The fact that many people today identify homosexuality with "gender deviance" (the butch has replaced the mannish woman, and "queen" and "fairy" are still common terms for gay men) reveals that the public has historically refused to abandon the traditional sex-gender system, despite arguments and evidence against it. As Kaja Silverman states, "the notion of inversion is probably as old as the hierarchical binarizing of 'man' and 'woman,' and . . . human culture has to date shown itself to be stubbornly resistant to conceptualizing sexual positionality—and, more recently, object-choice—apart from the binary logic of gender."[25] Under the dictates of this system, to disorder the conventional alignment among sex, gender, sexual practice, and desire is to produce unintelligible, queer bodies (hermaphrodites, homosexuals, lesbians, bisexuals, transsexuals, inverts) that are identifiable through their abnormal desire and practices (homosexuality, lesbianism, bisexuality, sodomy, cross-dressing).

These unintelligible, queer bodies were given a kind of intelligibility in the early twentieth century through their pathologization. Several sexologists at the turn of the century—especially the German physician Magnus Hirschfeld and Havelock Ellis—had attempted to decriminalize and normalize homosexuality by establishing its congenital basis, yet they still judged the condition a divergence from the norm. Ellis, for example, stated that homosexuality should "be classed with other congenital abnormalities which have psychic concomitants" ("Sexual Inversion," 322). Moreover, in distinguishing between female inverts who were born that way and another group of women who possessed only a temporary predisposition toward homosexuality, Ellis argued that these latter individuals could steer themselves away from homosexuality by staying within a heterosexual environment. Doing so would enable them to overcome their predisposition and become "normal" women.[26]

The most influential pathologization of homosexuality came from Freud and his American followers, who challenged the congenital theory by focusing on the psychic etiology of homosexuality. In its most radical formulation, Freudian theory asserts that all human beings are "capable of making a homosexual object-choice" (quoted in Silverman, 356) and that the turn toward heterosexuality demands as much explanation as the turn toward homosexuality. But despite Freud's declaration that many homosexuals do not need or desire treatment, he presupposed a preferred, healthier course of development by advancing the theory that the "aberration" of homosexuality resulted from the child's failure to resolve psychosexual relations with a parent (Chauncey, "Sexual Inversion," 137).[27] Freud explained this failure in several ways, but in his most expanded analyses, he located it in an inhibited development and narcissism.[28]

In summarizing Freud's theories about homosexuality, Juliet Mitchell writes that Freud contends that the homosexual chooses "not another of the same sex, but himself in the guise of another."[29] Such reasoning is exhibited in the word "homosexuality," suggesting sex with the same, love of the self. This equation has frequently been cited as evidence of the pathology of homosexuality, even though, as Michael Warner points out, such a formulation grows out of heterosexist assumptions, especially the assumption that gender is "our only access to alterity" ("Homo-Narcissism," 200). To quote Warner, "having a sexual object of the opposite gender is taken to be the normal and paradigmatic form of an interest either in the Other or, more generally, in others. That is why in our century it has acquired the name *heterosexuality*—a sexuality of otherness. . . . [A]ccording to this logic homoerotics is an unrecognized version of autoerotics, or more precisely of narcissism; both are seen as essentially an interest in self rather than in the other" (190).

As this brief historical overview suggests, by "inverting" their sex, Catherine and David set into motion a string of inversions having to do with gender and sexual orientation and thereby introduce a host of related questions regarding their normality, sanity, maturity, and depravity. Catherine, for example, displays many characteristics of the "mannish woman." She takes the man's part during sex, including being the penetrator;[30] she cuts her hair like a boy's; she wears fishermen's shirts and trousers; she names herself "Peter" and asks David to call her "brother." In addition, Catherine's actions and desires invoke the psychoanalytic paradigm that equates narcissism and homosexuality. She has the barber cut her hair like David's and later has him cut David's hair like hers; she asks David to become her girl "Catherine" so that she is, by inference, making love to herself; she urges David to bleach his hair to match hers and to become just as dark as she is; she has to remind herself to "stop thinking only about myself" (*Garden*, 143); and she wants to hang a mirror over the bar at Grau du Roi. In brief, to many of her contemporaries (and not a few of my own), Catherine looks like a lesbian.

The homosexual implications of David's "feminization" are equally visible. By playing the woman's role during sexual relations, especially by being the recipient in an act of sodomy, David aligns himself with the common conception of the homosexual man. Chauncey points out that during the 1919 investigation of homosexual activity at the Newport (Rhode Island) Naval Training Station, "the assumption of particular sexual roles and deviance from gender norms may have been more important than the coincidence of male or female sexual partners in the classification of sexual character" ("Christian Brotherhood," 205). In fact, before the middle of the twentieth century, Chauncey maintains, many men were labelled "queer" only if they demonstrated a much broader inversion of their gender status by "assuming the sexual and other cultural roles ascribed to women" (*Gay New York*, 13). In terms of Hemingway's novel, this means that each time David agrees to become the "girl," to be penetrated by the male member that Catherine has become, he puts himself into a position (so to speak) that makes him vulnerable to the diagnosis of homosexuality.

Because the scientific and social discourse of the time leaves little room between gender inversion, homosexual desire, and the homosexual body, Catherine and David are walking a thin line that stretches from acts to desire, from appearance to identity. If they go too far down this line, they not only call into question the stability of their heterosexual identities, they risk being the subjects of a transformation so complete it casts them from the garden of cultural acceptability into the hell of degeneracy—as the alternative title to Rodin's statue, *The Damned Women*, implies. The dilemma that faces both is not simply whether it is wo/manly, normal, moral, or sane to become a member of the opposite sex and to desire someone of the same sex. It is, more crucially, whether in *wanting* to become that person and in having this desire, one also "becomes" homosexual, an incarnation that raises the stakes on questions of wo/manliness, normality, morality, ego development, and sanity.

To maintain their balancing act between indulging their desires and instating an identity, Catherine and David create an elaborate system of defense mechanisms. Most important, they both work hard to keep from naming "the love that dares not speak its name" as their own. In fact, almost-but-not-quite naming this desire intensifies their excitement because it calls forth the eroticized prohibitive law without making them its targets. Catherine, for instance, refers frequently to male-male love. She declares that in her life as a boy she is learning the pleasures of homosexuality. "It's nice to be kissed when you're a boy," she says. "No wonder they made it a sin" (422.1–8, chap. 13, p. 10). Similarly, in front of David, she asks Andy Murray whether he believes the saying "women for breeding, boys for pleasure, and melons for delight?" This cultural epigram, Catherine declares, is what Kipling left out of his fiction because "he was ashamed of it," but she demands that David not omit this truth from their narrative (quoted in Eby, "Come Back to the Beach," 105).

Catherine can talk about discovering the pleasures of male homosexuality—talk that makes David nervous—because it is a pleasure to be found only in her imaginary life. She cannot admit to the reverse side of that discovery which is her attraction for other women. Because she has acted out her same-sex desire within the safety of a relationship that looks heterosexual, she can deny her feelings for other women even as she explores them. In the manuscript, however, soon after Catherine "makes the change" at night with David, Barbara Sheldon confronts her with the opportunity for a lesbian relationship. She flirts openly with Catherine, and later tells David that "You know no man ever looked at her that didn't have an erection. I don't know what women have but whatever it is I have it" (422.1–5, chap. 5, p. 7). Catherine refuses to acknowledge that the attraction is mutual. She claims to be fascinated only by Barbara and Nick as a couple and makes a point of telling Barbara that although she cut her hair to look like a boy, she doesn't like girls (422.1–4, p. 4).

Other evidence suggests just the opposite and implies that Catherine's observations about her male experience are, in part, projections of her lesbian desire. For example, Catherine recognizes her similarity to Barbara, admitting to David that she and Barbara are similar but in a different way (422.1–4, p. 9). Catherine thinks she's referring to Barbara's inclination to have her husband, Nick, grow his hair the same length as hers, an inclination that parallels Catherine's insistence that she and David get matching haircuts. But Barbara is much more insightful about the significance of their gender-bending. When David repeats Catherine's announcement that she doesn't like girls, Barbara snidely replies, "Of course. She just goes around perfectly innocently not knowing or careing (sic) whether she is a boy or a girl . . . " (422.1–5, chap. 5, pp. 7–8). Barbara is able to identify Catherine's motives because she has reached the point of being able to name them within herself even though she cannot believe that her desire for Catherine changes her sexual identity. "But I'm not a queer or I never was," she informs David (422.1–5, chap. 5, p. 8.1).

The day after meeting Barbara and Nick, Catherine returns from getting her hair cut and runs to tell David that she's a girl again and "we're not like them not prisoners of anything" (422.1–5, chap. 6, p. 13). Catherine is obviously afraid that they're exactly like Barbara and Nick, so afraid that she doesn't want to join Nick and Barbara at the café because "They look so Montparnasse. They look like everything I don't like" (422.1–5, chap. 7, p. 1). Montparnasse is the district in Paris where Hemingway lived and socialized in the 1920s, which was frequented by the avant garde, including many homosexuals. After reluctantly sitting at the Sheldons' table, Catherine seems determined to make an issue out of Barbara's attentions. She asks Barbara what she is looking at and brushes off Barbara's sarcastic statement that she sees Catherine's breasts "very<,> very well if that is what you're worried about" (422.1–5, chap. 7, p. 2). When Barbara declares her attraction, Catherine claims that she never intended to make Barbara feel that way and offers to leave in a few days so as not "to do anything to you or have any bad effect on you" (422.1–5, chap. 7, p. 4). She then slings what she considers the ultimate insult, asking Barbara why she doesn't let Nick cut his hair "so he won't be embarrassed looking like someone out of Montparnasse" (422.1–5, chap. 7, pp. 4–5).

Catherine's attacks on Barbara are apparently defenses against acknowledging her own homoerotic feelings and consciously admitting that the games she plays with David not only lead them into socially forbidden territory but threaten to leave them there. Despite telling David that her haircut was "a real invention. . . . Everybody will do mine and nobody will do hers but queers" (422.1–4, new chap. 2, p. 11), Catherine fears that her invention is, like Barbara's, simply a manifestation of same-sex desire. Before Catherine and David leave Hendaye, where Nick and Barbara are staying, Catherine insists on saying good-bye to Barbara even though David tries to dissuade her from doing so. Clearly, Catherine is fascinated by Barbara. Saying good-bye is a pretense that allows her one last chance to work her magic on Barbara, to tease her with a possibility that Catherine refuses to engage. In fact, Catherine refers frequently to Barbara after departing from Hendaye, saying that she misses her (422.1–11, p. 17) and telling Andy Murray that "it would be easy for anybody" to be in love with Barbara (422.1–6, chap. 9, p. 9).

Given Catherine's intense response to Barbara, the reader of the manuscript is hardly surprised when Catherine openly expresses her lesbian desire with the arrival of Marita. The night before they meet Marita, Catherine seems to announce her incipient lesbianism by telling David after they make love that she never changed from a girl to a boy, even though he changed into a girl. "I'm still a girl . . . . I never changed at all. That's why it's so complicated." In a telling response, David states, "Don't think about it [or] <nor> worry. It's always been complicated" (422.1–12, chap. 18, p. 19). Soon after meeting Marita, Catherine admits that she is "vulnerable," although "I wish I hadn't turned out to be." When David replies that everyone is vulnerable, Catherine states, "<Maybe to go through with it and get rid of it that way is best. . . .> Maybe we'll cure it. I had to say cure it" (422.1–14, pp. 28–29). Here Catherine uses the word "cure" in the sense of "get rid of," "purge," but given that she's talking about homosexual feelings, one cannot ignore the association of the word with illness, particularly mental illness. Even though Catherine assures David that "all this is nothing" (422.1–14, p. 29), she still asserts that "it's terrible when wrong is right" (422.1–14, p. 29). Catherine and David know that she has crossed an important societal line, bringing their nighttime, unnamed desires into the daylight.

It is no accident that references to her "madness" increase after admitting her desire for Marita.

During a day trip to Nice, Catherine kisses Marita and discovers that she likes the experience. Far from curing her, this kiss increases Catherine's desire. "You didn't forget why you were trying did you?" David asks her. "I did," she says. <"That was the trouble.> Once I started I forgot all about that because I liked it so much" (422.1–15, p. 12). Further, Catherine is able to differentiate between the games that she and David have been playing, and her affair with Marita. "I know I started it with us but it wasn't something that just I did. I did it to you but you [xx] understood and when I changed you <at Grau de (sic) Roi it was true> and you changed <in the night. Even the first time.> We both <changed> and we were each other and we're partners" (422.1–15, p. 19). Catherine thus suggests that her games with David have led her to this point; transgressions of gender rules inevitably involve transgressions of the heterosexual imperative.

Nonetheless, role-playing with her husband differs significantly from kissing a woman, because if the role-playing is more socially acceptable—it occurs within the boundaries of a heterosexual relationship—it's also not as physically exciting. As she tells David after sleeping with Marita, "It was what I wanted to do all my life and now I've done it and I loved it" (*Garden*, 120). Although Catherine continues to speak of David as her "true partner" (*Garden*, 115), she cannot resist the demands of her body. "I didn't know I'd ever be like this," she says (*Garden*, 114). Far from being cured, Catherine finds that she has tapped the source of her strongest desire.

But having finally arrived at this "truth" about herself and having brought the hidden/repressed desire of her sex-changing games into the light of day, Catherine discovers that she is suddenly in the minority. David, who participated in these games, and Marita, who was her first female lover, both align themselves with the voice of cultural prohibition and disapproval. Marita, who sought out Catherine (422.1–14, p. 17; 422.1–18, p. 23), leaving one woman to be Catherine's "girl" and David's too (*Garden*, 105), insists that "perversion" is "overrated and silly," "something girls do because they have nothing better" (*Garden*, 120). She refuses to engage in further lovemaking with Catherine, including the ménage à trois that Catherine proposes. David pretends to understand Catherine's feelings and claims that he will not apportion blame, but in private he thinks, "The worst was what had happened to Catherine" (*Garden*, 132). On David's scale of morality, Catherine's acting on her desire for women is worse than his falling in love with two women.

That David judges and condemns Catherine is most evident during a conversation he has with her in bed one night, a night that follows a morning when he makes vigorous love to Marita on the beach. David tells Catherine that it's not normal for a woman to want to share. "Who said normal?" Catherine retorts. "Who's normal? What's normal? I never went to normal school to be a teacher and teach normal. You don't want me to go to normal school and get a certificate do you?" (422.1–18, p. 33). David later claims that he has loved her in "all the ways" that she was, and so Catherine asks him to love her this way too. "I do," David claims. "But [it's] <there's> too many people." He wants to know why they can't be like they once were. Knowing that she cannot turn back, Catherine surrenders to this societal judgment, "Because I turned out wrong. . . . Just like a story" (422.1–18, pp. 36–37). "That's not true," David replies, a response that rings false with his accusation of abnormality still echoing in the room.

Although many critics assume that Catherine is unstable from the beginning of the novel and that her imbalance causes the breakup of her marriage, Catherine's decline escalates after she announces that she enjoys touching and kissing a woman, that it was what she wanted all along.[31] Her descent is propelled, if not precipitated, by Marita's and David's puritanism, a puritanism that is so sudden it is almost unbelievable and is certainly unearned, given their histories. In other words, Marita and David turn into societal police, imposing a heteronormative view onto Catherine. It is this pressure that reinforces prescriptives that Catherine has internalized but is challenging but that also intensifies Catherine's feelings of madness.

Catherine attempts to recover ground by restoring her significance in both Marita's and David's lives. She makes new plans and then, in desperation, tears up David's African stories in order to force him to return to work on their narrative. Yet they have relegated her to a different category of difference and abnormality that is apparently comprised of her desire for women and of her willingness to share her husband with another woman. Catherine rightly accuses them of hypocrisy. She tells Marita, "two days ago when you made passes at me it was simply dandy but today if I felt that way the slightest bit you had to act as though I was an I don't know what" (*Garden*, 134). Behind Catherine's back, Marita and David conspire to treat Catherine as if she were ill, agreeing that they must be "careful and good with her and only think about her" (*Garden*, 135). No wonder Catherine starts to feel unsettled and crazy and believes that she is "the one that's different" (422.1–14, p. 30). The two people who claim to love her the most are suddenly denying her sexual reality by reinscribing the societal boundaries that Catherine has tried to cross with their help.

Catherine's difficulty is that she has become too dangerous for David who has recognized the complexity of their nighttime games all along but has been even less able than Catherine to accept the presence, much less the enjoyment, of his own homosexual desire. As noted, in playing his part in their nighttime drama, a part that he often admits he enjoys, David has acted not only as a woman but as a homosexual man.[32] The possibility that his enjoyment of Catherine's penetration means he is a homosexual frightens him, as we see in his repeated reluctance to engage in the change. His fear is exacerbated by Catherine in several ways.

First, Catherine always demands that David return to work on their narrative, which she has designated as the place where male homosexuality will be brought to the surface. Significantly, David breaks off the narrative after writing about their experience in Madrid when Catherine tells Colonel John Boyle that she is a boy. This disclosure marks the point at which David's homosexual desire seems about to be made public or conscious, a near-revelation that David will have to repeat in writing the episode. After the encounter with Boyle, David tells Catherine that they cannot try to make the change if they're both boys (*Garden*, 67). But in this overreaction and in David's decision to leave "the ongoing narrative of their journey where it was to write a story that had come to him four or five days before" (*Garden*, 93), we sense David's panic not only that he might be perceived as homosexual but that he might actually be homosexual.

Catherine also threatens David's identification as heterosexual in her progress toward a lesbian relationship. Because Catherine explicitly connects this progress to their night games, it reveals to David how very close he too is to crossing the line between heterosexuality and homosexuality. In fact, Catherine's reading of Proust holds a clue to the way in which her lesbianism puts David's own sexual identity in crisis. In Proust's *Sodome et Gomorrhe*, a work known to Catherine and David (Jenks denies us this information), we are told that there are two broad categories of homosexuals—those who can love only men and those who can love lesbians as well as men:

the second sort seek out those women who love other women, who can procure for them a young man, enhance the pleasure they experience in his company; better still, they can, in the same fashion, take with such women the same pleasure as with a man. . . . in their relations with women, they play, for the woman who loves her own sex, the part of another woman, and she offers them at the same time more or less what they find in other men, so that the jealous friend suffers from the feeling that the man he loves is riveted to the woman who is to him almost a man, and at the same time feels his beloved almost escape him because, to these women, he is something which the lover himself cannot conceive, a sort of woman.[33]

By playing the part of a woman for a woman who, it turns out, desires other women, David casts doubt upon his own heterosexuality. He might very well be this second sort of homosexual.

Finally, David's anxieties about his sexual identity are reaffirmed when he agrees to bleach and cut his hair like Catherine's. In *All the Sexes: A Study of Masculinity and Femininity*, a book that Hemingway owned, George Henry announces, "One can say almost with certainty that any male who bleaches his hair is homosexual."[34] Although this book was published in 1955, several decades after Hemingway's novel takes place, the association of hair-dyeing and homosexuality had long been recognized. George Chauncey notes that in early twentieth-century New York, gay men "boldly announced their presence" through various insignias of the era, including bleached hair (*Gay New York*, 3, 54). Other Hemingway works reveal that Hemingway knew about this association of hair-dyeing with effeminacy and male homosexuality. For example, in "There's One in Every Town" (Item 743 in the Hemingway Collection), the narrator remembers the first time she saw one of the male homosexuals in the café, a man with hennaed hair. The narrator suspects that the man felt sexual excitement just by sitting there and showing off his hair.[35] In other Hemingway fiction, the hair salon serves as an important place for identifying homosexuals. In "The dark young man stood looking into the window . . . ," the main character is getting a permanent wave at a barbershop and corrects his opinion about the man who was sitting next to him, realizing that the man wasn't a pimp but an "upsidaisy" (Item 355a in the Hemingway Collection, 5). Finally, there's Hemingway's circumspect response to dyeing his own hair. As reported by Kenneth Lynn, when Hemingway gave his hair a henna rinse in 1947, he told the servants at the Finca that he had thought the bottle contained shampoo (Lynn, 543). His need to fabricate suggests that Hemingway was worried about how others would view him if they knew the truth.

David, in fact, sees the bleaching of his hair as a defining moment. Looking at himself in the mirror, he admits that he likes what he sees. "All right. You like it . . . . Now go through with the rest of it whatever it is and don't ever say anyone tempted you or that anyone bitched you" (*Garden*, 84). He concludes that he now knows exactly how he is, an assessment undercut by the narrator who claims, "Of course he did not know exactly how he was. But he made an effort aided by what he had seen in the mirror" (*Garden*, 85).

David's moment of self-understanding is obviated by Marita, whose name suggests (a little bit of) Mary in contrast to Catherine's Eve. Her conversion to heterosexuality and her adoration of David seem to provide him with a means for escaping from what he is learning about himself and to perform heterosexuality again. It is an escape that Jenks turned into a conclusion, ending his version of the novel with Marita and David naming themselves "the Bournes" (*Garden*, 243) and Marita asserting that she's not going to give David away to anyone the way Catherine did (*Garden*, 245). Such an ending reasserts the power of the dominant ideology in which the monogamous heterosexual relationship reigns supreme. Jenks's novel might thus be entitled *Paradise Regained*.

Hemingway's manuscript is more ambivalent, for it reveals that Marita knows about David's hunger for forbidden fruit. Not only has Marita read David's narrative about his and Catherine's activities, but she and Catherine have had lengthy discussions concerning David and his proclivities.[36] Catherine even sets David's next temptation in motion. Before leaving, Catherine tells Marita that she might start an affair with Barbara, who isn't a half boy like Marita. "I'm not attracted to the gamin type," Catherine states, but she encourages Marita not to change: "Go ahead and show David what sort of gamin you are. He'd like it" (*Garden*, 192).

This is precisely what Marita does. In fact, besides showing David what sort of gamin she is, she attempts to recreate all of Catherine's "tricks," including becoming David's Somali wife (422.1–29, p. 41). Her greatest trick is to become a non-threatening imitation of Catherine. After Catherine leaves, Marita cuts her hair short without David's knowledge, hoping to make herself look like an African girl but looking instead like an African boy. David is openly pleased with the outcome. He kisses her in front of their waiter and says that he felt excited when he saw what she had done. At their hotel, David finally states his desire, claiming that he wants to make the change and telling Marita, after they make love, that she didn't have to change back to a girl so soon (422.1–36, pp. 31–33).

But David has not returned to his moment of self-understanding prior to the relationship with Marita; rather, he has found a way to believe Marita's specious logic. Repeatedly, Marita claims she can do what Catherine did without causing David remorse, telling him: "You'll never have remorse because I'm your girl really and it never happened. It's not perversion. It's variety" (422.1–36, p. 5). With these words, Marita explains how David can enjoy sodomy with another "man" without ever having to worry about his heterosexual identity. All he has to do is remember that she's his "girl really" and "it" never happened. That way, "It's not perversion. It's variety."[37] This reasoning enables both Marita and David to differentiate themselves from homosexuals, "those people," as Marita calls them. "It's not for us. Anymore than queers would be for you," she tells David. David agrees, claiming that he always tried to understand and to be fair: "We've always had them and I'm never rude unless I have to be. But they give me the creeps" (422.1–37, p. 23). This is one of the last exchanges between Marita and David before the manuscript breaks off, and it is significant that the manuscript ends with yet another attempt to understand the meaning of the sex-changing, sodomy-engaging, role-playing games. Within this final perspective, what David does in bed does not make him homosexual and perverse; it makes him experimental, interested in "infinite variety" (422.1–36, p. 6).

Hemingway's Own Tangled Garden

In the recurrent attempts to neutralize David's anxiety about his sexuality, we sense the anxiety of Hemingway himself who, at the time he was writing this novel, was apparently involved in similar activities with his wife, Mary. We know most of this from Mary Hemingway's autobiography in which she includes several pages from her diary. The entry for 19 December 1953 describes Hemingway "clowning an interview" with an imaginary reporter from the imaginary magazine, *Recondite*. The reporter asks Hemingway whether it is true that his wife is a lesbian. "Of course not," Hemingway replies. "Mrs. Hemingway is a boy." The reporter then asks Hemingway to name his favorite sports, to which Hemingway responds: "Shooting, fishing, reading and sodomy." When the reporter wonders whether Mrs. Hemingway participates in these sports, Hemingway answers that she participates in all of them and then states that the diurnal sports must be distinguished from the nocturnal: "In this latter category sodomy is definitely superior to fishing" (425).

The next day, according to Mary Hemingway, Hemingway wrote an entry for her in which he states that

> Mary has always wanted to be a boy and thinks as a boy without ever losing any femininity. . . . She loves me to be her girls, which I love to be, not being absolutely stupid. . . . In return she makes me awards and at night we do every sort of thing which pleases her and which pleases me. . . . Mary has never had one lesbian impulse but has always wanted to be a boy. Since I have never cared for any man and dislike any tactile contact with men except the normal Spanish *abrazo* or embrace which precedes a departure or welcomes a return from a voyage or a more or less dangerous mission or attack, I loved feeling the embrace of Mary which came to me as something quite new and outside all tribal law. On the night of December 19th we worked out these things and I have never been happier. (426; ellipses in original)

Here Hemingway attempts to describe in his own life what he was working out in his novel.[38] Like the reasoning of his characters, Hemingway's reasoning evades reasoned logic. Hemingway states that because he has never cared for any man, he was excited by the embrace of Mary-as-boy. To be logical, he would have to state exactly the opposite: because he has always cared for men but has never been able to act on his feelings, beyond "the normal Spanish *abrazo*," he loved feeling the embrace of his boy-wife.

The best way to make sense of Hemingway's response to Mary's embrace is to view it within the logic of displacement and disavowal. Within Freudian theory, as Jonathan Dollimore notes, "disavowal always involves a simultaneous acknowledgement of what is being disavowed" (183). By dismissing homosexuality as the reason for his and Mary's behavior, Hemingway names the repressed desire that makes its way into consciousness only on the condition that it be negated. True to this notion, not only does Hemingway negate the possibility that his feelings are homosexual, he positions his desire "outside all tribal law." Through this move he normalizes his and Mary's desire—it's not homosexual—at the same time that he separates it from "civilized" sexual morality—it's outside tribal law and therefore instinctual and natural rather than socially produced.

Of course, Mary Hemingway's autobiography has its own biases, and her "Hemingway" is as much a construction as the Hemingway of other biographers. Any conclusions we draw from reading Mary's descriptions of Hemingway's life or from what she tells us in her diary are Hemingway's own words must thus be speculative. But whatever the personal history and dynamics, Hemingway's inability to name his desire and his correlative need to assert his and Mary's heterosexuality by denying their homosexuality are reflected not only in his characters, who are equally inconsistent and ambivalent, but in his text itself, which buckles under the weight of repeated acts and endless talk about the meaning of those acts. Finally, the text seems to be doubling back on itself, as Marita and David pick up where Catherine and David began. Such a text can end only where this one does, in the failure to end. The body of the text is an extension of the bodies of its characters and the body of its author. It wants to express transgressive desires but cannot figure out how to do so without seeming perverse, queer.

Yet the text is perverse not only in its unwieldiness and reiterations but also in its representations of gender as fluid and sexuality as polymorphous. To a great degree, Catherine and David demonstrate that gender is, to use Judith Butler's conception, performed. Butler argues that gender "is a compulsory repetition of prior and subjectivating norms, ones which cannot be thrown off at will, but which work, animate, and constrain the gendered subject, and which are also the resources from which resistance, subversion, displacement are to be forged."[39] Catherine and David do attempt to throw off gender at will, and their failure to completely do so verifies the power of the normative system, while their partial success attests to the vulnerability of that system. As the initiator of the change and as the one who seems to want it most, Catherine believes that the norms of femininity restrain her and that she cannot continue to repeat them. As she says, she tried to be a girl in Madrid, but "all it did was break me in pieces" (*Garden*, 192). Although Catherine reinforces the traditional gender system in her performance of masculinity, she questions the validity of that system by showing that it takes effort to align gender and sex, that the alignment does not come naturally.

Moreover, Catherine's and David's actions illustrate that sexual "orientation," too, is a performance.[40] Their bodies become sites of continual contestation and expression of desires that they attempt to negotiate into socially acceptable identities. In portraying the difficulty of this negotiation, they undermine the discourse of sexual orientation that inhibits their ability to transgress. Obviously, Catherine and David (and, to some extent, Barbara, Nick, and Marita) do not consciously enact a deconstruction of homosexual/heterosexual difference; to the contrary, they often work to retain the category of the heterosexual or at least of the non-homosexual. But as Wendy Hollway states, consciousness-changing "is not accomplished by new discourses replacing old ones. It is accomplished as a result of the contradictions in our positionings, desires and practices—and thus in our subjectivities—which result from the coexistence of the old and the new" (260). If nothing else, David and Catherine are contradictory bodies in which the old and the new coexist. In this embodiment, they represent the possibility for change.

In gauging the extent of this possibility, one must also take notice of the class status of the characters and emphasize their racism. Although both David and Nick are artists, and David frequently refers to his struggle to make a living from his writing and his intention not to let Catherine's money pay their way, these are people whose financial situation and white privilege provide them much leisure time and many luxuries. Having met their basic survival needs, Catherine, David, Marita, Nick, and Barbara can afford to explore their sexual desires. Their class status gives them access to any number of Edenic gardens, those isolated, romantic hideaways where they conduct their transgressions against normative models of gender and sexuality. This is not to dismiss the possibilities for change regarding gender and sexuality that are manifested through Hemingway's characters; rather, it is to emphasize that, in measuring the appeal of those possibilities, we must attend to the ways that they are linked to the whiteness and the upper-class status of the characters.

In light of an analysis of Hemingway's characters, it should be clear that I am not arguing that Hemingway himself was homosexual—repressed, latent, or otherwise. I am suggesting that homosexual desire was among the desires that he felt and depicted in his fiction, and we do a disservice to him and ourselves by not coming out and naming this desire for what it is. Hemingway's homosexual desire was, of course, complicated by many factors, including the homophobia and sexism for which he is famous as well as his famous persona which was, significantly, based on a kind of masculinity (homosociality) that must voice sexism and homophobia in order to retain its integrity and entitlement.[41] Hemingway worked intermittently on The Garden of Eden from 1946 to 1959, a period of extreme oppression and homophobia in America and a time during which Hemingway's public personality reached star status. As John Raeburn explains, "The commonplace of the 1950s that Americans had sacrificed their adventurous spirit and eagerness for challenge to become Organization Men made [Hemingway] stand out all the more as a supremely individualistic hero. Yet for all the emphasis on his uncompromising uniqueness, he was never portrayed as perversely eccentric or odd. The ubiquitous assertions that he was 'a man's man' were a shorthand way for journalists to assure readers that his heroism was of a familiar kind" (155).

Hemingway was undoubtedly aware of the chance he was taking in writing a novel that might suggest that he was perversely eccentric or odd—or simply perverse. The dilemma he faced is portrayed at several points in the *Garden* manuscript, most extensively in a tense scene near the beginning, a scene that Jenks includes only in part. Catherine becomes angry when David reads the reviews of his second book, telling him, "They make me feel as though I didn't know you at all and that we aren't us at all. You won't go away now and just live in the clippings will you?" (422.1–2, p. 6). Catherine wants to know how she and David can be "us and have the things we have and do what we do and you be this that's in the clippings?" (*Garden*, 24). David replies that the clippings are bad only if you subscribe to them (422.1–2, p. 7). This reply worries Catherine, for she understands that if David starts to be seduced by this public identity-construction, he will inhibit his ability to transgress societal prohibitions, to explore transgressive desires, to write texts that do not fit the public image of David Bourne (an image born into existence by critics and reviewers).

Hemingway's narrator even tells us that reading the press cuttings reminds David of his name (422.1–2, p. 5), implying that until this point, David has forgotten his history and his publicly constructed self and has been pursuing private pleasures and immediate desires. Although those pleasures are themselves mediated by the social, Hemingway reveals his awareness through the characterization of David of how the author's public persona can become a prohibition against acting or writing in a way that threatens the integrity of the public self. This is an almost inviolable prohibition because the public self, especially in Hemingway's case, has so much power to conceal, to impress, to make money, and to inspire imitation.

It is the threat to this power that forms the most serious prohibition facing Hemingway—and, to a lesser extent, David. Leo Bersani notes that "the moral taboo on 'passive' anal sex in ancient Athens is primarily formulated as a kind of hygienics of social power. *To be penetrated is to abdicate power.*" [42] This ancient equation still applies in most of the modern

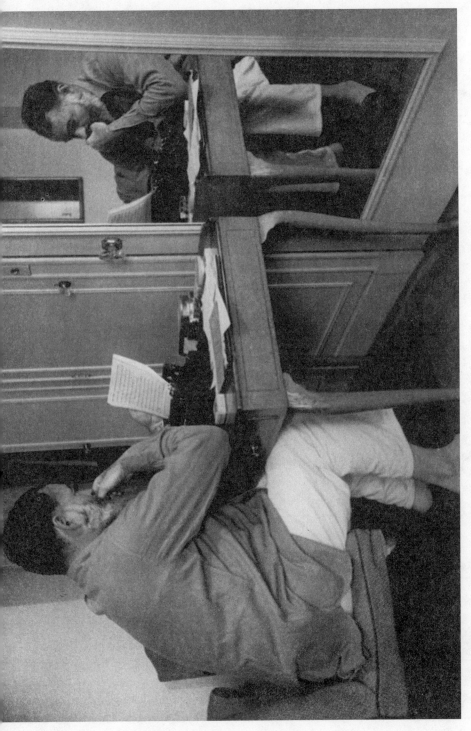

Desiring authors: Gazing on the writer at work. Hemingway writing at the Dorchester Hotel in 1940 (John F. Kennedy Library, photographer unknown).

Western world, which assumes that for a man, to be penetrated is to be feminized, to be homosexual. Such a man risks diluting the power of male privilege, the power that accrues from having a penis. By describing the mechanics of their unorthodox sex lives, whether explicitly as in the case of David with the personal narrative he is writing or obliquely in Hemingway's case with the *Garden* manuscript, both writers risk destroying not only their self-image as heterosexual men but the powerful public self that reinforces that self-image. Even more frightening, such a powerful, culturally admired self would be replaced by a powerless, scorned self.

Was Hemingway, then, as Jenks proposes, taking his biggest gamble with *The Garden of Eden*, acting and writing against his public identity? Possibly. The homophobia of his manuscript and his inability to finish or publish his story certainly suggest he understood the risk. However, his desire to return again and again to the *Garden*, to rewrite sections, to add, to make notes in the margin about what to do or cut, to produce a provisional ending, to write over 200,000 words—all this activity indicates that Hemingway was determined to write this story. He seems to have shared the position of his author-protagonist, David Bourne, to "never leave out anything because you are ashamed of it or because no one would ever understand" (quoted in Burwell, 123). In this insistence one gets the feeling not only that Hemingway was attempting to comprehend human sexuality, including his own, but that he was growing tired of the public mask that simplified the complexity of his own desire.

But Jenks's editing reduced the risk Hemingway was taking and restored the mask. Of all the changes Jenks made, the one that stands in greatest opposition to the movement of the manuscript is the cauterizing of the pages which reveal that Catherine's departure does not cure David's desire to engage in and enjoy actions that call into question his masculinity as well as his heterosexuality. To suggest that David's crisis is as serious as Catherine's, so serious that it compels him to force her out of his life, only to pick up again where they left off, was more than Jenks could allow or imagine. Such a suggestion does not fit the image we have of Hemingway as a writer who wrote in "the language that men use." In fact, it even threatens this image by supporting those recurring rumors that Hemingway's exhibitionist masculinity was simply a cover for his homosexuality. So Jenks removed the implicating pages, suturing the text into a model of heterosexual monogamy.

As dismayed as I am with Jenks's editing, it is not, of course, fair to say that he completely heteronormalized Hemingway's text; for as I have noted, Jenks's version of *The Garden of Eden* has been instrumental in convincing critics to reconsider Hemingway's identity and his collected work. Perhaps a better way to describe Jenks's editing is to suggest that it bears the marks of a contemporary crisis in the binary gender-sexuality system noted by several cultural theorists. For instance, both Rosemary Hennessy and Donald M. Lowe argue that the binary organization of gender and sexuality within late-capitalist societies has loosened—or shows signs of doing so—in the last 10–20 years. Hennessy proposes that the sex-gender bending of queer theory and activism "does seem to indicate shifts in the historical forces defining family, gender, and sexuality under advanced capitalism."[43] However, she questions the extent and radicalness of such shifts when they stand only as "an index of the discovery of new consumer markets where pleasure can be profitably appropriated and produced" rather than challenging heterosexual hegemony (108). Lowe confidently states that "bipolar sexuality is under assault by the commodification of sexuality and the sexualization of consumption in late capitalism."[44] Such an assault has led to "polysexuality, challenging and subverting the heterosexuality at the heart of the repressive regulation of sexuality" (137).

If it is true that we are beginning to see shifts in the dominant structuring of gender and sexuality, then Jenks's editing reveals how unstable and insecure those shifts are and how much capitalism is still entrenched in the traditional binary system. On the one hand, Jenks has retained enough of the gender-bending and same-sex desiring of Hemingway's original text to urge Hemingway's readers to reconsider his identity, however limited and anxiety-ridden that reconsideration might be. On the other hand, the parts of Hemingway's manuscript that Jenks (as Scribner's proxy) suppressed indicate that he and Scribner's are deeply loyal to the popular cultural image of Hemingway, given that capitalism is still invested in heterosexual normalization.

By containing the threat to Hemingway's public image, Jenks ensured that Scribner's would continue to cash in on the power of Hemingway's name. As Charles Scribner, Jr., has noted, Hemingway and Scribner's have been partners for seven decades, with 10 of Hemingway's works published posthumously.[45] The meaning of that partnership was not lost on Jenks who calls the association between Hemingway and Scribner's an outstanding record of "a publisher's long-standing commitment to honor a writer" ("Interview," 87).[46] More regretfully, by drastically editing Hemingway's novel, Jenks took away one of our best opportunities to reread both Hemingway and his work. Contrary to his claim that "*The*

Garden of Eden is out in the world to speak for itself" ("Interview," 87), it is actually sequestered on the shelves of the Hemingway Collection in the John F. Kennedy Library. Only scholars with time, the library's approval, and financial backing for travel to Boston may read Hemingway's novel. And no matter how much Jenks encourages "interested parties" to visit the library as well as to check "for odds and ends at the Princeton Library where the Scribner Archive is housed" ("Editing Hemingway," 33), the fact remains that it takes a Herculean effort and a sizable bankroll to implement this suggestion.

Even those who have the money and the time are likely to produce critical work, such as this chapter, which reaches mainly specialized readers of a scholarly community and not the general public. Although I don't want to discount the power of critical work to change minds or to enlarge perspectives, the difficulty of gaining access to Hemingway's text curtails opportunities for debate, dialogue, or even correction. Indeed, even bringing Hemingway's novel to undergraduate and graduate students is an almost impossible task. I have tried this, but much of my time was spent answering questions about what had been cut from the text, a frustrating experience for everyone. The fact that scholars are no longer allowed to even duplicate pages from the manuscripts places yet another barrier in the way of acquainting students with Hemingway's text.[47] I suppose one could pretend that Jenks's version is the only version and allow students to believe that the book they're holding in their hands was put together by Hemingway, but as I hope I have demonstrated, such an approach would amount to an act of collective repression. One might finally wish for a fuller version of the manuscript to be published, but for many reasons—its length, Scribner's investment, lack of a large market for such a text—that seems unlikely to happen. In sum, it will be a long time before *The Garden of Eden* will be out in the world speaking for itself, and that, I submit, is precisely what Scribner's, Jenks, and some Hemingway scholars want.

RE-EMBODYING HEMINGWAY'S FICTION AND LIFE

The fiction that having your ears pierced will make you a Kamba is an evasion of the reality that you can never be anything but an honorary Kamba, and it is out of harmony with your best character which is that of a wise thoughtful, realistic adult white American male.
—Mary Hemingway, letter to Ernest Hemingway, 4 October 1955
(quoted in Carl Eby, *Hemingway's Fetishism*)

My own wound had healed rapidly and well. . . .
—Ernest Hemingway, letter to Thomas Bledsoe, 9 December 1951

Like the place for which it is named, *The Garden of Eden* has achieved foundational status, even though it was one of the last novels that Hemingway worked on. Its publication has motivated a critical return to Hemingway and his texts for other signs of the desires that he explores through Catherine, David, Marita, Barbara, and Nick. As I have proposed, how one conducts this return depends, in part, on one's own desires and, more specifically, on how one desires to desire. Susan Beegel notes that Hemingway's critics writing in the wake of *Garden* have sought to uncover in the rest of Hemingway's fiction "themes" such as "feminine madness, male androgyny, bisexuality, and lesbianism" that are treated with such candor in *Garden*.[1] According to her, after the appearance of *Garden* in 1986, "[Mark] Spilka's prescient focus on Hemingway's androgynous impulses, and [Gerry] Brenner's psychoanalytic slant on the author's gender-bending relationships with his troubled father and strong-willed mother, once unusual points of view, were suddenly the order of the day" ("Conclusion," 291).[2] But, as I explained in Chapter 2, Spilka's androgynous approach and Brenner's homoerotic paradigm are invested in a system of compulsory heterosexuality and thus display a desire to maintain a normative Hemingway. Many critics who draw upon their work and hence these paradigms maintain the same desire.

In this chapter, I expand the argument that by reading Hemingway's life and fiction with an antifoundational desire to desire, we construct a different, more complex view of desire in both. Rather than reread all of Hemingway's fiction, I concentrate on several texts that critics, biographers, and editors have identified as central to the Hemingway canon: *The Sun Also Rises* (1926), "The Snows of Kilimanjaro" (1936), and "The Short Happy Life of Francis Macomber" (1936). In the final section, I examine descriptions of male and female bodies from a compilation of Hemingway's novels. To the extent that this chapter reveals the instabilities of desires associated with sexual orientation and gender identification in modern Western society, it provides support for my assertion that Hemingway's struggle with the homo-hetero binarism was lifelong. It also lends strength to the implication that by tracing this struggle, we might challenge the prevailing construction of Hemingway and its function in promoting heterosexism and homophobia. But given that modern forms of sexuality are always racialized and developed within a value system that categorizes bodies according to their desirability, this chapter also investigates the roles of race and of the able body in Hemingway's work and in the construction of him as a desiring subject.

Contradictory Bodies in *The Sun Also Rises*

With its attention to male bonding and rituals such as fishing, drinking, and bullfighting, *The Sun Also Rises* has become known as "classic Hemingway." Co-existing with these rituals is a thwarted heterosexual relationship—Jake and Brett's—a romantic situation that is also characteristic of Hemingway's fiction. The repetition of this pattern throughout Hemingway's work (e.g., *A Farewell to Arms*, *For Whom the Bell Tolls*, *Across the River and Into the Trees*, *Islands in the Stream*) suggests that Hemingway felt that the intense homosociality of his fiction demanded equally intense heterosexuality to deflect suspicions that either his male characters or he had homosexual tendencies.[3] Yet a closer look at *The Sun Also Rises* reveals that Hemingway's depiction of gender and sexuality is more complex than this description allows. Ironically, in mapping out this territory of interrogation, I will draw upon the very concepts that I claim Hemingway's work problematizes (masculinity/femininity, homosexuality/heterosexuality). As Gayatri Spivak observes, "There is no way that a deconstructive philosopher can say 'something is not something' when the word is being used as a concept to enable his discourse."[4] Despite this paradox, by tracing how Hemingway's texts bring traditional significations of gender and sexuality into conflict, I hope to illustrate that Hemingway's first novel (like one of his last, *The Garden of Eden*) exposes the intellectual limitations that result when "gender" and "sexuality" are read as innocent acts of nature and as fixed binaries.

Early in *The Sun Also Rises*, a scene occurs that seems to establish the gender and sexual ideologies upon which the story will turn: Jake Barnes and Brett Ashley's meeting at a dance club in which Jake is accompanied by a prostitute, Georgette Hobin, and Brett is accompanied by a group of homosexual men. In a poststructuralist reading that provides the starting point for mine, Cathy and Arnold Davidson observe that by switching dancing partners, these characters arrange themselves in different pairings: Jake and Georgette, Jake and Brett, the young men and Brett, the young men and Georgette. These partner exchanges initially suggest "the fundamental equivalence" of the women as well as of the men. Georgette and Brett are conjoined under the pairing of prostitution/promiscuity, just as Jake and the young men are linked under the pairing of sexually maimed/homosexual. Consequently, this episode reveals the contradictions in Jake's own life. Jake relies upon the homosexuality of the young men to define his manhood (at least his desire is the right kind), but that definition is tested by the joint presence of Georgette and Brett, neither of whom Jake has sex with.[5] As the Davidsons conclude, "The terrifying ambiguity of [Jake's] own sexual limitations and gender preferences may well be one source of his anger (it usually is) with Brett's companions, and another reason why he articulates his anger and hatred for them before he reveals his love for her" (92).

But this perceptive reading illuminates only one of the "fundamental equivalences" set up in this scene; further, it fails to recognize that as these equivalences multiply, the glue connecting the descriptive pair loses its adhesive power. Through a series of interchanges, Jake and Brett are equated differently; established relations dissolve and are rearranged into new relations. What began as an inseparable unit (sexually maimed-homosexual) ends up as free-floating terms (sexually maimed, homosexual), and the characters, particularly Jake and Brett, are revealed as bodies of contradictions. Ultimately these pairings challenge the validity of defining gender and sexuality in terms of binarisms—masculine/feminine, heterosexual/homosexual.

For instance, the pairing of Brett and Georgette, like the pairing of Jake and the homosexual men, is complex and multifaceted. The resemblance between the two women is underscored when Jake, half-asleep, thinks that Brett, who has come to visit him, is Georgette (32). Obviously such a correspondence reveals that both women sleep around, one because she believes it's the way she is made (55), the other because it's the way she makes a living. Yet this explanation of motives reminds us that women's outlets for their desires were closely intertwined with economic necessity in the years following World War I, even in the liberated Left Bank of Paris. As a white, heterosexually identified, upper-class woman, Brett still must depend, both financially and socially, on hooking up with one man or another. As Wendy Martin observes, "If Brett has gained a measure of freedom in leaving the traditional household, she is still very much dependent on men, who provide an arena in which she can be attractive and socially active as well as financially secure."[6]

Brett's self-destructive drinking and her attempts to distance herself from sexual role stereotyping—for example, her short hair is "brushed back like a boy's" (22) and she wears a "man's felt hat" (28)—indicate her resentment of this prescribed arrangement. Susan Gubar reminds us that many women artists of the modernist period escaped the strictures of socially defined femininity by appropriating male clothing, which they identified with freedom.[7] For such women, cross-dressing became "a way of ad-dressing and re-dressing the inequities of culturally-defined categories of masculinity and femininity" (Gubar, 479). Like Catherine Bourne of *The Garden of Eden*, Brett Ashley fits this category of women who were crossing gender lines by cross-dressing and behaving in "masculine ways." Although Brett's wool jersey sweater reveals her to be a woman, the exposure is not enough to counter the effect of her masculine apparel and appearance on the men around her. Pedro Romero's urge to both make her look more "womanly" (242) and marry her might be explained as the response of a man raised to demand clear distinctions between the gender roles of men and women. But the attempt of the more carefree Mike Campbell to convince Brett to buy a new hat (79) and to marry him suggests that Brett is dangerously close to overturning the categories upon which male and female identity, and patriarchal power, depend. The "new woman" must not venture too far outside the old boundaries.

Brett's cross-dressing conveys more than just a social statement about gender. It also evokes suggestions of the transvestism practiced by and associated with lesbians of the time (and since). As I described in Chapter 3, sexologists such as Havelock Ellis recognized the so-called mannish woman as only one kind of lesbian; nonetheless, the wearing of men's clothing by women was often viewed as sexual coding. Certainly many lesbians chose to cross-dress in order to announce their sexual preference.[8] One hint that we might read Brett's cross-dressing within this context comes in the parallel set up between her and Georgette. When Jake introduces Georgette to a group seated in the restaurant, he identifies her as his fiancée, Georgette Leblanc. As several scholars have pointed out, Georgette Leblanc was a contemporary singer and actress in Paris—and an acknowledged lesbian.[9] This association consequently deepens the symbolic relationship of Brett to Georgette, linking them in a new equation: independent/lesbian. Brett's transvestism crosses over from gender inversion to sexual sign: not only does Brett desire the lesbian's economic and social autonomy but she also possesses same-sex desire.

In fact, Brett's alcoholism and inability to sustain a relationship might be indications not of nymphomania, with which the critics have often charged her, but of a dissatisfaction with the strictures of the male-female relationship. Brett's announcement, for example, that she can drink safely among homosexual men (22) can be taken to mean that she cannot control her own heterosexual desire, though it could also reveal underlying anxiety toward the heterosexual desire of men. Such an anxiety might be related to her abusive marriage, but that experience need not be its only source. As Brett tells Jake after the break-up with Pedro Romero, "I can't even marry Mike" (242). Of course, soon after this, she declares, "I'm going back to Mike. . . . He's so damned nice and he's so awful. He's my sort of thing" (243). Yet even in giving her reasons for returning to Mike, Brett reveals her inner turmoil and ambivalence. Like Mike, she is both "nice" and "awful," and the novel ends before this promised reunion occurs.

We should be careful not to equate Brett's anxiety about male heterosexual desire with lesbian desire nor to presume that unhappy heterosexual relations are a necessary condition for lesbian desire. In fact, Brett's same-sex desire is hinted at in other ways than her cross-dressing and her frustrations with heterosexual men, namely, through her association with her homosexual companions. As Jake states three times, she is "with them," she is "very much with them" (20). This homosexual identification helps to explain Brett's attraction to Jake who, according to Hemingway in a letter written in 1951, has lost his penis but not his testicles and spermatic cord (*Ernest Hemingway: Selected Letters*, 745).[10] If we accept this explanation, Jake lacks the physical feature that has traditionally been the most important in distinguishing sex as well as male sexual desire.[11] He is a sexual invalid and, as a consequence, sexually in-valid.[12] Jake's maleness, masculinity, and heterosexuality, lined up and linked under the law of compulsory heterosexuality, are separated and problematized. Like a woman, Jake has no penis with which to make love with Brett. Instead, Brett ministers to him, "strok[ing] his head" as he lies on the bed (56), and recognizes that the absent male sex organ makes Jake different from other suitors.[13] In this context, Jake's notion that Brett "only wanted what she couldn't have" (31) takes on added meaning. Besides non-penile sex, she wants to find some way to accommodate the fluidity of sexual desire and gender identification that characterizes her condition.

Brett's affiliation with homosexual men and her transgendering complicate, in turn, Jake's relationship with her. Jake calls Brett "damned good-looking" and describes her hair as being "brushed back like a boy's" (22), two attributions that dissolve into one in Jake's later identification of Pedro Romero as "a damned good-looking boy" (167). Jake's attraction to Brett can be partially attributed to his homosexual desire, a desire that seems about to break through the surface of Jake's narrative at any time.[14] As the Davidsons observe and as I mentioned earlier, this desire can be seen in Jake's conflicted response to Brett's homosexual companions. It can also be seen in Jake's possession of *afición*, which must be confirmed by the touch of other men (132). To quote the Davidsons, there is something "suspect" in the aficionados vesting so much of their manhood in a boylike matador who woos a bull to death through "girlish flirtation and enticement." As a consequence, "the whole ethos of *afición* resembles a sublimation of sexual desire, and the aficionados— serving, guiding, surrounding the matador out of the ring and applauding him in it—seem all, in a sense, steers" (95).

Jake's descriptions of the meeting of the bull and bullfighter imply more than flirtation; the encounter evokes images of sexual foreplay and consummation. He states, "The bull wanted it again, and Romero's cape filled again, this time on the other side. Each time he let the bull pass so close that the man and the bull and the cape that filled and pivoted ahead of the bull were all one sharply etched mass" (217). Later Jake expresses the climax of the bullfight, the bull's death, in terms reminiscent of sexual climax:

[F]or just an instant [Romero] and the bull were one, Romero way out over the bull, the right arm extended high up to where the hilt of the sword had gone in between the bull's shoulders. Then the figure was broken. There was a little jolt as Romero came clear, and then he was standing, one hand up, facing the bull, his shirt ripped out from under his sleeve, the white blowing in the wind, and the bull, the red sword hilt tight between his shoulders, his head going down and his legs settling. (218–19)

Jake's relationships with Bill Gorton and Pedro Romero constitute two of the more important sources of sublimated homosexual desire. During their fishing trip to the Irati River, Bill tells Jake, "Listen. You're a hell of a good guy, and I'm fonder of you than anybody on earth. I couldn't tell you that in New York. It'd mean I was a faggot" (116). In expressing his fondness for Jake, Bill realizes the risk he takes in declaring strong feelings for another man. His words might be construed, by himself as well as by others, as an admission of homosexual love. To avoid being interpreted in that way, Bill must declare homosexual desire an impossibility. However, Bill's phrasing in this passage and his subsequent focus on homosexuality suggest that such desire is a very real possibility. For one, his statement "I'm fonder of you than anybody on earth" can be read as "I'm fonder of you than I am of anybody else on earth" or as "I'm fonder of you than anybody else is." Either reading elevates Bill and Jake's relationship to a primary position. It is a connection more binding and important than any other relationship Bill has formed.

In addition, Bill's worry that disclosing his affection for Jake would, in New York, mean that he is "a faggot" indicates Bill's awareness of the instability of the line separating homosocial and homosexual behavior and desire. Outside the geographic and psychological boundaries of New York and its taxonomy of deviance, Bill's feelings are platonic; inside those boundaries, they are homosexual.[15] Bill's concern about the boundaries for same-sex relationships indicates that he cannot be sure about the "purity" of his feelings for Jake or of Jake's for him. In an early draft of the novel, Bill's obsession and concern are even more apparent. Bill tells Jake that New York circles have marked him (Bill) as "crazy." "Also I'm supposed to be crazy to get married. Would marry anybody at any time. . . . Since Charley Gordon and I had an apartment together last winter, I suppose I'm a fairy. That probably explains everything." Bill also reinforces his awareness, and fear, of the instability of sexual identity when he attacks the literary world of New York by claiming that "every literary bastard" there "never goes to bed at night not knowing but that he'll wake up in the morning and find himself a fairy. There are plenty of real ones too" (quoted in Mellow, 312–13).

Even though Hemingway eventually cut this passage about fairies and the unstable sexual identities of "literary bastards," the anxieties it expresses remain in the published text. Having stated his fondness for Jake, Bill moves the discussion away from their relationship, but he cannot drop the subject of homosexuality: "That [homosexual love] was what the Civil War was about. Abraham Lincoln was a faggot. He was in love with General Grant. So was Jefferson Davis. . . . Sex explains it all. The Colonel's Lady and Judy O'Grady are Lesbians under their skin" (116). By identifying homosexual desire as the cause of all private and public action, a supposedly absurd exaggeration, Bill defuses the tension that expressing his affection for Jake creates. Yet homosexuality is still very much in the air—and "under their skin."

This homosexual current flowing through the text reaches its crisis at the same time that the heterosexuality of the text is also at its highest tension: during the liaison that Jake arranges between Brett and Pedro. As we have seen, Jake describes Pedro in terms that repeat his descriptions of Brett. Further, his first impression of the bullfighter is a physical one—"He was the best-looking boy I have ever seen" (163)—and his later observations continue this focus on Pedro's body. Jake tells Brett that Pedro is "nice to look at" (184), notices his clear, smooth, and very brown skin (185), and describes Pedro's hand as being "very fine" and his wrist as being small (185). Considering the way Jake gazes upon Pedro's body (a body that, like Brett's, blends male and female, masculine and feminine), the moment when Jake brings together Pedro and Brett is also the moment when the text reveals its inability to separate heterosexual from homosexual desire within the desiring body.

This scene has typically been read as the tragic fulfillment of a traditional love triangle in which two men want the same women and desire moves heterosexually: Jake wants Brett who wants Pedro who wants Brett. Yet given the similarity in the way Jake describes Brett and Pedro, given Jake's homoerotic depictions of the bullfighter's meeting with the bull, and given the sexual ambiguities embodied by Brett and Jake, it seems more accurate to view this relationship not as a triangle but as a web in which desire flows in many directions. When Brett and Pedro consummate their desire for each other, Pedro also becomes Jake's surrogate, fulfilling his desire for Brett and hers for him, while Brett becomes Jake's "extension" for satisfying his infatuation with Pedro. Although Jake is physically and phallically absent from Pedro and Brett's "honeymoon" (190), his desire is multiply and symbolically present. Of course, the inadequacy of a figurative presence is disclosed when Brett persists in telling Jake the details of her relationship with Pedro, a verbal reenactment that drives him to overeat and overdrink.

The final scene of the novel situates Jake between the raised baton of the policeman, an obvious phallic symbol and representative of the Law, and the pressure of Brett's body. Such a situation suggests that the novel does not stop trying to bridge the multiple desires of its characters. However, Brett's wishful statement—"we could have had such a damned good time together"—and Jake's ironic question—"Isn't it pretty to think so?" (247)—reveal that at least part of the failure, part of the "lostness," conveyed in the novel is that such a bridge cannot be built. The prescriptions for masculinity and femininity and for heterosexuality and homosexuality are too strong to be destroyed or evaded, even in a time and place of sexual and gender experimentation.

As my analysis suggests, to explore the fundamental equivalences implied in the dancing club scene and their reverberations throughout *The Sun Also Rises* leads to constructing a network of ambiguities and contradictions pertaining to sexuality and gender. As I admitted earlier, in creating such a construction, I have had to draw upon the very concepts that I claim Hemingway's novel calls into question (masculinity/femininity, homosexuality/heterosexuality). But by refusing to qualify or resolve the contradictions surrounding these categories and by focusing attention upon the points at which they conflict, we see that Hemingway's novel puts gender and sexuality into constant motion. Although modern society attempts to stabilize conduct and appearance as masculine or feminine, and desire as homosexual, heterosexual, or bisexual, it is still not easy to contain and categorize desire and behavior. Actions, appearance, and desire in *The Sun Also Rises* spill over the "normal" boundaries of identity and identification so that categories become destabilized and merge with one another.

This is not to say that Brett and Jake have discarded society's scripts for femininity and masculinity, or for heterosexuality and homosexuality, in favor of more contemporary concepts such as transgendered or queer. Their actions, particularly Brett's flirtations and Jake's homophobia, show that they know these scripts well. Nevertheless, as we see by following the several parallels suggested in the club scene, both Jake and Brett continually stray from the lines the scripts demand. The text asks us to suspect, and finally to critique, those systems of representation that are insufficient and hence disabling to efforts to comprehend the human body and its desires.

The Race of Desire and Hemingway's World-Traveling: Re-Placing Africa in "The Snows of Kilimanjaro" and in Hemingway's African Safari, 1953–54

If the cultural construction of Hemingway as ultra masculine and therefore ultra heterosexual (or vice versa) has been predominant during and after his life, equally predominant is the construction of him as a white American. Yet rarely have critics studied the race of Hemingway or of his white characters, nor have they thought much about the ways in which whiteness intersects with his desires, the desires of his white characters, or the desires of his few characters of color.[16] The paucity of such study reflects the tendency of many scholars to view race and difference in terms of those who are non-white, to study the deviant "other" rather than the normed white. It might also suggest a tendency on the part of Hemingway scholars to infer that Hemingway's world-traveling and world-residing obviated, or at least reduced, the importance of racial and national identity in his makeup or that of his characters.[17] But rather than precluding these matters, surely Hemingway's world-traveling is tied to his Americanness as well as to his whiteness. Mobility, one of the distinguishing components of critical and popular constructions of Hemingway, is also a characteristic of wealthy white Americans and white economic, intellectual, and social privilege. That this mobility is also a constituent element of maleness, heterosexuality, and the "able" body underscores the difficulty of speaking of identity categories in isolation of one another.

By "mobility" I mean both a conceptual mobility as well as a physical mobility. Conceptual mobility refers not only to the power that white Americans, and whites in general, have had to name the terms of existence and to conceptualize the world from their viewpoint, but it also alludes to the ability of whites to inhabit different places on a conceptual continuum without risking social power. For instance, as we saw in Chapter 3, Catherine Bourne's attempt to darken her skin, to change her race, does not signal her recognition of the arbitrariness, complexity, and fluidity of racial designations; instead, it signifies her desire to inhabit the erotic conceptual space that whites have traditionally assigned to black

Africans and Americans of African descent. Unlike the racial movement in, say, Nella Larsen's *Passing*, where light-skinned black women pass as white at the risk of social ostracization or worse, Catherine's desire to pass as Kanaka contains little physical or social risk, and actually originates in the racist fantasy of the sexual desirability of the African woman. Kate Davy contends that white women's privilege can be understood in terms of our potential to traverse the nature/culture continuum, moving away from savagery toward enlightenment.[18] As we see, however, from Catherine's situation and from the fascination of many whites with "primitivism" (especially popular in the early twentieth century but also prevalent in recent movements such as New Age spirituality), the mobility of white people is even greater than Davy envisions.[19] We can also move away from enlightenment toward savagery, revaluing these concepts in the process. This is not to say that people of color are completely immobile with respect to this continuum, nor do they lack power to revalue the terms of domination. Rather, the historical production of social knowledge about race has been controlled by whites, and as David Theo Goldberg demonstrates, this knowledge is not just information about a racial Other but permeates "the principal formative developments in modernity's self-understanding and expression" (1).

The physical mobility of white Americans is obviously connected to our conceptual mobility. With important exceptions and restrictions (class-based but also body-based), whites in the United States move freely from business establishment to business establishment. We expect to be upwardly mobile in terms of jobs and places of residence, we can travel throughout much of the world without trouble, and we have access to most modes of transportation. White people take much of this mobility for granted, though Toni Morrison reminds us that white privilege is often not simply defined but indulged through reference to people of color:

Freedom (to move, to earn, to learn, to be allied with a powerful center, to narrate the world) can be relished more deeply in a cheek-by-jowl existence with the bound and unfree, the economically oppressed, the marginalized, the silenced. The ideological dependence on racialism is intact and, like its metaphysical existence, offers in historical, political, and literary discourse a safe route into meditations on morality and ethics; a way of examining the mind-body dichotomy; a way of thinking about justice; a way of contemplating the modern world. (64)

The junction of physical and conceptual mobility is prominent in constructions of Hemingway's identity and in discussions of many of his white characters who possess similar mobilities. One of the more interesting sites for viewing this junction can be found in the critical construction of Hemingway in the 1930s and in the related interpretations of "The Snows of Kilimanjaro" (1936), since this site brings together many aspects of white mobility and American ideology, thereby revealing the ethical repercussions and limitations of both.

To be specific, in this section I will show how the construction of Hemingway as a "great American writer" who revived his reputation with the writing of "Snows" has subtended most readings of his male protagonist, Harry. My point is that the reasoning that underlies this image of Hemingway is complicit with the reasoning that allows Harry to stage his life drama on the backs of African Others without realizing he is doing so or having to contemplate what that means for his moral stocktaking. Paris, Constantinople, Austria, Italy, Wyoming, and Michigan might be the locations to which Harry returns in his imagination, but the true setting of his story is the plains of East Africa with capitalist-imperialism so permeating the stage as to be invisible, as is any ideology for those whose behavior is structured by it. Having exposed the way in which a story of American individualism has been written over a story of capitalist-imperialism, I will then show how the privileged behavior exhibited by Hemingway's white characters in "Snows" is intimately connected to Hemingway's whiteness, his desire for the African Other, and his cultural status as world-traveler.

Scholars such as Sacvan Bercovitch (*The American Jeremiad* [1978]) and Rob Wilson have argued that in their very form biographies of American men and women reproduce the ideology of America. According to Wilson, the "self" the American biographer feels compelled to construct is "typically a 'representative self' . . . incarnating American social codes and norms and thereby affirming the power of liberal ideology to sacralize its own goals."[20] In American biographies, the individual embodies a mission of America originally defined by white men, and affirms, "if at times castigating, the virtues, freedoms, and goals of [the] American way" (Wilson, 171). In particular, Wilson argues, American biography is grounded on "assumptions of selfhood as a conflicted drama of individuation." Such assumptions involve the idea of America as a space where the individual and the nation are "metaphorically conjoined in the quest for economic and cultural capital" (172–73).

To support his thesis, Wilson examines the construction of selfhood in selected biographies of four American writers—Wallace Stevens, William Carlos Williams, Langston Hughes, and Emily Dickinson. He could just as easily have chosen the biographies of Hemingway, even those written by biographers such as Carlos Baker and Kenneth Lynn, who seem to construct Hemingway's identity from divergent perspectives. Indeed, the biographical construction of Hemingway during the time he wrote "Snows" demonstrates Wilson's thesis in miniature. Nearly every description of Hemingway at this time portrays him as caught between fearing that his artistic powers and individuality were being corrupted by a rich wife and her rich friends and proving those fears to be unwarranted by writing "The Snows of Kilimanjaro."

Through this understanding, Hemingway emerges as *the* representative American in that his Puritan work ethic redeems him from sloth and a failure to live up to his potential. This redemption tautologically proves him to be worthy of the success he achieves and reaffirms the merits of American democracy. Hemingway distinguishes himself from the lazy, undeserving rich by proving that hard work and discipline *do* pay off, given that America is considered a meritocracy. Moreover, because Hemingway's particular form of personal success has to do with "art," his breakthrough implies that the American political system produces great artists.

The critics who depict Hemingway as (at least partly) redeemed by writing "Snows" are numerous. Here I enlist only a few to speak for the majority. Consider, for instance, John Raeburn's description of this time in Hemingway's life. Hemingway, Raeburn claims, "had reached a crossroads [in the 1930s], and 'The Snows of Kilimanjaro' reviewed the course which had led him there and, more important, indicated a new direction. It signified Hemingway's determination to avoid Harry's fate, to resist the seductions of the comfort and security his sale of vitality to the unworthy had gotten him, and to devote himself to scaling the peaks of Art, where one might with luck and dedication create something so mysterious and imperishable as the frozen leopard found near the summit of Mount Kilimanjaro" (207). Kenneth Lynn notes that "Many factors in Hemingway's own life lay behind [Harry's] self-condemnation—his guilty sense of spending too much time playing instead of working, his fear of drinking, his consciousness of how many of the new friendships he had formed were with millionaires, his pained awareness of the inadequacy of his recent books, his realization of the destructiveness of publicity. But perhaps the most significant of all the similarities between author and protagonist was symbolized by that phrase of Harry's about trading on his talent" (430). Nonetheless, Lynn assures us, when Hemingway wrote "Snows" and "Macomber," two brief masterpieces, he was working as well as he ever had and was "again in touch with who he actually was" (429).

Robert Fleming paints a similar picture, maintaining that Hemingway had to be aware when he wrote "Snows" that "his own career had taken a wrong turn since those days in Paris when he was considered the most promising writer of his generation."[21] But, according to Fleming, "Snows" is a "major short story" that documents his *"real* growth during the 1930s" (47; emphasis added). Finally, James Mellow expresses what is by now the common representation of Hemingway, claiming that "Snows," "unquestionably the great masterpiece among his short stories" (449), was written at a time when Hemingway's reputation was "suffering at the hands of critics who complained of the effect of the Hemingway legend on his work and style" (442).

The pattern by which critics have characterized Hemingway is the pattern of success as defined by the American political system. In effect, Hemingway struggles to save himself from the temptations of laziness, self-indulgence, and unproductivity, and succeeds by writing an American literary masterpiece. As can be seen from their accounts, many critics have given weight to this construction by comparing Hemingway with his protagonist, Harry, who typically serves as the failure contrasting to Hemingway's success.[22] But in centering their discussions of "Snows" around this drama of success/failure, cultural production/nonproduction, and temptation/redemption, critics have invariably overlooked the imperialist implications of Harry's story, for such implications are suppressed by the very ideology used to measure Harry and Hemingway.

It might seem odd to hear that Harry, his story, and his critics have remained oblivious to the nuances of American ideology when all three seem explicitly to critique capitalism, especially as it manifests itself in a fascination with accumulating material comforts and wealth. Admittedly, Harry is acutely aware of the way in which money can corrupt a person, dulling one's ability and softening the will to work so that finally one does no work at all.[23] This awareness motivates his return to Africa, "where he had been happiest in the good time of his life," for he wants to "start again." He and Helen have made their safari "with the minimum of comfort," because Harry believes that without luxuries he can "get back into training" and "work the fat off his soul" (44). His attacks on Helen, their wealthy friends, and "poor Julian," obsessed with the rich and identified in the original printing of the story as F. Scott Fitzgerald, seem to distinguish Harry from those who are used to a life of riches or who stand in awe of those who have them. "Your damned money," he snarls at Helen (43). Twice he calls her a "rich bitch" (43, 45). He even associates Helen's small amount of fame, her commodification by the magazines *Spur* and *Town & Country*, with death: "as he looked and saw her well-known pleasant smile, he felt death come again" (49). The rich, Harry concludes, "were dull and they drank too much, or they played too much backgammon. They were dull and they were repetitious" (53).

In his more reflective and self-conscious moments, Harry relieves Helen of blame and places it on himself. He thus determines that, ultimately, the villain in his own morality play is himself. Isn't it strange, he asks, in what is clearly a rhetorical question, that "when he fell in love with another woman, that woman should always have more money than the last one?" (45). In such moments, Harry locates the center of his value system by gauging how far he has wandered from it: "He had destroyed his talent by not using it, by betrayals of himself and what he believed in, by drinking so much that he blunted the edge of his perceptions, by laziness, by sloth, and by snobbery, by pride and by prejudice, by hook and by crook" (45). In depicting his "fall from grace," Harry establishes the moral center of the story as a critique of wealth and a celebration of hard work.

This critique has been taken up by critics as they have attempted to decide whether Harry is a successful artist, a failure, or something in between. In making this decision, most critics have focused on three elements. The first is the status and function of the italicized passages that represent Harry's thoughts but can also be seen as evidence of his artistic abilities or his lack of them. In studying these passages, critics have asked such questions as: Is writing in his head "all the stories that he meant to write" (52) the same as actually writing down these stories for others to read? Is the writing in these passages good writing, or is it maudlin and melodramatic? Are these stories, or are they simply fragments of stories? Another place where critics have looked for indications of Harry's redemption is the story's epigraph, which describes the mysterious situation of a leopard's carcass found near the western summit of Kilimanjaro. Is Harry leopard-like in reaching the "summit" of his artistic promise? If so, is it important that the leopard is found close to the summit but not actually at it? Can we explain, as no one else has been able to, what the leopard was seeking at that altitude? Finally, critics have sought evidence of Harry's status as artist in his penultimate vision of the mountain. Does his approach to Mount Kilimanjaro equate to Harry's apotheosis as artist, or is it a cruel delusion?

As my account of these three elements suggests, critics have taken both sides in developing their arguments for or against Harry's artistic redemption. But my point is that by becoming entrenched in the effort to measure Harry according to the American ideology of hard work, productivity, and success, we miss the larger picture. Critiquing wealth and celebrating hard work are not the same as critiquing an economic system that produces wealth at the expense of those who labor. While critics have sought to explain what the leopard was seeking near the western summit of "Ngàje Ngài," the House of God, they have ignored the plight of the Africans laboring below on the East Plains of Africa and Harry's relation to them.

When we look more closely at Harry's situation, we find that those who labor are at his beck and call; they are "personal boys" and a "half-baked Kikuyu driver" (41), black Africans whose subordination to the white American travelers reminds us of the intricate connections among imperialism, capitalism, and racism.[24] The most prominent African laborers in "Snows" are the personal boys who slip in and out of the picture to ensure that even if Harry and Helen's safari contains no luxury, it also contains "no hardship" (44). When Harry does suffer the hardship of gangrene, these men continue to fulfill his and his wife's needs in order to minimize their discomfort. Whether lifting his cot, accompanying Helen on a shoot, carrying her "kill," fixing dinner, lighting a fire, or changing Harry's dressing, the African "boys" are present to take care of Harry and Helen. The extent of their caretaking function is characterized in one small scene when Molo, Harry's "personal boy," is sitting by the side of Harry's bed and asks, "Does Bwana want?" "Nothing," Harry replies, but the offer defines their relationship (44).[25]

The importance of the black African servant to the white American tourist is made clear in the final pages of the story. In the penultimate scene, the rescue plane arrives with Compton ready to fly Harry to a hospital where his leg can be treated. We discover later that this scene represents Harry's final moments alive and takes place solely in his mind. In his imagination, Harry envisions "the boys" running out to the landing area and lighting fires "at each end of the level place" (55) so that Compton will know where to set down the plane. Even Harry's death requires the aid of African servants who prepare the way. In the final scene, this death has occurred, with Helen finding Harry's lifeless body and shouting for Molo to come to her aid. Only when she sees that Harry is beyond help does she plead for Harry to help her—or himself— which he can no longer do.

The black African servant is always in the background, coming into sight only when Harry or Helen calls to him, their voices carrying the authority of commanding his presence. Reflected in this dynamic is the economy of a colonial situation in which, to quote David Spurr, "one race holds, however provisionally and uneasily, authority over another."[26] Further defining this dynamic is the fact that the black man rarely speaks, and when he does, it is in response to Harry's needs: "Yes Bwana," Molo says twice (40), and once he tells Harry, "Memsahib's gone to shoot . . . . Does Bwana want?" (44). Significantly, in the final scene, when Harry is dead, the black servant is unavailable, an absence that confirms, once and for all, the relationship of dependency that exists between the white master and the "personal boy" who cares for him. Once the master is gone, the servant disappears as well, his existence defined by the existence of the white man.

The imperialist economy of Harry and Helen's situation is suggested not only in the instant availability of the black African servants but also in the way they inhabit the country. It is ironic—and telling—that Harry believes he has stripped himself of luxuries on this safari. He and Helen never have to cook a meal, and they apparently eat well; there is liquor available; there is a bath within the camp; and they have proper clothing (Helen wears jodhpurs and mosquito boots). Helen and Harry have, as far as possible, imported their home and lifestyle to Africa. As Harry says, surveying the place he and Helen have made their home, "This was a pleasant camp under big trees against a hill, with good water, and close by, a nearly dry water hole where sand grouse flighted in the mornings" (40).

One also finds imperialist thinking in Helen's and Harry's attitudes toward Africa itself. For Helen, Africa has been, with the exception of Harry's sickness, a playground: "I love Africa. Really. If *you're* all right it's the most fun that I've ever had. You don't know the fun it's been to shoot with you. I've loved the country" (46; original emphasis). For Harry, Africa is "where he had been happiest in the good time of his life," a place to start again, "to work the fat off his soul" (44), in other words, a kind of fat farm where Harry can sweat out the excess of American and European decadence and wealth. Through such metaphors we come to understand the ideology of capitalist-imperialism that fuels

Harry and Helen's trip to Africa. Africa is described only to the extent that it has "use value" for the white travelers: a good place to camp, a park with plenty of game, a space for writing and righting one's life. The only things that Harry and Helen lack are the antiseptics that will restore Harry's health. But they do have access to a plane that might arrive in time to take Harry to a hospital. When the going gets too rough, the white American travelers can arrange to go.

One might argue that this is the point of the story: that Harry cannot work the fat of money off his soul because he has sold his soul to that very devil. Such a point seems to be implied when Harry states that the rich "were dull and they drank too much, or they played too much backgammon. They were dull and they were repetitious" (53). In repeating the idea that the rich were dull, Harry implicates himself. He repeats himself; he is rich. He is rich; he repeats himself. That this implication comes in the very act of critiquing the rich indicates the internal battle that Harry is waging. He wants to believe he is different from the rich, but in fact he is fully ensconced within an ideology of wealth. Harry is as obsessed with the rich as is "poor Julian."

But if this is the story's point—that wealth corrupts and especially corrupts the artist—then we must recognize how that point has caused, perhaps even permitted, both Harry and his readers to miss the larger picture in which capitalist-imperialism is complicit with the ideology of self-reliant individualism. As much as Harry might compare himself to the self he once was and to find his present self lacking, at no time does this soul-searching consider that his trip to Africa might rely on questionable ethics. Harry perceives his return to Africa as an attempt to resuscitate that former, more desirable self that he was when he was young, poor, and disciplined. But Harry never sees the Africans who surround him and wait on him as anything other than beings trained to service his needs; equally important, the story gives no indication that a younger Harry saw them differently. Africa is simply "where he had been happiest in the good time of his life, so he had come out here to start again" (44).

This lack of sight—and insight—indicates the extent to which Harry's view of Africa is structured by the ideology of capitalist-imperialism. We find the most blatant sign of this structuring in the terms the indigenous Africans apply to Harry and Helen: "Bwana," a Swahili term meaning "master" or "boss," and "memsahib," which means "madame boss." One might contend that these African men are servants and, as such, have no part to play except to attend those who pay their wages. Yet that, too, makes the point that under capitalism, especially in its imperialistic form, the laborer becomes visible and meaningful only to the extent that he or she can produce for the capitalist boss.

As in so much American and British literature written by white men, Africa thus becomes the stage for the white male's drama of individuation in which black African natives serve as stage hands without histories or scripts of their own. It is a dynamic mirrored in another story Hemingway published in 1936 and that, along with "Snows," he identified as one of his favorites: "The Short Happy Life of Francis Macomber." Once again, a white American man plays out his drama of self-actualization on African soil, this time in Kenya. Like Harry and Helen, Francis and Margot Macomber rely on the native Africans for their survival and comfort but do not question the economic system that makes these men, in effect, indentured servants.

This servitude is highlighted most clearly in a scene where Francis's "personal boy" gives Francis a curious look for having bolted from the charging lion, a visible transgression of the colonized/colonizer relationship that the white hunter Robert Wilson notices and immediately handles by warning the worker that he will be whipped if he continues his rude behavior. This warning foregrounds the ideology of dominance that sustains imperialism even as it points to the instabilities of that dominance. Wilson's warning makes clear that the colonized Other must never return or initiate the gaze; he or she is supposed to be the object of the gaze, never its instigator. In addition, Wilson's warning exposes the master-slave dynamic that underlies the colonialist system and reminds us that under British colonial rule in Kenya, the contractual relationship between employer and employee was subject to the force of criminal law.[27] When Francis asks, "Do you still have them whipped?" Wilson admits that it's illegal to beat the African workers but insists that they don't complain because they prefer the beatings to the fines, which are legal.[28] The colonial master can administer punishment with impunity simply because he is the colonial master.

In this analysis of "Snows" and "Macomber," I am not claiming that any of the characters has an imperialistic relationship with Africa. As individuals, they cannot have such a relationship, for imperialism is a relationship between nations. In addition, in the 1930s, when "Snows" takes place, such a relationship did not exist between Africa and the United States, although Tanganyika in which "Snows" is set—called Tanzania today—and Kenya, the setting of "Macomber," were under the colonial rule of Great Britain, one of the closest allies of the United States.[29] When I claim that Harry's attitude toward Africa is complicit with capitalist-imperialism, I am not suggesting that he literally wants to acquire or control African territory or that he directly supports American imperialistic policies. Rather, I am referring to a state of mind that is produced by and in turn helps to produce imperialistic attitudes toward another nation and thus subjects its people to dependency and domination. It is a state of mind that is shared, as I have shown, by the white characters of "The Short Happy Life of Francis Macomber."

Connecting this state of mind to the logic of capitalist-imperialism is crucial since we have a history in the United States of believing that our country does not support imperialist policies or behavior.[30] Harry, Helen, Francis, and Margot (not to mention Robert Wilson, who is British) all have a colonial relationship with the Africans who serve them, a relationship made possible by national ideologies in which the subjugation of a foreign land and its people is seen as just and ethical. To ignore this situation is to reproduce in our reading the position of dominance that lies at the heart of the colonial relationship.

Although this reading of "Snows" and "Macomber" has benefitted from recent critical work done in the field of postcolonial studies, it is important to note that anti-imperialist sentiments have circulated in both the United States and Great Britain throughout the nineteenth and twentieth centuries. A conceptual framework for critiquing the imperialist economy of "Snows" and "Macomber" has, therefore, been available ever since they were written.[31] As I mentioned earlier, our ability to apply such a framework has been obstructed by the particular biographical construction of Hemingway as a writer who was struggling with his own artistic individuation when he wrote these stories. Perhaps a better way to say this is to state that our vision has been constrained by our national ideology, for the life of Hemingway and those of his characters, Harry and Francis, have been read through that most representative of American plots in which the attainment of selfhood and success is seen as "a conflicted drama of individuation" (Wilson, 172).

By going outside the lines of this plot, beyond the individual to the relational and the international, we enlarge the ethical scope for reading Hemingway's stories. This suggests that a similar enlargement is required for analyzing critical constructions of Hemingway and for possibly formulating a counter-construction. Beyond the fact that Hemingway spent some time in Africa and called it the "place where it pleased

[him] to live; to really live,"[32] what exactly was his relationship to Africa? As a white American writer, did it serve him metaphorically and artistically in the way that it literally serves Francis and Harry? Moreover, given that the public interest in Hemingway has been based in large part on his world-traveling, what role do his travels to Africa play in that image?

At the time he was writing "Snows" and "Macomber," Hemingway referred to them as his African stories.[33] In a letter to his editor, Max Perkins, dated 9 April 1936, Hemingway states that he has finished a long "very exciting story *of* Africa," tentatively titled "A Budding Friendship" (renamed "Macomber"), and he also has "another story *of* Africa" called "The Happy Ending" (renamed "Snows"). His phrasing here is intriguing and suggests a realignment of our critical vision away from the two protagonists, Francis and Harry, and toward Africa itself. Is it possible that Hemingway wanted us to see Africa as the primary subject of both stories? As noted above, there were those in the 1930s who articulated anti-imperialist sentiments. In fact, in 1922, when Hemingway was working as a journalist for the *Toronto Star Weekly*, he reviewed René Maran's novel *Batouala*, which contained a preface attacking French colonialism in Africa. Of this book, Hemingway wrote, "you see the white man as the black man sees him."[34] Was Hemingway himself, fifteen years later, seeing the white colonizer as the colonized black African sees him? Should we view Hemingway as anti-imperialist?

Hemingway certainly realized the way in which colonial foreigners destroy countries that they invade. He expresses such sentiments in *Green Hills of Africa*, the fictionalized non-fiction he published a year before "Snows" and "Macomber," which recounts his own African safari taken in 1933–34. Near the end of this work he states that "A continent ages quickly once we come," explaining,

The natives live in harmony with it. But the foreigner destroys, cuts down the trees, drains the water, so that the water supply is altered and in a short time the soil, once the sod is turned under, is cropped out and, next, it starts to blow away as it has blown away in every old country and as I had seen it start to blow in Canada. The earth gets tired of being exploited. A country wears out quickly unless man puts back in it all his residue and that of all his beasts. When he quits using beasts and uses machines, the earth defeats him quickly. The machine can't reproduce, nor does it fertilize the soil, and it eats what he cannot raise. *A country was made to be as we found it.* We are the intruders and after we are dead we may have ruined it but it will still be there and we don't know what the next changes are. (284–85; emphasis added)

Although Hemingway acknowledges that natives live in these invaded countries, and live harmoniously with the land, they disappear from his account so that the land is left as the only victim of the invasion. The conflict is between the land and "us," the foreigners who "intrude" on the land and ruin it. In portraying the confrontation in this way Hemingway reveals his own inability to see the natives of the invaded country and to question the ethics of foreign invasion itself. He sees the wrong done to the land—and, I agree, it is a terrible wrong—not to the people. By removing the natives from the scene, Hemingway thus transforms a foreign invasion into a narrative of discovery ("A country was made to be as we found it") and restricts his view of the unethical action to environmental destruction.

Hemingway repeats this logic later in the same paragraph when he states, "*Our* people went to America because that was the place to go then. It had been a good country and we had made a bloody mess of it" (285; emphasis added). This description reflects thinking in which the colonizer simply eliminates indigenous peoples (in this case, Native Americans and Mexicans) from the field of vision. America has been ruined, Hemingway states, and now he will go somewhere else—like Africa. What we see in these two passages from *Green Hills of Africa* is that even though Hemingway has a rather admirable view about the need for humans to develop an ecologically sound relationship with the environment, his approach to Africa does not critique capitalist-imperialism but emanates from it. At the time that he wrote "Snows" and "Macomber," Hemingway apparently did not hold anti-imperialist views toward Africa, at least not as expressed in his non-fiction about Africa.[35]

His position is not so clear-cut in "Snows" or "Macomber." Because both stories criticize their white characters for embracing an American ideology of wealth, materialism, and commodification, one could argue that this critique also covers their imperialist attitudes. Both stories disparage the effects of entitlement—being served, being shielded from unpleasantness, commanding others—exhibited by wealthy, white American and British citizens with authority over the colonized Africans. From this point of view, both stories can be read as anti-imperialist.

In opposition to this anti-imperialist position, one might maintain that the critique of wealth and materialism in "Snows" and "Macomber" does not include a critique of imperialism per se, since the target of both stories seems to be people who act imperially rather than the economic and political system that oppresses racialized others for the benefit of white-dominated nations. For example, "Snows" suggests that the younger Harry was exemplary in his poverty and work ethic, yet as I've pointed out, this younger Harry, like the older Harry, was unaware of his immersion in imperialist doctrine. From this point of view, Hemingway's African stories have to do not with capitalist-imperialism but with two quintessential American vices: a lack of integrity regarding work (Harry) and a lack of bravery (Francis). By calling these works his "African stories," Hemingway is not attempting to redirect the reader's vision but is advocating a kind of artistic imperialism. Africa serves Hemingway as an imaginative space onto which he can project white characters and conflicts without considering the ethics of their occupation of Africa or the humanity of the black people who stand before them.

Africa continued to serve Hemingway as an imaginative space for much of his life, especially in his final decade when he took his second African safari (1953–54), worked on "the African book,"[36] and developed the white characters of *The Garden of Eden* who were obsessed with "becoming" African and going to Africa. By this time, his reputation as a literary star (he won the Nobel Prize for Literature in 1954) and world-traveler was fully established. Moreover, Hemingway's second safari took place primarily in Kenya, which at the time was in the middle of the Mau Mau rebellion of colonized natives seeking economic reforms and political freedom from British rule. We might look, therefore, to these later years for additional instruction regarding Hemingway's stance on capitalist-imperialism and the relation of that stance to his desire and his cultural image as world-traveler.

When Hemingway embarked on his safari to Africa in 1953, he was famous in large part because of his reputation as a world-traveler and man of action. According to John Raeburn, "Hemingway's return to Africa in 1953 was an event of public note, reported to curious readers by newspapers, gossip columnists, and *Time*" (145). Whereas his first safari had been financed by a wealthy uncle-in-law, Hemingway's second safari was underwritten by *Look* magazine, who also sent along a photographer to record his experiences. In addition, the Kenya Game Department and the Nairobi Game Department welcomed Hemingway to the country, for they hoped that the publicity surrounding Hemingway's excursion would divert international attention from the Mau Mau rebellion and encourage other rich Americans to take their own safaris.[37] As

Rose Marie Burwell puts it, "Hemingway's name on the cover of a popular magazine had enormous power to draw serious, moneyed readers eager to follow in his footsteps" (136). Thus, Hemingway's second safari was set up as a money-making (ad)venture with other white Americans as the market audience.

The pictorial-article that recounted Hemingway's safari appeared in the 26 January 1954 issue of *Look*. As was consistent with the magazine's name, the piece gave more space to photos than to Hemingway's text. Many of the photos picture Hemingway killing animals, posing with animals he had supposedly killed, and demonstrating various Western skills to Kenyan natives (how to box, how to treat a case of skin disease). The emphasis of the piece is thus on Hemingway's expertise (whether shooting a gun, reporting the habits of animals, teaching boxing techniques, or dispensing medical advice). This emphasis is strengthened by the cover photo in which a wise-looking Hemingway looks to his left, his gaze followed by that of a smiling, black African man who stands in the shadowed background over Hemingway's left shoulder. Hemingway's wife, Mary, is also featured in the photo layout, and she has her own kind of expertise. In one photo, she inspects a young Masai woman while the accompanying text refers to a village "where the girls varied in their beauty." The implication is that Mary knows how to detect such aesthetic variations. The photo next to this one shows a child covered with flies, but the text notes that Mary gave the child's mother "an insecticide bomb," so concerned readers can presume the child will recover.[38] One full page of photos and text is devoted to Mary's adoption of a newborn gazelle (named Baa) who had been abandoned by his mother when she and her herd were frightened by lions (31). In the other two photos in which Mary appears, she stands next to or nearby Hemingway as his companion. In only one of these photos does she hold a gun, and here she is simply carrying it, not using it. The sense one gets from these pictures is that Mary has brought to Africa the expertise of white feminine domesticity. To clinch the point that both Hemingways possess superior expertise, the magazine commentary reports that, *"The Masai, tall warriors and wanderers, had a problem and asked the Hemingways for help"* in killing the lions that had been attacking their cattle (24; original italics).

The superiority of white expertise is also found in the text where, for example, Hemingway tells us that he knows something of the Kikuyu war (the Mau Mau rebellion) being fought in Kenya, but that it is "no part of this picture story." The reference to the war in Kenya conveys yet another important side of Hemingway's competence—his ability to size up the dangers of Africa for the white traveler. Hemingway tells his readers that "the Mau Mau might be going on for a considerable time" and he hopes to return some day "to study them" (20). In the meantime, he assures us, any "foreigner" who comes to Africa need not worry about the war. "Nairobi for a foreigner with no one with a grudge against him is safer than New York, five times safer than parts of Memphis, West Memphis or Jacksonville, infinitely safer than many parts of Chicago and most certainly safer than Brooklyn, the Bronx, Central Park at night or Cooke City, Montana, on the date of the celebration of the Old Timers Fish Fry" (20). Further, visitors need not worry about "the bush" so long as they have a white hunter as guide, an added expense that Hemingway wholeheartedly recommends (20). So detailed is Hemingway's discussion of safety that Mary interrupts his text with a parenthetical insertion—"This seems to be excessive emphasis on safety, a fickle friend" (20)—an observation that ironically increases the representation of both Hemingways as experts on safety.[39] The overall impression of the essay and its photos is that prospective white travelers need not fear either tall natives or big game. Africa not only waits for them, it needs them.

Considering the attention given to the expert knowledge and skills of Ernest and Mary Hemingway, and their benefit to the African people, the account in *Look* ends rather oddly. The final photo portrays a hawk killing a guinea fowl. Hemingway's text describes the guinea's unsuccessful effort to escape the hawk's persistent attacks, concluding that the hawk and the guinea were "obviously of different tribes. Watching this action I was not wholly sure of the white man's role in Africa" (34). Hemingway's ambiguous observation fails to specify whether the hawk is the white man or Africa. However, when the emphasis on white people's interventions in African affairs is set against the background of the Mau Mau rebellion, it seems that Hemingway aligns the predatory, devouring hawk with whites.[40] Although the note of doubt is brief and completely overshadowed by the rest of the piece, which carves out a clear and safe space for white people's presence in Africa, it indicates that Hemingway continued to feel ambivalent toward white intrusion in African territories and cultures.

If we are to understand fully the consequences of this ambivalence, we must shift our eyes from the pages of *Look* where we find another image of Hemingway, one that the magazine did not include and that Hemingway himself failed to narrate. While on safari, Hemingway "shaved his head, painted himself and sometimes went native in dress; and he took young Wakumba women to his tent" (Burwell, 136); he imagined that he would take a new Wakumba wife, a woman named Debba, who would bear him children, as his white wife, Mary, could not (Burwell, 142–43). Hemingway also started hunting with a spear, and once when tracking a leopard, he found a piece of the leopard's shoulder blade and "popped it into his mouth like a savage talisman" (Baker, 518). He even "started ceremonies for face-cutting and ear-piercing" (Mary Hemingway, 451). In short, what *Look*'s readers were prevented from seeing is what Burwell calls "the Africanization of Hemingway" (140) or what Baker refers to as Hemingway's "going native with a vengeance" (518).

Although they might seem worlds apart, the Hemingway pictured in the pages of *Look* and the one who isn't found there are actually joined by an important logic. In referring to whites in Africa as predatory hawks, Hemingway seems to recognize the potential unethicalness of white imposition of Western attitudes, practices, and beliefs on native Africans. Rather than deal with the responsibility such recognition brings, he divests himself of that imperative by "going native," by attempting to align himself with the black Africans rather than with the white travelers who form his safari party.[41] In this case, deflection of responsibility for racist and/or colonialist ideology becomes a kind of mental counterpart to the physical mobility that plays such an important role in Hemingway's cultural image. When the ethics of white presence in Africa become too much for him to bear, Hemingway simply moves—into the colonial fantasy regarding black primitiveness and desire. Significantly, Hemingway's description of whites as predatory hawks who devour Africans in the guise of guinea fowls recalls bell hooks's concept of "eating the other," and thus it is not surprising that she provides insight into Hemingway's movement away from whiteness and toward blackness. According to hooks, the desire of whites to make contact with bodies deemed Other with no apparent will to dominate "establishes a contemporary narrative where the suffering imposed by structures of domination on those designated Other is deflected by an emphasis on seduction and longing where the desire is not to make the Other over in one's image but to become the Other" (25).

In light of hooks's explanation of white people's desire to become the Other, it is interesting to note that at the same time Hemingway was pursuing Debba, whom he called his fiancée, he was also working out the specifics of a transgendered sexual relationship with Mary Hemingway. As we saw in Chapter 3, in this interaction Hemingway played the part of Mary's girl, yet another way of becoming Other. Hemingway denied that this role reversal had anything to do with homosexual desire, labeling it instead as "something quite new and outside all tribal law" (quoted in Mary Hemingway, 426). However, in rejecting same-sex desire as the driving force behind his and Mary's cross-sexual sex, Hemingway actually names the desire that underlies his attraction to Mary-as-boy. The discourse of the primitive thus serves double duty for Hemingway. It not only heightens his experience of heterosexual desire by engaging the taboo racialized Other; it also makes possible the circulation of homosexual desire by substituting for it a desire that is "outside all tribal law." The tension between homosexual desire and heterosexual desire is here, in Africa and in Hemingway's "Africanization," revealed to be imbricated in the tension between intraracial and interracial desire.

Like his white characters in "Snows" and "Macomber," Hemingway also can physically leave Africa, which he did in 1954 after two well publicized airplane crashes.[42] His actions in Africa reveal, then, the way in which white mobility can prevent white Americans from understanding not only the culture and people of other nations but also the ethics of our behavior in and occupation of those lands. For one thing, white Americans' contacts with other cultures and people—especially cultures and people deemed "Other"—are typically transitory. On safari, on vacation, on spiritual retreat, on military assignment, in our media, in our classrooms, we seldom stay away from the United States for long. For another, this mobility reflects the fact that many American whites come to know the "colored Other" through an internalization of racist and colonialist tropes about both Other and Self. This knowing is difficult to reject completely, because it so thoroughly influences how we see the world, because it can be easily obscured by concepts of American ideology such as self-reliance and self-actualization, and because whites so often align racism and imperialism solely with discrimination against people of color rather than also with white privileges. Consequently, although we are not literally agents for capitalist-imperialism, we can still act according to the dictates of its thinking even when we consciously endeavor to identify ourselves with the colonized Other, as Hemingway sometimes did in his work and life. From this perspective, Hemingway's world-traveling ironically signifies its opposite: immobility, arrogant perception,[43] lack of knowledge about Other and thus about Self.[44]

In a recent memoir, David Mura, who is Japanese American, writes about his experience of watching the film *Out of Africa* while visiting Japan. His primary emotion, he says, was boredom:

I'd seen the great white bwana story and the romance of Europeans in Africa a hundred times before. What I wanted to know about, what I knew little about were the minds of the Africans around [Karen] Blixen, the Kenyans who, two decades later, would organize the Mau Maus and the revolt which gained independence for Kenya. What was the interior life behind those black faces? I found I couldn't keep both the Meryl Streep character [Blixen] and the black faces at the center of my attention at the same time. I had to choose. Indeed, I had been choosing all my life. Only now I was withdrawing attention, affection, curiosity, from the white face at the center of the picture and giving it to the black faces. I was striking a new balance. And the world looked differently. I saw that this was a form of cultural and political power, the almost unconscious and instantaneous granting of priority to faces of one skin color over another.[45]

Mura describes a habit of looking ingrained into many of us in the United States, regardless of our color. It is a habit of looking that I have shared even though I work to resist it. In writing this section on how we might construct Hemingway's whiteness as it relates to his desire for the African Other as well as his desire to be the African Other, I have become increasingly conscious of the way in which I might be perceived—or want to be perceived—as a white person who lacks such desires. Examining the way in which Hemingway's sexual desires are connected to race might simultaneously imply a particular construction of me—as someone who is unambivalent about capitalist-imperialism and whose desires are unaffected by racist tropes. I have thus wondered whether my critique of Hemingway's behavior might serve me in the same way Hemingway's "Africanization" served him. The act of exploring the ethics of Hemingway's actions in Africa and his ambivalence toward capitalist-imperialism could be my way of deflecting responsibility for my own part in perpetuating racism, for benefitting from white American privilege, and for understanding how my own desire is structured by racist colonialist discourse. I am also aware of how a focus on whiteness can ironically have the unintended effect of putting whiteness in the center of the picture again.

I want to look at these possibilities; however, this is not the same kind of looking that Mura objects to. Rather, it is a kind of looking that takes into account the relational and asks us to examine the ways in which desires are connected to the power relations in which they are formed and in which power is manifested through our acts of desiring. It is a kind of looking that forces me to recognize the way in which my desire, like Hemingway's desire as I have constructed it here, is caught up in a complex relationship to race and racism. Consequently, while I would never argue that we should accept racism wherever we find it or that we should exclude racism (or other dehumanizing practices) from our aesthetic evaluations, our constructions of authors, or our own critical practices, reading racism—or imperialism, or sexism, or homophobia, or anti-Semitism—is not always a simple matter. Perhaps this is particularly so for those who have never suffered from the oppression or violence of these attitudes and have, in fact, perpetuated them, often unknowingly. The first step in eliminating such attitudes is for the perpetrators to learn how to read them, to learn how to see themselves and others differently.[46] As this section has shown, an important way to expand one's vision is to bring the relational into American paradigms of individualism, hard work, success, and world-traveling; from there, one can begin to see the larger ramifications of his or her encounters with diverse peoples and with a complex ecosystem.

The Disabled Able Body and White Heteromasculinity

It is impossible to explore the intersections of mobility and desire without also examining the body and its capacity for being mobile and desirable. In mentioning Hemingway's mobility, one undoubtedly recalls some famous images and stories of his attractive and capable body in action, for example, Hemingway hunting, boxing, fishing, running with the bulls, swimming, skiing, supposedly carrying an injured soldier to safety during battle, or busting his way out of a crashed and burning airplane.[47] Always, one sees Hemingway walking—through the streets of Paris, across the plains of East Africa, in the woods of Upper Michigan, up the snow-covered mountains of Switzerland and Austria. But Hemingway's active life took a toll on his body as well, and almost as famous as the images of his body in motion are images of his body in pain.[48] Some idea of the pain Hemingway endured—and of the legendary status his body in pain has acquired—can be found at the end of Jeffrey Meyers's biography of Hemingway where a three-page appendix lists Hemingway's accidents and illnesses. The appendix begins with a childhood accident in which Hemingway fell with a stick in his throat and gouged his tonsils and concludes with a 14-item list of ailments suffered during the last two years of his life, everything from skin rash to hepatitis to severe depression. Another measure of both Hemingway's body in pain and the legend surrounding it appears in a letter Hemingway wrote while he recuperated from two plane crashes in Africa in 1954 and after he had read the obituaries erroneously announcing his death. "Ruptured kidney (much blood and pieces of kidney in urine). The hell with the rest of it. It goes on from there. It is all much better but it hurts and people aren't indestructible even if the journalists say so" (2 February 1954; *Ernest Hemingway: Selected Letters*, 828).

Of course, both desirability and mobility are culturally and historically determined. What one culture finds beautiful, another finds repulsive; the body that one society views as blessed with special powers, another labels crippled, deformed, or retarded. In regard to modern Western nations, Lennard Davis argues that Western Europe and the United States have formed their identities upon a notion of normalcy that is "intricately tied up with eugenics, statistical proofs of intelligence, ability, and so on."[49] According to Davis, this hegemony of normalcy is the driving force behind Western imperialism which has evolved standards of normal behavior and normal bodies based on the white, able (and, I would add, heterosexual) body. Indeed, Davis claims that this hegemony of normalcy is so pervasive in modern Western culture that it shapes our literature as well. For example, the form of the novel tends to be normative, "ideologically emphasizing the universal quality of the central character whose normativity encourages us to identify with him or her" (41). Most novels, Davis contends, rely upon characters with disabilities, characters who are "lame, tubercular, dying of AIDS, chronically ill, depressed, mentally ill, and so on" to reinforce the normalcy of the primary characters (44). As Rosemarie Garland Thomson states, "main characters [in literature] almost never have physical disabilities."[50]

Given that Hemingway assumed this ideology of normalcy and that he had first-hand experiences with all kinds of illnesses and injuries, we can construct him as having intimate knowledge of the culturally determined line separating the able body from the disabled body. His fiction supports such a portrayal, filled as it is with characters who suffer illness, accidents, and, most of all, injury in the line of duty, especially duty related to military service, hazardous occupations, and sporting events. Contrary to Davis's and Thomson's assertions about the physical normalcy of main characters in literature, Hemingway's disabled characters are not secondary, deviating and deviant characters; they are the central characters, Hemingway's male heroes. As Philip Young insisted years ago, rare is the Hemingway novel whose white male protagonist lacks experience with serious injury, usually injury related to his participation in war-time activities.[51] Not surprisingly, given the masculine arenas in which these characters sustain their injuries, their scars or disabilities do not detract from their masculinity or their ability to perform successfully. Peter Lehman notes that in the cinema, a scar on a man's face "frequently enhances rather than detracts from his power, providing a sign that he has been tested in the violent and dangerous world of male action and has survived. He is not easily defeated or killed."[52] Such an observation can be extended to Hemingway's work as well. But as I argue in this section, the scarring of Hemingway's heroes, which occurs more often on their bodies than their faces, operates in several ways. Not only is it an index of their toughness, their ability to endure a harsh and cruel world (a common characterization of Hemingway's male protagonists), but it also serves as a visible marker of their white, masculine heterosexuality, as if the white male body were incapable of doing that work by itself. However, as I will also show, the wound ultimately increases rather than appeases the anxieties it was meant to deflect, moving the heteromasculine body into the realm of the female, the feminine, and the homosexual.

Let us begin with a simple inventory of the injuries, accidents, and health problems suffered by the male heroes of Hemingway's novels. Jake Barnes has lost his penis during World War I, a "rotten way to be wounded" (*The Sun Also Rises*, 31). While delivering food to Italian troops in that war, Frederic Henry endures "Multiple superficial wounds of the left and right thigh and left and right knee and right foot. Profound wounds of right knee and foot. Lacerations of the scalp . . . with possible fracture of the skull"; he also gets jaundice and has recovered from gonorrhea.[53] Harry Morgan is shot and loses his right arm while running liquor between Cuba and Key West but continues to transport contraband and revolutionaries until he is fatally shot (*To Have and Have Not*). Robert Jordan is healthy for the first two days of *For Whom the Bell Tolls*; on the third day, he breaks his left thigh bone while fleeing Fascist soldiers in Spain and determines to make a final stand, disabled but armed, in order that his Loyalist compatriots and lover, Maria, might escape. Colonel Richard Cantwell (*Across the River and Into the Trees*) admits to having had ten concussions, has a bad leg which hurts him always, takes medicine for a bad heart, and has a misshapen right hand (the result of his hand being shot twice during war).[54] Santiago of *The Old Man and the Sea* has skin cancer and "deep-creased" scars on his hands from handling heavy fish on the cords, and his lower leg was once paralyzed by a sting ray.[55] While battling the enormous marlin that makes up the bulk of his story, he suffers a cut below his eye, rope burns on his hands, and a painful cramp that temporarily disables his left hand. Patrolling for German submarines off the shore of Cuba during World War II, Thomas Hudson (*Islands in the Stream*) is shot in his left leg, a wound that eventually causes his death. The only Hemingway male who seems to be without injury is David Bourne, at least in the published text; the manuscript of *Garden* reveals that David was wounded and trepanned during World War I.[56]

The obvious explanation for the recurrence of the wounded hero in Hemingway's work is that the wound marks a character's inner worth, especially his virility. We can hardly miss this meaning of the wound since these men or members of their circle repeatedly assert it. For instance, after speaking to Arnaldo, "the glass-eyed waiter," Richard Cantwell comes to the following understanding about himself: "He only loved people . . . who had fought or been mutilated. Other people were fine and you liked them and were good friends; but you only felt true tenderness and love for those who had been there and had received the castigation that everyone receives who goes there long enough. So I'm a sucker for crips . . . . And any son of a bitch who has been hit solidly, as every man will be if he stays, then I love him" (*Across the River*, 71). Expressing a similar philosophy, Thomas Hudson refuses to intervene when his son, David, attempts to catch a huge fish, even though David's feet and hands are bloody: "there is a time boys have to do things if they are ever going to be men. That's where Dave is now."[57] If David catches this fish, "he'll have something inside him for all his life and it will make everything else easier" (131). In *To Have and Have Not*, Harry Morgan, a man who has stayed and been hit solidly, determines that a lost arm signals no loss of manhood: "You lose an arm you lose an arm. There's worse things than lose [*sic*] an arm. You've got two arms and you've got two of something else [testicles]. And a man's still a man with one arm or with one of those."[58] As a final example, when Brett Ashley brings Count Mippipopolous to Jake Barnes's room, the count displays scars on his ribs and back, the result of being wounded by arrows while on a business trip to Abyssinia at age twenty one. Jake is impressed, and Brett proudly asserts, "I told you he was one of us. Didn't I?" (*Sun*, 60).

Given the wound's function as a measure of character worth and manhood, it is no surprise that the wound never prevents Hemingway's male heroes from leading active lives, except when it kills, and even then, the character never dies immediately but performs one or more acts of heroism before dying. Hemingway's wounded heroes ski, fish, hunt, ride bicycles, walk, swim, row themselves and their lovers to safety, lead troops, get into fights, play tennis, and do their work. Moreover, with important exceptions (i.e., when the wound is fatal or in the case of Jake Barnes's destroyed penis), the injury does not obstruct the hero's ability to make love, but can actually improve it. Even though Hemingway's leading men often worry, especially when older, that their wounds might make them less sexually desirable, the women they take up with assure them otherwise. Renata is practically obsessed with Richard Cantwell's misshapen hand, wanting to touch it and dreaming about it, telling him, "I love your hand and all your other wounded places" (*Across the River*, 141). When Harry Morgan asks his wife, Marie, whether she minds his amputated arm, she replies, "You're silly. I like it. Any that's you I like. Put it across there. Put it along there. Go on. I like it, true" (*Have*, 113). Marie sexualizes Harry's disability, asking him as they make love to "Put the stump there. Hold it. Hold it now. Hold it" (114). Here disability enhances ability, the ability to please a woman. The disabled hero's body performs as an able one, as "normal."

The full meaning of this normality, its status as "the norm," becomes clearer when we recognize that the men in Hemingway's novels who are identified as men of color or as homosexual generally lack the wound or react to it in despicable ways. For instance, Mr. Sing, the Chinese man who engages Harry Morgan to transport unfortunate Chinese "compatriots" (32), is about "the smoothest-looking thing" Harry has ever seen, an observation that applies to Mr. Sing's dress and English manner but also implies unblemished features. Similarly, the white homosexual men who accompany Brett to the bal musette in *The Sun Also Rises* are distinguished by newly washed white hands, wavy hair, and white faces (20). These are men who are unmarked by the effects of dangerous situations, hard work, or even the sun—and thus are to be read as unmasculine.

When a man of color or a homosexually identified man *is* wounded, he generally responds in a weak and cowardly way or his bravery is undercut. For instance, as Toni Morrison emphasizes, when Wesley, the black crewman in *To Have and Have Not*, is wounded, he whines and calls attention to his pain, a reaction that contrasts sharply with the impassive response of the more critically wounded Harry (Morrison, 74–75). More conventionally heroic is "the great negro from Cienfuegos" who arm wrestles Santiago until blood comes out from under the fingernails of both men. However, this wound is temporary, superficial, and Santiago not only defeats this black man but also breaks his confidence (*Old Man*, 76–78). In David Bourne's elephant story in *The Garden of Eden*, the native African guide, Juma, keeps his "pain in contempt" after he is mauled by an elephant (200), but because David despises him for killing this animal, his stoic response never achieves the status of bravery associated with Hemingway's wounded white heroes. Finally, in *Across the River and Into the Trees*, Renata points out "a boy with [a] wave in his hair" who is a very good painter but has false teeth in front "because he was a little bit *pédéraste* once and other *pédérastes* attacked him." The boy, she concludes, "is a man now, of course, and goes with very many women to hide what he is" (96). Here the wound is a brand that announces what the character seeks to hide, his lack of heterosexuality and virtue.

In delineating the structure of war and how nationality and nationalism become insignificant at the moment of the soldier's injury, Elaine Scarry notes that the wound "is empty of reference, though its intended referent can be inferred by the uniform over which the blood now falls, or by some other cultural insignia, a symbol and fragment of disembodied national identification."[59] Although Hemingway's protagonists typically receive their wounds during war, the inferences to the nation and its politics that Scarry mentions are often unavailable to readers since the male protagonist either does not wear the uniform of the state (e.g., Robert Jordan, Thomas Hudson) or renounces the patriotism that motivated his military participation (e.g., Frederic Henry). Through such actions, the wound loses its connections to state politics and becomes a vehicle for signifying the virtue of the body it marks. But as I pointed out, these virtuous bodies are all white, male, and heterosexually identified. Such men are the only ones in Hemingway's fiction who consistently respond with bravery and integrity to injury (besides Hemingway's protagonists, one thinks also of many of his Spanish bullfighters). The wound can thus be read as a way of asserting the physical and moral superiority of white normative masculinity and heterosexuality. At the same time, the need to repeat this pattern reveals an underlying hysteria about this superiority. It is as if white heteromasculinity requires some kind of physical mark to confirm its identity and affirm its dominance.

Clearly, the wound in Hemingway's fiction is overdetermined. One clue to understanding Hemingway's obsession with the wound and its meaning lies in the portrayal of his heroes' bodies. In most Hemingway novels, the male hero's injury is described in more detail than are the features of the man who endures it. One tries in vain to develop a mental picture of the bodies and faces of first-person narrators such as Jake

Barnes and Frederic Henry. A reader might have more success in imagining Richard Cantwell, Thomas Hudson, Robert Jordan, and Santiago, but not much more. All these men are described at some point, but their portraits are vague generalities: suntanned skin, streaked hair, a thin or big body, steel eyes, an occasional broken nose. This information marks these men as outdoor types and as Anglo—their skin and hair are colored by the sun—but the details that might individualize them are scanty and, significantly, often mixed in with references to their scars.

For instance, the only information we get about Thomas Hudson's features is that he is "a big man and looked bigger stripped than he did in his clothes. He was very tanned and his hair was faded and streaked from the sun. He carried no extra weight and the scales saw that he weighed 192 pounds" (*Islands*, 12). We learn a bit more about Richard Cantwell, most of it centered around his scars. Looking at himself in the mirror, he sees the welts and ridges on his head, the result of plastic surgery after head wounds, and determines that his tan mitigates some of the ugliness. The narrator then relates what the colonel doesn't notice, but the information is sketchy: "the old used steel of his eyes," "the small, long extending laugh wrinkles at the corners of his eyes," "his broken nose [that] was like a gladiator's in the oldest statues," and "his basically kind mouth which could be truly ruthless" (*Across the River*, 111–12). Later, when Richard looks in the mirror again, he decides that his "gut is flat" and his "chest is all right except where it contains the defective muscle. We are hung as we are hung, for better or worse, or something, or something awful" (180).

The Old Man, Santiago, is "thin and gaunt with deep wrinkles in the back of his neck. The brown blotches of the benevolent skin cancer the sun brings from its reflection on the tropic sea were on his cheeks. The blotches ran well down the sides of his face and his hands had deep-creased scars from handling heavy fish on the cords. Everything about him was old except his eyes and they were the same color as the sea and were cheerful and undefeated" (*Old Man*, 9–10). He also has "strange shoulders, still powerful although very old" and a strong neck whose "creases did not show so much when the old man was asleep and his head fallen forward" (19–20). Finally, Robert Jordan is portrayed as a young man, "who was tall and thin, with sun-streaked fair hair, and a wind- and sun-burned face," wearing a "sun-faded flannel shirt, a pair of peasant's trousers and rope-soled shoes" (*Bell*, 5). That's it. Although we learn a great deal about what these men do and, to a lesser extent, about how they feel, we don't receive further information about their looks.

The only Hemingway hero whose face and body are developed into a clear image is Harry Morgan, and how those features come into existence is instructive. Harry is as nondescript as his counterparts in other Hemingway fiction until his wife, Marie, watches him leave their house for what turns out to be the last time:

> She watched him go out of the house, tall, wide-shouldered, flat-backed, his hips narrow, moving, still, *she thought*, like some kind of animal, easy and swift and not old yet, he moves so light and smooth-like, *she thought*, and when he got in the car she saw him blonde, with the sunburned hair, his face with the broad mongol cheek bones, and the narrow eyes, the nose broken at the bridge, the wide mouth and the round jaw, and getting in the car he grinned at her and she began to cry. "His goddamn face," *she thought*. "Everytime I see his goddamn face it makes me want to cry." (*Have*, 128; emphasis added)

The reiterated "she thought" is unnecessary yet purposeful. It reminds us, as if we might forget, that we are seeing Harry's body and face through the eyes of a woman. Harry's case is exceptional because Marie's reverie constitutes one of the few times a narrator in Hemingway's fiction looks at the world through a woman's eyes. Such an exception suggests that Hemingway resists lingering on the male hero's body because he worries that turning the narrator's male gaze on these men will not only feminize them but produce homosexual implications.

This suggestion is supported by the fact that, in contrast to Hemingway's heroes, his female protagonists are described frequently and specifically, albeit stereotypically. For instance, as we have already seen, Jake describes Brett as "damned good-looking. She wore a slipover jersey sweater and a tweed skirt, and her hair was brushed back like a boy's. . . . She was built with curves like the hull of a racing yacht, and you missed none of it with that wool jersey" (*Sun*, 22). We also view her white face and "the long line of her neck" (25), and later Jake tells us that she wears "a black, sleeveless evening dress. She looked quite beautiful" (146). In *A Farewell to Arms*, when Frederic Henry first sees Catherine Barkley, he relates that she "was quite tall. She wore what seemed to me to be a nurse's uniform, was blonde and had a tawny skin and gray eyes. I thought she was very beautiful" (18). After they become lovers, he tells us that she had "wonderfully beautiful hair, and I would lie sometimes and watch her twisting it up in the light. . . . She had a lovely face and body and lovely smooth skin too" (114).

Even more detail is provided about Maria in *For Whom the Bell Tolls:* "[Robert Jordan] noticed her handsome brown hands. Now she looked him full in the face and smiled. Her teeth were white in her brown face and her skin and her eyes were the same golden tawny brown. She had high cheekbones, merry eyes and a straight mouth with full lips. Her hair was the golden brown of a grain field that has been burned dark in the sun but it was cut short all over her head so that it was but little longer than the fur on a beaver pelt. . . . She has a beautiful face, Robert Jordan thought. She'd be beautiful if they hadn't cropped her hair" (*Bell,* 25–26). When Maria sits opposite him, Robert notices her legs "slanted long and clean from the open cuffs" of her trousers and "the shape of her small, up-tilted breasts under the gray shirt" (26). He looks at her face and body frequently, focusing on her "smooth skin," "the cup of her breasts," her "tawny brown face," full lips, "cropped sun-burned hair," and lovely body (48, 173–74, 176). In fact, one of Robert and Maria's last conversations before he bombs the bridge concerns her hair and body. She worries that he might prefer beautiful women of his own culture and determines to take care of her figure since Spanish women tend to gain weight easily. Robert allays these anxieties by telling Maria how to cut her hair to even out its choppy ends and reassuring her that her figure will maintain its fine shape for many years (371–76).

Specifics about Marie in *To Have and Have Not* are also plentiful. Despite her minimal role in the novel, Marie is described not only by her husband, Harry, but also by the visiting writer, Richard Gordon. When Marie gets into the car, Harry sees her as "a big woman, long legged, big handed, big hipped, still handsome, a hat pulled down over her bleached blonde hair" (116). In contrast, Richard is impressed by her ugliness. Passing her on the road after Harry is wounded, Richard observes "a heavy-set, big, blue-eyed woman, with bleached-blonde hair showing under her old man's felt hat, hurrying across the road, her eyes red from crying. Look at that big ox, he thought. . . . Wasn't she an appalling looking woman. Like a battleship. Terrific" (176). Although we are meant to understand that his impressions indicate his insensitivity and obtuseness, undesirable qualities in a writer, these details give extra weight and shape to Marie's face and body.

In *Across the River and Into the Trees,* Colonel Richard Cantwell watches Renata come into the room, "shining in her youth and tall striding beauty, and the carelessness the wind had made of her hair. She had pale, almost olive colored skin, a profile that could break your, or any one else's heart, and her dark hair, of an alive texture, hung down over her shoulders" (80). Later when he kisses her, he feels "her wonderful, long, lithe and properly built body against his own body, which was hard and good, but beat-up" (109). Richard also sees her in the street "with the lovely long-legged stride and the wind doing anything it wants to her hair, and her true breasts under the sweater" (179). Like Robert Jordan, he presents himself as an expert on the preservation and deterioration of women's beauty and bodies, determining that Renata "could hold the pace and stay the course. The dark ones last the best, he thought, and look at the bony structure in that face" (247).

Two attractive white women come into Thomas Hudson's life during the course of his story, and his gaze moves over them both in similar ways. Like most female love interests in Hemingway's novels, Audrey Bruce has a beautiful face, smooth brown skin, tawny hair, good legs and breasts, and a lovely mouth. Thomas's first ex-wife (never named) is described similarly, although her features are more finely defined. "The high forehead, the magic rolling line of hair that was the same silvery ripe-wheat color as always, the high cheekbones with the hollows just below them, the hollows that could always break your heart, the slightly flattened nose, and the mouth he had just left that was disarranged by the kissing, and the lovely chin and throat line" (*Islands*, 306). And, finally, the two female protagonists in the published version of *The Garden of Eden* resemble their counterparts and, thus, each other as well. Catherine has "long brown legs," "a beautiful body tanned evenly," "laughing eyes," a "golden face with tiny freckles," and "breasts [that] show beautifully against the worn cloth" of her fisherman's shirt (12, 6). Readers are also privy to every intricacy regarding the color, shape, and length of her hair. The description of Marita is nearly a carbon copy, except that her skin is naturally dark—"almost Javanese," David thinks (236)—and her hair is dark as well (205).

This comparison between the descriptions of Hemingway's female and male protagonists suggests that in his fiction the body is identified as female (and simultaneously feminized) in part by the intensity of the male gaze, a pattern that mirrors a dynamic of the larger society. Equally important, the other way that Hemingway's female protagonists are marked as female is through the "perfection" of their bodies, the complete absence of physical scarring or wounds. Although these women might suffer psychological wounds—and, indeed, they have to suffer in some way in order to be worthy of the wounded men who love them—they rarely carry the physical scars of that suffering. The one exception to this rule is Maria of *For Whom the Bell Tolls*. Maria's chopped hair is a visible reminder of her imprisonment at Valladolid and her abusive treatment by the Falangists. Further, as Robert comes to know her more intimately, he speculates that her rapists might have scarred her genitals, causing her some pain (371). She also asks him to feel a small scar on her ear, the result of a razor cut made by the rapists. But except for her hair, which will grow to a "normal" length soon, Maria's physical scars are either too small to notice or hidden from view. Her body and skin are smooth; she has a perfect figure and no disabling or distracting disfigurements.

In Hemingway's fiction, then, the wound marks a body as white, male, masculine, and heterosexual, whereas the lack of the wound means that the body is most likely female, feminine, racialized, and/or homosexual. This arrangement reflects the cultural choreography of gender concisely described by John Berger: "men act and women appear" (quoted in Thomson, 110). But this is only half the story. For the wound to perform its classifying functions, it must be recorded, verified, *seen*. This requirement justifies turning the male gaze on the male body, a turn that places the body in the position traditionally occupied by the female, the feminized, the colonized, and/or the homosexual. An unresolvable tension arises wherein the wound that is supposed to preclude the gaze actually demands it. Further, the more the gaze lingers on the body, the more that body risks being re-marked as female, feminine, and homosexual.[60] This risk is heightened, rather than defused, by the hero's lack of distinct body imagery and features, for this ambiguity opens up that body to the re-marking of gender, sex, and sexuality. Other circumstances increase this risk, such as a female lover who wants to switch sexes or seeks to merge her identity with the hero's identity, as happens not just in *The Garden of Eden* but in almost every Hemingway novel,[61] or the fact that the male protagonist spends so much time with other men, or finally, the wound's implicit associations with castration, as in the associations with respect to Jake Barnes's injury.

A scene from *The Sun Also Rises* provides an excellent illustration of the dilemma I have just outlined. Undressing in his Paris hotel room, Jake looks at himself in the mirror, compelling the reader's gaze to follow his (30). Jake does not tell us what he sees, although his wry statements ("Of all the ways to be wounded. I suppose it was funny") and other evidence in the novel allow us to speculate that what he sees is, in fact, nothing: the penis is missing. Or, rather, Jake sees the lack which, in psychoanalytic terms, signifies the female and, in societal terms, indicates the diminishment of privilege and power. The wound is here revealed to be a castration, a revelation that is confirmed by the fact that, with the gaze turned on him, Jake occupies both the masculinized and the feminized position. He is not only the seer but the seen, spectator and spectacle.

Michael S. Kimmel reminds us that "masculine identity [which appears simultaneously with heterosexual identity] is born in the renunciation of the feminine, not in the direct affirmation of the masculine, which leaves masculine gender identity tenuous and fragile."[62] As I have argued in this section, the recurrence of the wound in Hemingway's fiction can be read not merely as a sign of heteromasculinity but, more crucially, as an attempt to stabilize that masculinity and to validate white hegemony. But, as I have also shown, the wound ultimately falters in that task. And it is in this faltering that I would propose one last meaning for the wound in Hemingway's work. The metonymic substitution of the wound for white heteromasculinity inevitably suggests that this particular form of masculinity is itself a wound, a disabling of the man who possesses it. That Hemingway himself carried the physical markings of many woundings, and that he required his heroes to pass the same test, simply emphasizes that he felt a constant need to prove his heteromasculinity. Yet because the wound in his fiction magnifies the very anxiety it is meant to deflect, it clarifies the logic of that need and supports the construction of Hemingway that I have been advancing here, a Hemingway who both rebuffed and desired the gaze of other men, whose desire never found a resting place on either side of the homo-hetero binary.[63]

5

CRITICAL MULTICULTURALISM, CANONIZED AUTHORS, AND DESIRE

> But the problem is, precisely, to decide if it is actually suitable to place oneself within a "we" in order to assert the principles one recognizes and the values one accepts; or if it is not, rather, necessary to make the future formation of a "we" possible, by elaborating the question. Because it seems to me that the "we" must not be previous to the question; it can only be the result—and the necessarily temporary result—of the question as it is posed in the new terms in which one formulates it.
> —Michel Foucault ("Polemics, Politics, and Problemizations")

> Even to begin with the body I have to say that from the outset that body had more than one identity. . . . Two thoughts: there is no liberation that only knows how to say "I"; there is no collective movement that speaks for each of us all the way through.
> —Adrienne Rich (*Blood, Bread, and Poetry*)

Defining desire as a tension toward the other (or others) that exists through fantasy—a definition that locates desire in both the social and the psychic—I have endeavored to go beyond an essentialist, modernist vision that equates sexual desire with sexual orientation. I have sought to explore how desire inheres not only in sexual orientation but also in identity structures such as gender, race, class, (dis)ability, and nationality. In taking this approach, I am suggesting that we understand the subject, in Wendy Brown's words, as "an effect of an (ongoing) genealogy of desire, including the social processes constitutive of, fulfilling, or frustrating desire" (75). Because subject formation is a complex, ambiguous, and continual process, any attempt to reconstruct Hemingway (or any author) and his desires will be not entirely adequate. Moreover, we should not forget that this attempt at reconstruction involves its own process of narrating a specific representation that constructs the author. In engaging in this process, the critic, I have argued, engages his or her own desire. The critic might not completely transform the author into his or her object of desire, but he or she will construct a figure that reflects a particular understanding of the desiring subject that is not simply intellectual but actually part of that critic's desire.

My reason for focusing on gender, race, class, sexual orientation, nationality, and (dis)ability is that these categories of identification and identity are the most crucial for explaining the cultural and critical fascination with Hemingway—our desire for him. Why they are so is clear. These categories have been the most politically charged and powerful concepts in shaping identities and desires in the twentieth-century United States. In this century, these categories have gained prominence through social movements, legislation, scientific investigations, educational reforms, America's rise as a world power, changing demographics, representation in the media, among many other factors. Moreover, as educational institutions have also been shaped by the political and social movements of the twentieth century, these identity categories have acquired increasing importance in literary studies and general education. They are now the identity structures most frequently invoked under the rubric of multiculturalism, that variably defined political project which has been transforming literary studies as well as public education at all levels in the United States.[1]

In this final chapter, I ask how my approach to reading Hemingway, the author, and desire might contribute to the ongoing effort to articulate U.S. literary multiculturalism and, within that articulation, to reshape American literary studies. I restrict my focus to U.S. literary multiculturalism for a number of reasons. Although I agree with those critics who conceive multiculturalism as breaking down disciplinary and national boundaries within educational studies, I still find valid reasons for invoking these boundaries. Most obviously, to break down such boundaries, we must necessarily invoke them. In addition, because certain paradigms are specific to geographical, historical, or disciplinary configurations, we can critique those paradigms only by comprehending these parameters. The Chicago Cultural Studies Group points out, for instance, that "the politics of identity-formation is less effective institutionally in anthropology than in the humanities."[2] But concentrating on U.S.

literature does not mean restricting one's vision to U.S. borders, as can be seen in my analysis of "The Snows of Kilimanjaro" as well as in critical interpretations before mine (e.g., Toni Morrison's *Playing in the Dark* or many of the essays in *Cultures of United States Imperialism*, ed. Pease and Kaplan). Our national identity is constructed in relation to the identities of other nations and in relation to identities of nations that were conquered or assimilated within U.S. borders.[3] Our relations are global, complicated by our own brand of imperialism and the transnational reorganization of capitalism.

In asking how my work in this book might be relevant to multicultural studies, I want to make clear that I am not proposing that U.S. literary multiculturalism situate so-called canonized writers at its center, nor am I contending that such writers have completely lost their privileged place in American literary studies.[4] As many polls have shown, these writers still dominate curricular choices. In fact, according to Susan Beegel, Hemingway's critical reputation is stronger today than at any time since his death ("Conclusion," 294). What I am interested in analyzing is the uneasy relationship that multiculturalism has with canonized writers, the uncertainty about what to "do" with them, about whether and how they fit in the project of multiculturalism.

Distinguishing Multiculturalisms

In its most popular form, U.S. literary multiculturalism has concentrated on drawing attention to creative works written by people of color, an outgrowth of the effort to "revise the canon, exposing and correcting its ethnocentric and class biases."[5] Within this framework, "multicultural" becomes synonymous with visibly ethnic peoples, as can be seen in the common usage of "multicultural literature" and "multicultural syllabus" to describe texts and courses organized around works written by African American, Asian American, Latino/a American, and Native American authors. In its more liberal pluralistic form, U.S. literary multiculturalism refers to literature written not only by people of color but also by white women, working-class citizens, and less consistently, people with disabilities, Jewish people, and people who self-identify as gay and lesbian.

This move toward diversifying the subjects of study in the literary classroom has many motives behind it. A primary stimulus, as Biddy Martin writes, has been the understanding that "traditional canons of literature have been shaped by exclusions based on gender, race, ethnicity, nationality, and sexuality, and that those exclusions produce structures of intelligibility, legitimacy, and value that do not include all kinds of experience."[6] Although the canon has never been set in stone, as writers that one generation admires lose their appeal for another generation, recent critique has exposed the racist and sexist politics of these choices. For Martin, the reorganization of literary study and classrooms underscores the importance of "provisionally reversing the hierarchical oppositions between valuable and unimportant" (15). This is a multiculturalism based, in part if not in whole, on a politics of representation or what Charles Taylor calls "the politics of recognition," the idea that "the withholding of recognition can be a form of oppression."[7]

Much has been written by now, in both the public and academic press, about this identity- and rights-based literary multiculturalism. While many agree that the motives behind this particular form of curricular and canonical change are well-intentioned, a growing number of critics voice concern over its premises, goals, and effects. The most constant criticism is that this kind of multiculturalism is unreflective. In its drive for inclusiveness and full representation, it reproduces the political structures (and failures) of liberal pluralism rather than analyzing the causes of social and economic inequities, and imagining alternative forms of social organization. Further, as John Guillory argues, by centering on aspects of identity—such as race and gender—pluralistic multiculturalism has encouraged critics to perceive writers as being representatives of the identity they have assumed or been assumed by (e.g., Hemingway represents Euro-American heterosexual men, Zora Neale Hurston represents African-American heterosexual women). Pushed to its logical end, this reasoning makes it difficult to "define a progressive rationale for the teaching of canonical texts" since such texts must be seen as disseminating hegemonic values.[8] Within this perspective in which identity and culture are fixed in both meaning and content, the only thing for multiculturalists to "do" with canonical writers, according to Guillory, is to expose and resist the hegemonic values inscribed in their texts.

Guillory is right to suggest that the tendency to stabilize identity and cultural categories has caused difficulties for multiculturalists. Such stabilization simplifies the enormous differences among the people who occupy these identity positions. For instance, the category "Asian American" elides the many cultural differences among ancestries as various as Japanese, Chinese, Filipino, Vietnamese, Korean, and Indian, to give only a partial list. Stabilizing identity can also obscure the way in which identities are imbricated and not simply stacked on top of each other like building blocks. Some black feminists, for example, have insisted that black women experience racism not as blacks but as black *women*, and conversely, they experience sexism not as women but as *black* women. Once we start to account for these imbrications, both identity and culture grow in complexity. A third problem with stabilizing identity is that it can limit consideration of the myriad ways that an identity might be inhabited, performed, and/or resisted, the variations on a theme. Finally, such categorizations function best when an identity category is clearly delineated; when a writer's identity blends delineations—as in the case of the racial identity of the American-born poet, Ai—pluralistic multiculturalism is less equipped to deal with the hybridity.

The problem, however, is not that multiculturalists have stabilized identity, since that move occurred long before multiculturalism came on the scene. In fact, one reason why multiculturalism so easily slides into identity politics is that such politics at least acknowledges, as liberal humanism often fails to, that differentiated identities matter. As Wendy Brown puts it, "Contemporary politicized identity in the United States contests the terms of liberal discourse insofar as it challenges liberalism's universal 'we' as a strategic fiction of historically hegemonic groups and asserts liberalism's 'I' as social—both relational and constructed by power—rather than contingent, private, or autarkic" (64). Identity politics highlights the roles that identities play in social positioning, that is, in the location that subjects assume in fields of power. This interrelation between identity and social positioning is not necessarily one of power over others but refers more specifically to often invisible social and economic privileges that are a form of power and domination.

So the problem isn't that pluralistic multiculturalism fixes identity. Rather, the problem is that pluralistic multiculturalism hasn't figured out a way to account for the stability and materiality of identity while also allowing for its artificiality, its fluidity, its hybridity and how to turn that accounting into a practice of reading, of organizing curricula, of transforming education and, possibly, of changing social realities. This is the same political and theoretical problem that has recently troubled feminists in their efforts to determine whether a representational politics can embrace the diversity and flux of the category "woman." As the problems of representation and identity politics have become more and more apparent, a number of literary critics have attempted to rework a rights-based multiculturalism into a more radical form, one that aims, according to Wahneema Lubiano, "at critical engagement with the entire process of information creation as well as political, economic, and social de-cision-making."[9] One of the primary questions these critics are asking is "Can the language of multiculture begin with a recognition of the am-bivalence of meaning and the detours of representing identities that are always already overburdened with meanings one may not choose but, nonetheless, must confront and transform? What if education that is multicultural is also education that is anti-essentialist?"[10]

So while the popular, pluralist form of multiculturalism has built its pedagogy and practice upon stabilizing identity and culture—turning both into entities to be recovered, celebrated, and respected—critical multiculturalism makes the difficulties of representation part of its frame-work. It seeks to explain how identity and culture are made to seem es-sential and how that imaginary state functions materially. It sees identity and culture, along with nation, as overdetermined notions whose bound-aries and processes are problems to be expounded. Power might be de-ployed through culture and identity, but culture and identity are also power's effects. Critical multiculturalism thus attempts to establish the social imperatives that encourage subjects to experience an identity as the truth of their being, that pushes them to reduce the differences upon which identity grounds itself into falsities or evils (Connolly, 83), that authorizes the U.S. government among other institutions to regulate subjects according to their identity, that, in short, enables identity and culture to serve as dense transfer points for power relations.

It is in terms of the conflict between seeing identities and cultures as unstable configurations and seeing them as stable sites of power that I pose the question of how my work on Hemingway fits into the project of critical multiculturalism. I will address the importance of analyzing Hemingway's identity *as* a white, heterosexual, American male while also making space to critique that analysis. Insofar as Hemingway's hetero-masculine identity has been sustained by the desires of critics, editors, biographers, publishers, booksellers, the media, and the general public, I will also suggest that critical multiculturalism should look more closely at the matter of desire, how it figures into our constructions of authors and our readings of their texts.[11]

The Importance of Being and Not Being Ernest

One of the most important reasons for including white, male canonized writers in a multicultural perspective is that their presence can help to counter the presumption that whiteness, masculinity, heterosexuality, middle-classness, and able-bodiedness, should be the standard, and that all other identities should be deviations that constitute difference.[12] The common assumption in the United States is that race, gender, class, sexuality, and even the body itself belong to people of color, women, poor people, gays and lesbians, and people with disabilities and are not part of the identity structuring of all subjects. Even educators who express full awareness of this assumption and attempt to eliminate it from their critical practices can still fall back on it. For instance, in explaining his pedagogy for a Fictions of Multiculturalism class offered at the University of Wisconsin-Milwaukee, Gregory Jay asks his students to analyze their own cultural identity, an assignment designed "to explore what a cultural identity might be, where we might get one, and how we might feel about the ones we have or that others have."[13] Jay clearly understands, as he is trying to get his students to, that we all have such identities, including those people associated with dominant groups such as whites and men. Jay then relates the dilemma of trying to make his classroom a place that supports the expression of formerly silenced subjectivities, yet feeling that it's unfair to "make the sexual orientation of [his] students a matter of pedagogical manipulation" (118). In this wording, Jay makes clear that by "sexual orientation" he means gay, lesbian, or bisexual; he thus misses an opportunity to point out to his students that heterosexuals also have an orientation. Not "outing" heterosexuality is as much a pedagogical manipulation as is encouraging gay or lesbian students to out themselves.

Failing to interrogate dominant identities *as* identities not only perpetuates their status as the norm but also ensures that they remain undertheorized. As Lisa Kahaleole Chang Hall explains, "the only people perceived to experience the dynamics of race, class, gender, and sexuality are those who are *marginalized* by those dynamics because the theoretical scholarship on the institutionalized privileges of men, white people, and heterosexuals has, with rare exception, not been written."[14] Although the recent formation of men's studies and white studies have made some strides in addressing these information gaps, much remains to be done, especially in terms of how to incorporate this theory into the classroom. AnnLouise Keating tells of her efforts to integrate analyses of whiteness into her U.S. literature and composition courses, relating that both she and her students have been baffled as to "what this 'whiteness' entailed."[15] In my classrooms, I've experienced similar confusion. My white students especially are unable to name social positionings or privileges that white people have. Their ability improves only slightly after I suggest some privileges, such as mobility, or hand out Peggy McIntosh's famous list of white privileges.[16] Because the naturalized standards in U.S. society are white, male, heterosexual, middle-class, and able-bodied, these identities can easily remain invisible and unexplored, a situation that is furthered if critical multiculturalism directs its focus only on "the other."

United States literary multicultural studies is especially uninformed about the relation of these identities to the "isms" (racism, sexism, heterosexism, etc.) and the privileges (white, male, heterosexual, etc.) that help to secure oppression of certain identities. We need to investigate more fully the connections among whiteness, white racism, and white privilege; among maleness, masculinity, sexism, and male privilege; among heterosexuality, heterosexism, homophobia, and heterosexual privilege; and so forth. We also need to explore the interconnections among these groupings, how white privilege works in conjunction with male privilege or heterosexual privilege or able-bodied privilege. This is particularly true for those of us who occupy one or more dominant identity-positions yet are attempting through our criticism and teaching to engage in anti-racist, anti-homophobic, anti-sexist work. Often we unknowingly perpetuate the very attitudes we oppose because we reassert our privilege in the act of opposition. For example, Christine Sleeter points out that white teachers perceive racism as "the unfair application of (probably) accurate generalizations about groups to individuals, in a way that biases one's treatment of them" rather than as the distribution of resources across groups or the ideology of equal opportunity.[17] In addition, we have yet to understand completely how identity-based privileges and discriminations are embedded in our political and social institutions, including educational institutions, and how they help to sustain the operations of capitalism, imperialism, and patriarchy. For instance, the institution of marriage, which is reserved for two people of the opposite sex, carries tax breaks, health benefits, hospital visitation rights, child adoption opportunities, among other privileges that are routinely denied to individuals who partner with someone of their same sex. As Lisa Duggan notes, through such policies and practices, the state has actually established a "state sexuality."[18] Comprehending the full range and depth of identity-based privileges and discriminations within our political and social institutions will obviously be an immense task, but it cannot be accomplished if U.S. multicultural studies fails to scrutinize identities that occupy dominant social positions.

Excluding writers who occupy dominant social positions also runs the risk of implying that sexism, racism, homophobia, and so forth will be found only among those people who benefit most from the current social structure. This implication overlooks the ways in which these attitudes are part of the social fabric in which all identity construction takes place. The danger here is that such a notion might lull us into falsely believing that we escape such attitudes when occupying identities—female, person of color, gay, lesbian, poor, disabled—that are the targets of those discourses. As Gloria Anzaldúa once said in a public lecture at Ohio State University, all of us (even white men) have a white man running around inside our heads, by which I understood her to mean that we do not evade status-quo thinking simply because we are oppressed by it or oppose it.

There are, of course, risks that come with including white, male, heterosexually identified canonized writers within the project of U.S. literary multiculturalism. For one, these writers have been used by literary scholars and publishers to set standards of aesthetics, acceptable subject matter, and norms of characterization. They have also, as part of what Guillory calls the "school culture," helped to fashion understandings of human beings, social realities, and American national identity. Concentrating on them at all can reaffirm these standards no matter how actively we attempt to critique them, to measure their limits, and to replace them with other possibilities. Linda Singer's warning to feminist scholars who read against the grain of canonized philosophers is worth noting here. Singer suggests that reading against the grain can actually lead to replacing the myth of authorial intentionalism with that of "the good father under another guise." Such readings, she concludes, "despite their intention to do otherwise, end up revalidating the force of the canon, by attributing to it more power and authority than it has or deserves."[19] This caution gives one pause, especially when writing on a figure with the nickname "Papa." Whiteness, maleness, masculinity, middle-classness, heterosexuality, and able-bodiedness have powerful leverage in our society, and are thoroughly tied up with national ideologies of individualism, self-reliance, upward mobility, and equal opportunity. Efforts to interrogate them or to show their antifoundational status might not only fail but end up relocating them as the norm, or at least as the place from which the discussion about gender, class, race, sexuality, desire, the body, and literature should begin.

But, to repeat what I said earlier, investigations of whiteness as a race, of heterosexuality as a sexual orientation, of masculinity or maleness as a gender, of middle-classness as a class in a supposedly classless society have not been fully incorporated into multicultural studies. To approach

these identity categories not as standards but as socially devised and politically potent narratives is a necessary step for comprehending social
power and relations. Such an approach is especially crucial, I believe, for
those of us who speak from one or more of these privileged identities
(and surely there aren't that many of us in the profession or among our
students who don't occupy at least one of these categories) and who are
committed to developing a critical multiculturalism. We need to ask, as
honestly and self-reflexively as possible (and I admit this kind of inquiry
will always be qualified) how our desire is caught up in this commitment.
Leslie G. Roman writes convincingly about the way in which white critics, teachers, and students can develop "white fantasies of identification
with those rendered 'racial' or 'subaltern others'" and, in the process,
produce their own "redemption discourses."[20] Her point is that whites
often identify with the texts of "racial others" as a way of aligning themselves with their struggles against racism and colonialism rather than examine "the white privileges built into putatively race-neutral liberal social democratic reforms" (274). Although Roman considers multiple
consequences of such identification, she warns that one effect is that these
fantasies can become a way of sustaining our possessive investment in
whiteness, our claims as the original and deserving citizens of the nation
(274–75).

This process of identification with—and, as I will argue shortly, desire for—the oppressed other occurs not only within the realm of racial
relations. When teaching gay and lesbian literature, I have witnessed
heterosexually identified students make a similar move. These students
will identify with gay and lesbian others as a way of distancing themselves from homophobic thinking and rejecting heterosexist narratives
of desire. They thereby hope to prove their progressive politics and even
to re-identify themselves as queer, an identity that allows them to be
straight without being straight-laced. They often start to "dress gay," to
recommend gay films they've seen, to deplore that more mainstream
theaters don't show these films, and to bring up narratives about their
own experiments with a same-sex partner, their experiences with a "sissy"
brother or lesbian aunt, or even the ways in which their own (hetero)sex-
ual practices go against the norm. Perhaps because their identification is
across explicitly sexual lines, it reveals how easily identification and desire blur. As Judith Butler states, "The heterosexual logic that requires
that identification and desire be mutually exclusive is one of the most
reductive of heterosexism's psychological instruments" (*Bodies*, 239). Because identification *with* the gay other is not such a long leap from

identification *as* or desire *for* this other, these students also often show signs of ambivalence about their identification. As with the experiences of Hemingway's characters in *The Garden of Eden*, their identifications constantly run up against their internalized homophobia and their heterosexual privilege, to which they are more strongly wedded than they are capable of admitting. To put this another way, these students need homophobia and heterosexism, for without both, their identification might reveal itself as desire.

Identification with and desire for "the oppressed other" can thus be a way for members of dominant groups to downplay or sidestep their complicity in oppressive social relations. Becoming aware of these seductions can help us and our students to explore the complexities of social positioning, the ways in which subjects, including readers and authors, interact in fields of power. However, while the preceding arguments have focused on the politics of identity, they have also treated Hemingway and other canonized white male writers as if their identity were stable and its meaning automatically known. This is a necessary initial move if we are to examine the conditions for changing social and political relations in the United States as well as to recognize how literary studies and educational institutions perpetuate these relations. But the problem with focusing on fixed identities is that this approach fails to ask how identities are formed, where the congealing of an identity might fail, and whether the power deployed through identity-formation is something that can or should be resisted. Such a focus can lead to a rights-based understanding of politics where the goal is simply to ensure that historically oppressed groups attain the same civil and social rights as dominant groups, for instance, granting same-sex partners the right to marry. But this approach misses the opportunity to advance more systematic critiques of our political, economic, and social system. It also leads to a multicultural pedagogy that operates as if an author's identity is fixed, transparent, and self-evident.

In short, these arguments fail to take notice of the way in which an identity is a construction, and in the case of literary authors, a construction drawn by readers from historical-textual materials and mediated by desire. To put this differently, these arguments operate as if stabilizing an author's identity were obvious when such stabilization actually provokes a series of questions for critical investigation. How is it that the author's identity can be fixed in this way and not another? Which representation of history and the social is being used to shape this coherent construction? How is the critic's desire invested in this process? And which power structures are supported by this construction? These questions lead, in other words, to the examinations I have undertaken in this book: analyzing the process of authorial construction as generated by literary critics, including myself, as well as by other readers.

Duplicating all the arguments and analyses provided throughout this study in the classroom would be an impossible pedagogical strategy, although I hope these investigations provide literature teachers with some ideas about how to approach Hemingway from a critical multicultural perspective. Almost without fail, students come to the college classroom with impressions of Hemingway and his work. And why not, since, like us, they have been influenced by the critical-biographical-media-educational nexus that I have examined in this study? Asking students to summarize their images of Hemingway before they (re)read his work will help to specify the representations of his identity that inform their reading. Most students to whom I give this assignment describe Hemingway either as a macho, overbearing, sexist, racist, womanizing, pugnacious alcoholic whose fiction treats women, blacks, Jews, and animals with equal disdain or as a hard-drinking, woman-loving sportsman / adventurer who lived life to the fullest and wrote honestly about it. While one can spend some time asking students for evidence to support these interpretations—and can thereby illustrate how the media, booksellers, literary critics, and teachers themselves have helped to circulate such images—the ultimate goal should be to help students see that both are constructions of Hemingway that solidify his identity around heterosexuality, masculinity, and perhaps nationality and artistry.

This can be a good starting place for introducing students to the politics and ethics involved in authorial construction and textual interpretation. If some of the students' evidence comes from Hemingway's texts, one can also ask about the connection between his fiction and these constructions. Students usually point to Hemingway's more famous novels or short stories for their proof: *The Sun Also Rises, A Farewell to Arms, For Whom the Bell Tolls,* "Hills Like White Elephants," "The Short Happy Life of Francis Macomber," some of the Nick Adams stories, and *In Our Time.* When this happens, I ask how many students know the following works: *The Garden of Eden,* "The Sea Change," "A Simple Enquiry," "A Lack of Passion," or "The Mother of a Queen." Most students say they've never heard of these narratives, which opens the door to a discussion about why Hemingway's fiction dealing explicitly with homosexuality is not usually taught or anthologized.

In pursuing this topic, we can talk, first, about imposed restrictions, such as Scribner's requirement that anthologies may use only one of Hemingway's stories and no more.[21] This condition places a burden on editors who want to select a "representative" story. But even if editors refuse to buy into this notion of representativeness, no editor, to my knowledge, has selected any of the Hemingway stories named above for his or her anthology. Why not? It's not enough to say that these are inferior Hemingway stories. Notions of inferiority have historically been projected onto any text that deals with homosexuality. This is not to argue that all, or any, of these Hemingway narratives subvert heterosexual or gendered norms or even that they all treat homosexuality with sympathy, but their absence from educational settings and resources raises questions about the politics of editing and teaching. What would the inclusion of such texts do to the traditional image of Hemingway that still circulates in our schools and that has helped to authorize the teaching of his texts? What would their inclusion do to our reading of his more well-known works, almost all of which include some reference to or hint of homosexual attraction between central characters (e.g., Frederic Henry and Rinaldi, Catherine Barkley and Helen Ferguson, Jake Barnes and Bill Gorton, Jake and Pedro Romero, Maria and Pilar)?

The ultimate point of this exercise, though, is not to engage students in a quest to uncover Hemingway's hidden sexuality or the hidden sexualities of his characters. In fact, after students learn that many of Hemingway's writings deal with the topic of homosexuality, one or two will often confide that they have heard that Hemingway was a latent or closeted homosexual or that (perhaps repeating what they've read in Ann Landers's column) his mother dressed him as a girl and that this "messed him up" for life. Ending with this conclusion forces students to choose between a homosexual and a heterosexual Hemingway. But rather than ask students to make such a choice, the goal should be to make them more aware of the presumptions of our sexual system, to encourage them to think about how identities are constructed, and to help them to consider the cultural, pedagogical, and personal uses to which such constructions are put.

There are other ways for teachers to introduce students to the issues I've explored in this book without undertaking an extensive study of a single author. For example, I frequently present the following works for class discussion: Roland Barthes's "The Death of the Author"; Eve Sedgwick's Axiom 6 from *Epistemology of the Closet* (48–59), which reviews different reasons educators give for not looking at same-sex desire in literature; and W. H. Auden's poem, "Law Like Love." In Auden's poem, an unnamed narrator assembles various definitions of the law, all of them derived from the perspective of the people offering them (gardener, scholar, grandfather, grandchildren, priest, and judge). The poem ends with a direct address to a beloved in which the narrator compares law to love:

> Like love we don't know where or why,
> Like love we can't compel or fly,
> Like love we often weep,
> Like love we seldom keep (ll. 57–60).[22]

Most of my students are unfamiliar with Auden and his poetry but presume that Auden's narrator is heterosexual, and therefore Auden must have been too. Most students make this presumption about any author or work of literature unless there is clear evidence to suggest otherwise. When I've questioned students, they've argued that, in Auden's case, their heterosexual presumption is justified by the intensity with which the narrator addresses his lover and the fact that he calls the lover "dear" (l. 35). They also presume that the narrator is white and able-bodied, and that the addressee is as well. These are not innocent or incidental presumptions but starting places for interpreting Auden's poem as well as for discussing the issues that Barthes and Sedgwick deal with in regard to the author, his or her body, and the place of both in interpretation.

Significantly, my students also make presumptions about the sexuality, race, gender, and able-bodiedness of Barthes and Sedgwick. Because Sedgwick writes in favor of attending to the author's sexuality, many students assume that she is a (white) lesbian. These students' assumptions about Sedgwick's sexuality emanate from an unspoken *rule of vested interest* which predicts that a critic/reader who focuses on marginalized others does so because he or she is one. The opposite rule operates in the case of students' assumptions about the sexuality of Barthes, as well as his racial and able-bodied status. Because Barthes never mentions such "issues" as race and sexuality, indeed removes them almost completely from the reader's sight, students presume that he is a (white) heterosexual. The basis for and effect of these assumptions can be pursued in class, not to determine once and for all the sexual preferences of Sedgwick, Barthes, and Auden but to help students see that such assumptions are operating in their reading practices. Which interpretive possibilities do they enable and which do they foreclose? What kinds of power structures do such assumptions support, and how do students' own desires become invested in these suppositions?

Although combining these three works always generates fascinating discussions in my classes, their potential to introduce challenging questions about authorship, identity, and desire occurred most memorably a few years ago when several students in a Critical Writing class misread the bibliographical information and came to class thinking that Eve Sedgwick was *Steve* Sedgwick. That "mistake" led us immediately into the heart of the matter regarding identity, identity construction, and authorship that I anticipated these works would precipitate. The students who read Eve as Steve read her as a gay man rather than as the lesbian that the rest of the class presumed her to be. In discussing these different readings of Sedgwick's gender and sexuality, I pointed out that at one time in her life Sedgwick announced that she was "a queer but long-married woman whose erotic and intellectual life were fiercely transitive, shaped by a thirst for knowledges and identifications that might cross the barriers of what seemed my identity."[23] Most students were unsure of Sedgwick's meaning, not understanding how someone can identify as "queer" but also be married or "thirst" for identifications that cross traditional boundaries. Their uncertainty allowed us to talk briefly about the fluidity of desire and identity, their inability to stay always within the confines of the social categories we give them.

This discussion proved to be the perfect starting place for investigating Auden's poem and the difference it would make if we read it as a gay or heterosexual love poem. Most students insisted that love is universal, that the sexual orientation of the speaker—and of Auden—doesn't matter. Then one student remarked that even if the poem *were* spoken by one man to another, that didn't mean that "we" heterosexuals couldn't appreciate it as well. In the middle of her comment, this student realized the presumption she was making about the sexual desires of the members of the class, including the teacher. Her realization altered the direction of the discussion as some students began to argue that the heterosexism and homophobia of the class had actually erased rather than foregrounded the gay possibilities of the poem. In opposition, other students referred us back to our earlier conversation about the fluidity of desire and identity, suggesting that the poem's ambiguity regarding the gender of both the speaker and the listener opens up desiring potentialities in the reader so that the lines between heterosexuality and homosexuality are blurred. We consequently had a productive discussion about

the politics of identity, who is empowered in a "love-is-universal" interpretation of Auden's poem, and how "the Law" in the poem might be
connected to desire. That is, we focused finally on the politics of the
erotic. Such a focus allowed us also to consider the racial dynamics of
the poem as well as other identity-linked possibilities: for example, what
difference does it make if both speaker and listener are white, middle-
class, and able-bodied?

Asking such questions will not lead to definitive portraits of the author or final interpretations of texts but should move us and our students
more deeply into political as well as ethical issues. Within the constraints of the postmodern condition, no one can claim that his or her
construction of an author is absolutely real; we can make claims only
about our representations of the real. But these are not peripheral or
harmless claims. As Tony Bennett has argued, such claims must be
framed *politically* in terms of their ability to organize the consciousness
and practice of historical agents (paraphrased by Hennessy, 28). In constructing an author's identity we do not simply reflect the power structures we want to enforce or subvert, but we undertake those very acts of
enforcement and subversion. That is why in reconstructing Hemingway's identity, my approach has not been to redeem him from the homophobia, sexism, racism, and brutishness for which he has so often
been condemned, nor has it been to join with those who would elevate
him to heroic status or construct him as androgynous. Such constructions emanate from and perpetuate heterosexist and homophobic narratives of desire. Rather, I have attempted to ask where we might find
Hemingway's desire once we overturn the heterosexist politics that have
motivated other constructions of his identity and once we open up the
space in which his—and our own—desire might be read. This is a question we can ask our students as well.

NOTES

Introduction

1. Nancy Comley and Robert Scholes, *Hemingway's Genders: Rereading the Hemingway Text* (New Haven: Yale University Press, 1994), 94.

2. Many commentators have recently questioned this theoretical divide between identification and desire, a divide most famously inferred by Freud. As Diana Fuss notes, for Freud identification is the wish to be the other, whereas desire is the wish to have the other. Fuss provides an extended critique of the view that identification and desire are mutually exclusive and that, consequently, any subject's sexuality is structured in terms of pairs. In *Identification Papers*, she demonstrates that even Freud was unable to disambiguate desire and identification. Fuss asks, "What is identification if not a way to assume the desires of the other? And what is desire if not a means of becoming the other whom one wishes to have?" The critical displacement of the identification/desire opposition opens up, according to Fuss, "a new way of thinking about the complexity of sexual identity formation outside the rigid thematics of cultural binaries," *Identification Papers* (New York: Routledge, 1995), 11–12.

3. Eve Sedgwick, *Epistemology of the Closet* (Berkeley: University of California Press, 1990), 53.

4. Of course, Sedgwick herself does not suggest that the outcome of a gay-centered inquiry will be the outing of canonized—and presumably heterosexual—authors. This is a presumption made by those who know little about her work or queer theory. I also want to note that Carl Eby's book, *Hemingway's Fetishism: Psychoanalysis and the Mirror of Manhood* (Albany: State University of New York Press, 1999), appeared after my deadline, so I was unable to factor its portrait into my formulation of critical constructions of Hemingway's desire and identity. Had I had access to Eby's entire study before completing my own, I would have modified my argument that critics have been hesitant to imagine a per-

verse or queer Hemingway. Indeed, Eby's work would have inspired me to draw an important distinction between "the perverse" as defined by psychoanalysis and "the queer" as employed by queer theorists and political activists. Because Eby employs a psychoanalytic framework, which views perversion as a compulsive and fixated sexuality largely devoid of erotic freedoms (9), the desires of his Hemingway are interpreted according to the value system of psychoanalysis. Despite Eby's best efforts to intervene in some of the more obviously biased claims of Freudian and Lacanian psychoanalysis, his Hemingway is mired in a fetishistic frame that organizes all of his non-traditional (read: queer) desires into a sexuality unfamiliar to and unshared by the majority of people. Thus, while there are many merits to a psychoanalytic approach to sexuality—for example, it encourages us to consider psychic processes such as repression, displacement, projection, and transference—I, like many queer theorists, want to challenge psychoanalytic explanations of desire. From the antifoundational perspective that I employ in this book, psychoanalytic narratives about desire are a means by which desire is socially coded rather than the ultimate judge of desire's meaning. One of the moves that can then be made is to queer these narratives, that is, to reveal the perversions of a psychoanalytic understanding of desire and to re-value perverse desires.

5. Emma Wilson, *Sexuality and the Reading Encounter: Identity and Desire in Proust, Duras, Tournier, and Cixous* (Oxford: Clarendon Press, 1996), 6.

6. Wilson acknowledges that the poststructuralist challenge to the author's authority over the text might change the power structure between author and reader rather than remove the author's presence completely. She concludes, "Stripped of control of his text, the paternal author may very well be prey to his reader. The hierarchical relation of author to reader is permanently troubled, and this will be seen to have important implications for questions of reading and sexuality" (8). Wilson's view that the relations between text and reader have been democratized, leading to new configurations of how the reader's desire enters a text, seems accurate. As I argue in this book, however, the loosening of the author-reader relationship does not mean that readers should, or can, do away completely with the historical author. Indeed, Wilson recognizes that readers face certain constraints on the liberties they can take with a text, although, for her, the author is not one of those constraints. From Wilson's perspective, a primary constraint on the reader is "the function of texts in representing, replicating, or even creating the cultural and social matrix within which and against which we are more or less obliged to live. By this token the reader is considerably less free than the death of the author might lead us to suppose" (57).

Chapter 1: Reading Hemingway After the Author's Death and Return

1. Leonard Kriegel, *On Men and Manhood* (New York: Hawthorn, 1979), 99.

2. Jackson J. Benson, "Hemingway Criticism: Getting at the Hard Questions," in *Hemingway: A Revaluation*, ed. Donald R. Noble (Troy, N.Y.: Whitson, 1983), 19.

3. For an examination of Hemingway's appeal to advertisers as a product endorser both during his life and after his death, see Nina M. Ray, "The Endorsement Potential Also Rises: The Merchandising of Ernest Hemingway," *The Hemingway Review* 13.2 (1994): 74–86. Ray suggests that Hemingway's endorsement potential in the category of "trustworthiness" would be low today because of his current status as "politically incorrect": "With his reputation as a misogynist, anti-Semite, and heavy drinker, Hemingway may not be perceived as trustworthy by present-day consumers" (79). However, she also observes that marketers have not found a significant relation between celebrity trustworthiness and "purchase intention," so Hemingway's status as politically incorrect may not significantly affect his overall endorsement potential. Indeed, Hemingway is still featured in his fair share of ads. Besides the Gap ad, which I describe below, Hemingway's name

has recently been used to market a Montblanc fountain pen (the Montblanc Meisterstück Hemingway) and a holiday to Spain or Mexico, offered by Toros Travel (Chula Vista, Calif.) to experience the bullfights. He is also named by Harry Cipriani, owner of Harry's Bar in Venice, Italy, in an ad for American Express (1993). Finally, a recent television ad for Calvin Klein's "Obsession" (a perfume) featured the tortured words of Jake Barnes as he thought about Brett Ashley.

4. Valerie Ross, "Too Close to Home: Repressing Biography, Instituting Authority," in *Contesting the Subject: Essays in the Postmodern Theory and Practice of Biography and Biographical Criticism*, ed. William H. Epstein (West Lafayette, Ind.: Purdue University Press, 1991), 137–38.

5. Nancy Miller, "Changing the Subject: Authorship, Writing, and the Reader," in *Feminist Studies/Critical Studies*, ed. Teresa de Lauretis (Bloomington: Indiana University Press, 1986), 116–17.

6. Cheryl Walker, "Persona Criticism and the Death of the Author," in *Contesting the Subject: Essays in the Postmodern Theory and Practice of Biography and Biographical Criticism*, ed. William H. Epstein (West Lafayette, Ind.: Purdue University Press, 1991), 114.

7. David Saunders and Ian Hunter, "Lessons from the 'Literary': How to Historicise Authorship," *Critical Inquiry* 17 (1991): 486.

8. Michel Foucault, "What Is an Author?" trans. Josué V. Harari, in *The Foucault Reader*, ed. Paul Rabinow (New York: Pantheon, 1984), 119.

9. Roland Barthes, "The Death of the Author," trans. Stephen Heath, in *Image-Music-Text* (New York: Noonday Press, 1977), 142.

10. Jackson J. Benson, "Ernest Hemingway: The Life as Fiction and the Fiction as Life," in *Hemingway: Essays of Reassessment*, ed. Frank Scafella (New York: Oxford University Press, 1991), 156.

11. The A&E film was directed by Hemingway's granddaughter, Mariel Hemingway, and was shown in the fall of 1998. See James Brady, "In Step with Mariel Hemingway," *Parade Magazine* 18 January 1998: 17. Information about Hemingway and "Jeopardy" is referenced in Kelli A. Larson, "Introduction," *Ernest Hemingway: A Reference Guide, 1974– 1989* (Boston: G. K. Hall, 1991), vii.

12. Wendy Brown, *States of Injury: Power and Freedom in Late Modernity* (Princeton: Princeton University Press, 1995), 119.

13. Here I am drawing from Althusser's idea of the hailing of the subject, wherein ideology transforms individuals into subjects. Althusser notes that even before its birth, the child is a subject, "appointed as a subject in and by the specific familial ideological configuration in which it is 'expected' once it has been conceived." This subject who is yet to be born will eventually have to find its place, that is, "'become' the sexual subject (boy or girl) which it already is in advance." Louis Althusser, "Ideology and Ideological State Apparatuses," in *Lenin and Philosophy and Other Essays*, trans. Ben Brewster (New York: Monthly Review Press, 1971), 176. I am following Althusser's formulation in agreeing that ideology hails or interpellates subjects, but I am specifying that act as, in part, a series of hailings (or a complex process of being taken up) by various identity structures.

14. William Connolly, *Identity/Difference: Democratic Negotiations of Political Paradox* (Ithaca, N.Y.: Cornell University Press, 1991), 64; emphasis added.

15. Of course, this self-conscious construction is itself mediated. I am talking about kinds and degrees of agency. For instance, the subject who consciously reconstructs his/her identity is still bound by the available identity discourses as well as by the workings of the unconscious.

16. Judith Butler, *Gender Trouble: Feminism and the Subversion of Identity* (New York: Routledge, 1993), 147.

17. In exploring the status of the author in anti-authorial work, I am especially indebted to Burke who, in a compelling analysis of anti-authorial theory and theorists, concludes that the return of the author takes place almost instantaneously with the announcement

of his departure. The death of the author, Burke insists, emerges as "a blind-spot in the work of Barthes, Foucault, and Derrida, an absence they seek to create and explore, but one which is always already filled with the idea of the author." In short, "the concept of the author is never more alive than when pronounced dead." Seán Burke, *The Death and the Return of the Author: Criticism and Subjectivity in Barthes, Foucault and Derrida* (Edinburgh: Edinburgh University Press, 1992), 154, 7.

18. In "Signature Event Context," Derrida spells out the dynamic as follows: the writer's obsolescence is prescribed by the very functioning of language. The absence of the author belongs to the structure of all writing since it is impossible for the subject who writes to be fully present at the scene of his writing's consumption. Further, because words are signs whose meanings proliferate beyond the moment of their inscription, writing gives rise to iteration "in the absence and beyond the presence of the empirically determined subject who, in a given context has emitted or produced it." The author's consciousness, intentions, and responsibility for his writing are subsumed by textuality. *Glyph* 1 (1977): 177, 181-82.

19. Maurice Biriotti, "Introduction: Authorship, Authority, Authorisation," in *What Is an Author?*, ed. Maurice Biriotti and Nicola Miller (Manchester: Manchester University Press, 1993), 4.

20. Several years after publishing "The Death of the Author," Barthes seems to have realized that he could not, finally, erase the personal features of the subject writing. In *Sade, Fourier, Loyola* (1971), he sets forth the conditions for the historical author's return, and significantly, these conditions are grounded not in the rules of language per se but in the reader's subjectivity. "The pleasure of the Text also includes the amicable return of the author," Barthes asserts, but he also warns, "the author who returns is not the one identified by our institutions (history and courses in literature, philosophy, church discourse); he is not even the biographical hero. The author who leaves his text and comes into our life has no unity; he is a mere plural of 'charms,' the site of a few tenuous details, yet the source of vivid novelistic glimmerings, a discontinuous chant of amiabilities, in which we nevertheless read death more certainly than in the epic of a fate; he is not a (civil, moral) person, he is a body," *Sade, Fourier, Loyola*, trans. Richard Miller (Berkeley: University of California Press, 1976), 8.

The conditions under which Barthes welcomes the author back into the interpretive theater are postmodernist and explicitly not modernist. His author is not a biographical hero, for to be such, his life would have to be mapped onto a narrative line that would verify current social arrangements and morality. Against this paradigm, Barthes reduces the author's life and body to "a few details, a few preferences, a few inflections," which he terms "biographemes" (*Sade*, 9). Thus, what Barthes takes from Sade's life is not the spectacle of "a man oppressed by an entire society because of his passion"; it is the way in which Sade says "*milli*" (mademoiselle), but also indicating "his white muff when he accosts Rose Keller, his last games with the Charenton linen seller" (8). In a final section called "Lives," Barthes reduces Sade's life to 22 biographemes and Fourier's life to 12. These fragments consist of everything from where Sade was born, baptized, and imprisoned to his predilection for theater costumes and his fondness for dogs.

Significantly, Barthes does not attempt a "life" of "Loyola" for the simple reason that he lacks sufficient material since details about Loyola's body have not been recorded in history or biographies (11). But in explaining this omission, Barthes hints at how deeply he relies on traditional biography, despite his claims to the contrary. As much as he seeks to dispense with such biography wherein the "facts" of an author's life are emplotted onto a narrative line, he cannot do away with, or without, it. He depends on it not only when telling us what he refuses to do with the lives of his three authors (e.g., present Sade as the spectacle of a man oppressed) but also in his notes listing the biographies—or in Loyola's case, the lack of any biographies—from which he extracts his biographemes (11).

Barthes's concept of the biographeme turns out to be uniquely "personal," a product of the critic's own preferences, predilections, and passions. Whereas the reader in "The Death of the Author" seems primarily heuristic in that he is simply "*someone* who holds together in a single field all the traces by which the written text is constituted" (148), the reader in *Sade, Fourier, Loyola* is Barthes himself, or Barthes's representation of himself. Those fragments of the lives of Sade, Fourier, and Loyola that stand out for Barthes, those details that resonate with his own pleasures, images, ideology, and history—those are his biographemes. Barthes submits that he would love it if his life, "through the pains of some friendly and detached biographer," were to be reduced in the same way. He encourages others to break down an author's life into a few biographemes and to find them dispersed within the author's texts, like the "barely written darkness of the intertitles" in a film (9). According to these rules, then, any detail can be transformed into a biographeme. In this way, Barthes returns the entirety of an author's life—or at least the imaginary field that represents that entirety—to the reader's consideration. Behind the reader-derived postmodernist biographeme stands the author-centered modernist biography.

This personal and desiring connection of reader with author will flourish in Barthes's later work, particularly *The Pleasure of the Text* (1973). In this series of meditations on the pleasures that readers seduce from a text, Barthes claims that "in the text, in a way, I *desire* the author: I need his figure (which is neither his representation nor his projection), as he needs mine," *The Pleasure of the Text*, trans. Richard Miller (New York: Hill and Wang, 1975), 27. This pursuit of the author is not, however, a regression to the kind of biographical criticism of which Barthes spoke so disparagingly in "Death of the Author." To the contrary, the author's presence in the text becomes part of the bodily pleasure experienced by the reading reader rather than a fixed source monitoring the text's meaning. As Burke puts it, the author reappears as a desire of the reader's, a spectre spirited back into existence by the critic himself (30).

Barthes's progress back to the bodies of both the reader and the author, however fragmented he might perceive those bodies to be, connects at several points with my own exploration of the author's status in the act of reading. For one, with his emphasis on the reader's part in creating the author and dispersing signs of that author throughout the text, Barthes opens the way for examining the circulation of desire between the reader and the author. Further, in formulating his biographeme, Barthes acknowledges that the author is situated in history, even though his fragmentation of the author's life into images can often have the (undesirable, I believe) effect of lifting the author out of a particular construction of history and making him solely the reader's contemporary. Finally, Barthes is well aware of the ethics of authorial constructions, for he expects (wrongly, I think) that by segmenting the author's life into glimpses of experience, like frames in a film, that he will resist dominant moral paradigms.

21. Foucault does include one female author, Ann Radcliffe, along with the many male authors he discusses, but he mentions her only to explain why she cannot be a founder of discursivity. The singularity of her presence in his essay, and the under-representation of other women authors in literary history, goes unremarked.

22. Seán Burke reaches a similar conclusion, but on different grounds, in discussing Foucault's theorization of the "founders of discursivity" in "What Is an Author?" These are authors, such as Marx and Freud, who can lay claim to having authored a transdiscursive discourse. Their status as founding authors of this discourse is manifested in the perpetual returns to their work as primary coordinates. As Burke puts it, Foucault provides the most extreme example of why authorial identity matters: "The discovery of a text like Freud's 'Project for a Scientific Psychology' will modify psychoanalysis if and only if it is a text by Freud. Over and above the text's contents, the fact of attribution—in and of itself—is the primary factor in establishing its significance for the psychoanalytic field" (93).

1. For information on the opening of Hemingway's papers to the public, see Susan Beegel, "Conclusion: The Critical Reputation of Ernest Hemingway," in *The Cambridge Companion to Hemingway*, ed. Scott Donaldson (Cambridge: Cambridge University Press, 1996), 283, 286. Jo August notes that The Hemingway Collection was officially opened at the Kennedy Library on July 18, 1980, but parts of the Collection were accessible beginning in 1975. "A Note on the Hemingway Collection," *College Literature* 7.3 (1980): introductory note.

2. Aaron Latham, "A Farewell to Machismo," *The New York Times Magazine*, 16 October 1977, 99.

3. John Raeburn, *Fame Became of Him: Hemingway as Public Writer* (Bloomington: Indiana University Press, 1984), 7.

4. Quoted in Michael Reynolds, *Hemingway: The American Homecoming* (Oxford: Blackwell, 1992), 46.

5. Virginia Woolf, "An Essay in Criticism," in *Ernest Hemingway: The Critical Reception*, ed. Robert O. Stephens (New York: Burt Franklin, 1977), 54.

6. Aaron Latham and Carlos Baker were apparently the only critics allowed to see *The Garden of Eden* manuscripts before the publication of the novel in 1986. Since then, any individual with permission to visit the Collection may study them, but in 1990, scholars were prohibited from photocopying any published material, including the manuscripts of "Garden." This is a curious and contradictory prohibition since, as I discuss in Chapter 3, only a small portion of the manuscripts was actually published.

7. Susan Beegel, "Introduction," in *Hemingway's Neglected Short Fiction: New Perspectives*, ed. Susan Beegel (Ann Arbor: UMI Research Press, 1989), 11.

8. As I will discuss shortly, Mark Spilka's exploration of androgyny in Hemingway's life and work preceded and then overlapped *Garden*'s publication. Moreover, in 1978, Georges-Michel Sarotte looked at both androgyny and homosexuality, concluding that Hemingway's work contains three facets of latent homosexuality: "the cult of pure male friendship, the contempt for women (the counterpart to blatant promiscuity), the constant, conscious effort to be a man among men." "Ernest Hemingway: The (Almost) Total Sublimation of the Homosexual Instinct," trans. Richard Miller, in *Like a Brother, Like a Lover: Male Homosexuality in the American Novel and Theater from Herman Melville to James Baldwin* (Garden City, N.Y.: Anchor Press, 1978), 276. Even earlier, in 1965, Richard Drinnon proposed that Hemingway's fiction was blatantly homoerotic and that "Hemingway's real problem was not the innocent emotions other men stirred in him but the intolerable psychic burdens they imposed." "In the American Heartland: Hemingway and Death," *The Psychoanalytic Review* 52.2 (1965): 27. Other pre-1986 criticism that deals with homosexuality includes Charles Stetler and Gerald Locklin, "Beneath the Tip of the Iceberg in Hemingway's 'The Mother of a Queen,'" *The Hemingway Review* 1.1 (1981): 27–32; and Ernest Fontana, "Hemingway's 'A Pursuit Race,'" *Explicator* 42.4 (1984): 42–45.

9. Marcelline Hemingway Sanford, *At the Hemingways* (Boston: Little, Brown, 1962), 62, 109.

10. Carlos Baker, *Ernest Hemingway: A Life Story* (New York: Scribner's Sons, 1969), 3.

11. Madelaine Hemingway Miller, *Ernie: Hemingway's Sister "Sunny" Remembers* (New York: Crown, 1975), 98.

12. Part of the difficulty of accepting Sunny's version is the existence of photographs that show Ernest and Marcelline dressed alike and sporting matching Dutch-bob haircuts. As Gerry Brenner points out, Sunny's story is actually refuted by the "generous swarm" of photographs that she includes in her book, *Concealments in Hemingway's Works* (Columbus: Ohio State University Press, 1983), 240. In 1977, Scott Donaldson referred to the twinning episode as fact, citing it as a source for Hemingway's hypermasculinity and his

dislike of "effeminate men" and his mother, *By Force of Will: The Life and Art of Ernest Hemingway* (New York: Viking Press, 1977), 190.

13. Mark Spilka, "Hemingway and Fauntleroy: An Androgynous Pursuit," in *American Novelists Revisited: Essays in Feminist Criticism*, ed. Fritz Fleischmann (Boston: G. K. Hall, 1982), 341.

14. Mark Spilka, *Hemingway's Quarrel with Androgyny* (Lincoln: University of Nebraska Press, 1990), 57. From this point on, I quote from Spilka's book rather than the articles themselves since the book is the more readily available work and incorporates the articles with little or no change.

15. Kenneth Lynn, *Hemingway* (New York: Simon and Schuster, 1987), 10.

16. James Mellow, *Hemingway: A Life Without Consequences* (Boston: Houghton Mifflin, 1992), 11.

17. Jeffrey Meyers, "Hemingway: Wanted by the FBI," in *The Spirit of Biography* (Ann Arbor: UMI Research Press, 1989), 222.

18. Joan Scott, "The Evidence of Experience," *Critical Inquiry* 17.4 (1991): 792.

19. Hayden White, *Tropics of Discourse: Essays in Cultural Criticism* (Baltimore: Johns Hopkins University Press, 1978), 60.

20. The question of where ideology lies in historical representation is complicated, and I have, of course, implied a false dichotomy by referring to narrative and ideology as separate entities. As White observes, it is conventional "to use ideological designations of different 'schools' of historical interpretation ('liberal' and 'conservative' or 'Whig' and 'Tory') and to speak, for example, of a Marxist 'approach' to history when one intends to cast doubt on a radical historian's 'explanations' by relegating them to the status of mere 'interpretations'" (67). But because one can find ideological implications in narrative forms themselves (as Roland Barthes does in "The Discourse of History"), in the strategy the historian uses to structure his or her story, and in the facts themselves (and what counts as a fact), one can say that historical representation is permeated by the ideological. Consider Michel de Certeau's position: "every 'historical fact' results from a praxis, . . . it is already the sign of an act and therefore a statement of meaning," *The Writing of History*, trans. Tom Conley (1975; New York: Columbia University Press, 1988), 30.

21. William H. Epstein, "(Post)Modern Lives: Abducting the Biographical Subject," in *Contesting the Subject: Essays in the Postmodern Theory and Practice of Biography and Biographical Criticism*, ed. William H. Epstein (West Lafayette, Ind.: Purdue University Press, 1991), 219.

22. Quoted in Denis Brian, *The True Gen: An Intimate Portrait of Hemingway by Those Who Knew Him* (New York: Grove Press, 1988), 189.

23. Earl Rovit and Gerry Brenner, *Ernest Hemingway*, rev. ed. (Boston: Little, Brown, 1986), 141.

24. Gerald Kennedy, *Imagining Paris: Exile, Writing, and American Identity* (New Haven, Conn.: Yale University Press, 1993), 137. Kennedy also works out his argument in an earlier essay, "Hemingway's Gender Trouble," *American Literature* 63 (1991): 187–207.

25. Robert Gajdusek, "Elephant Hunt in Eden: A Study of New and Old Myths and Other Strange Beasts in Hemingway's Garden," *The Hemingway Review* 7.1 (1987): 14–19.

26. John Gaggin, *Hemingway and Nineteenth-Century Aestheticism* (Ann Arbor: UMI Research Press, 1988), 78. Kennedy, Gajdusek, and Gaggin do look at sexuality in Hemingway's works, but their approaches do not fully avoid the problems I am focusing on. Kennedy proposes that while *A Moveable Feast* "portrays a writer secure in his gendered identity and advances a rigorously heterosexual view of relationships," *Garden* explores "the unstable terrain of sexual ambivalence, exposing the multiple forms of desire and the seemingly arbitrary nature of gender," *Imagining Paris*, 133. This is a promising statement, but Kennedy deflates it by insisting that Hemingway's "secret" has to do with androgyny and not sexuality.

For his part, Gajdusek mentions that bisexuality and sexual inversion are, like androgyny, important concerns in Hemingway's fiction; however, he uses these terms to describe the desires and actions of Hemingway's women, not his men. Gaggin is more inclusive, looking at both lesbianism and male homosexuality, but his investigation is bound by his aim of showing Hemingway's links to nineteenth-century decadence. His analysis of homosexuality is thus connected to the way that nineteenth-century decadent writers viewed androgyny. Although such a view allows him to examine sexuality as well as gender—in many cases, very perceptively—it limits his scope.

27. Michael Reynolds, *Hemingway: The Paris Years* (Oxford: Blackwell, 1989), 99.

28. Mary Hemingway, *How It Was* (New York: Knopf, 1976), 297.

29. Adrienne Rich, *Of Woman Born: Motherhood as Experience and Institution* (New York: Norton, 1976), 76.

30. Daniel Harris, "Androgyny: The Sexist Myth in Disguise," *Women's Studies: An Interdisciplinary Journal* 2 (1974): 171–72.

31. Carolyn Heilbrun, "Androgyny and the Psychology of Sex Differences," in *The Future of Difference*, ed. Hester Eisenstein and Alice Jardine (1980; New Brunswick: Rutgers University Press, 1985), 265.

32. For an excellent overview of the rise and fall of androgyny within feminism, see Sandra Lipsitz Bem, *The Lenses of Gender: Transforming the Debate on Sexual Inequality* (New Haven: Yale University Press, 1993), 121–27.

33. Robert Crozier, "The Mask of Death, The Face of Life: Hemingway's Feminique," *The Hemingway Review* 8.1 (1984): 6. Crozier does not use the term "androgyny" but does divide traits according to masculine and feminine.

34. Sukrita Paul Kumar, *Man, Woman and Androgyny: A Study of the Novels of Theodore Dreiser, Scott Fitzgerald and Ernest Hemingway* (New Delhi: Indus Publishing, 1989), 118.

35. Rarely do Hemingway critics even cite feminist work that introduced androgyny as a revolutionary paradigm for the second wave of feminism. Two critics who do refer to this work are Kennedy and Sukrita Paul Kumar. Both mention Carolyn Heilbrun's *Toward a Recognition of Androgyny* (Kennedy in his article only, not in his book), and Kennedy also cites June Singer's *Androgyny: Toward a New Theory of Sexuality* (1977). However, both critics fail to consider the work criticizing androgyny or Heilbrun's own abandonment of the term.

36. Catharine Stimpson, "The Androgyne and the Homosexual," *Women's Studies: An Interdisciplinary Journal* 2 (1974): 242.

37. Indeed, contrary to Stimpson's claim that the androgyne is nothing more than an idea, the androgyne has actually "existed" in the past. For instance, in two books that were published by the *Medico-Legal Journal* of New York, *Autobiography of an Androgyne* (1918) and *The Female Impersonators* (1922), Ralph Werther writes about his life as an androgyne, by which he means "a person with a male body but a feminine soul and mind—and even some physical traits of the female—a somatic-psychical situation that involves attraction to other men." Or as Alfred W. Herzog, the editor of *Autobiography of an Androgyne*, states, androgynes are "that class of homosexuals in whom homosexuality is not an acquired vice but in whom it is congenital" (1919; rpt. New York: Arno Press, 1975), ii. Within this medical lexicon, gynaders are the female counterpart to androgynes.

This association of androgyny with homosexuality is more true to the classical roots of the concept, but as Kari Weil points out, "Plato's myth . . . comes down to us with the androgyne's homosexual kinship banished . . . . From the Renaissance to the present, as Jean Libis tells us, philosophical commentaries on the myth have displayed a common prudishness, turning the opportunity to discuss sexuality to an occasion to consider our transcendental origins instead," *Androgyny and the Denial of Difference* (Charlottesville: University of Virginia Press, 1992), 63–64.

38. See Michael Reynolds, *The Young Hemingway* (Oxford: Blackwell, 1986), 81.

39. Ernest Hemingway, *Death in the Afternoon* (New York: Scribner's, 1932), 204.

40. There are some recent signs of a shift in critical attention. For example, one of the sessions of the Hemingway Society at the 1997 Modern Language Association Convention dealt with "Gay and Lesbian Issues in Hemingway's Work," and Carl Eby's work certainly does not try to protect Hemingway from a psychosexual analysis that might reveal unorthodox desires.

41. A number of biographers and critics have discussed the fact that Hemingway knew many lesbians. Kenneth Lynn, for example, reviews some of the famous lesbians that Hemingway met while in Paris, concluding, "Hemingway was not only acquainted with a remarkable number of lesbians, but, far more remarkably, was able in his imagination to identify himself with them. It was no accident that from 'Soldier's Home' to 'The Last Good Country' he would write about tomboyish girls, or that he was sexually attracted to Jinny Pfeiffer and Gertrude Stein, or that he valued Hadley—as he would his other wives—as a good buddy who could drink with him and share his sporting enthusiasms," *Hemingway* (New York: Simon and Schuster, 1987), 320–22. Typical of Hemingway criticism, this passage expresses a number of stereotypes (the tomboyish girl is presumed to be [a proto] lesbian), and Lynn also insists that Hemingway's fascination with "the ambiguities of feminine identity" came from his "firsthand experience of knowing how it felt to look like a girl but feel like a boy" (322), thus erasing the possibility that Hemingway's lesbian "identification" might be a displacement of his own homosexual desire.

One critic who does consider the possibility that Hemingway's close friendships with lesbians, especially Gertrude Stein and Janet Flanner, were related to his homosexual desire is Shari Benstock, who writes, "the importance of these two friendships for Hemingway may lie in the other direction—that lesbian women (no doubt without his conscious knowledge) affiliated him with his feared and repressed other, the Hemingway whose womanizing was the means by which latent homosexuality was repressed," *Women of the Left Bank: Paris, 1900–1940* (Austin: University of Texas Press, 1986), 173.

42. Several Hemingway biographers have recently shown awareness of their positionality and bias in writing their versions of Hemingway's history. For example, Michael Reynolds acknowledges the "limits of [biography] and the fictive nature of [the] trade," "Up Against the Crannied Wall: The Limits of Biography," in *Hemingway: Essays of Reassessment*, ed. Frank Scafella (New York: Oxford University Press, 1991), 170. However, so far this acknowledgment has not appeared as part of Reynolds's biographical approach (Reynolds has published four volumes of his biography on Hemingway). In his biography, he not only constructs the story of Hemingway's life but presumes to know what Hemingway and other people in his life were thinking when certain events occurred. James Mellow also reveals self-consciousness about his role as recorder of Hemingway's life, stating, for example: "The biographer . . . retouches the picture, patches up the damage, tries to restore the fixed, fascinating moment out of a once continuous narrative. And the unwilling and, more likely, ambivalent subject—like Hemingway, who became the prey of resolute biographers—might justifiably dismiss the effort as a lost cause, 'just one faded snap-shot more compared to what truly happened on a given day'" (458). Nonetheless, Mellow does not question the "authority" of his own particular restoration of Hemingway's portrait, maintaining that Hemingway's philosophy was to live a life without consequences (see 125, 138, 542, and title).

43. Cheryl Walker, "Feminist Literary Criticism and the Author," *Critical Inquiry* 16 (1990): 569.

44. In reformulating and redistributing Foucault's notion of power, Wendy Hollway (along with her co-authors) refers to the "investment" that an individual makes in a particular discourse, "Gender Difference and the Production of Subjectivity," *Changing the Subject: Psychology, Social Regulation and Subjectivity* (London: Methuen, 1984), 227–63. As de Lauretis summarizes Hollway's argument, "If at any one time there are several competing, even contradictory, discourses on sexuality—rather than a single, all-encompassing or monolithic, ideology—then what makes one take up a position in a certain discourse

rather than another is an 'investment' . . . , something between an emotional commitment and a vested interest, in the relative power (satisfaction, reward, payoff) which that position promises (but does not necessarily fulfill)," *Technologies of Gender: Essays on Theory, Film, and Fiction* (Bloomington: Indiana University Press, 1994), 16. Hollway thus attributes our positioning within a discourse to the combination of our emotions and a commitment to a promised conferral of power. But as de Lauretis notes, Hollway's delineation does not specify *how* someone develops the particular combination of emotions and vested interest needed to occupy a specific position (17). I also do not have a definitive answer to this question, nor do I think that one answer would fit all situations or individuals. In focusing on the social construction of desire, I do not deny the possibility that our desires have an innate component. But even if they do, that does not contradict the view that they are conditioned by social discourses and practices.

45. Here I am using "material" in the sense that Rosemary Hennessy proposes, "as that which intervenes in production of the social real by being *made* intelligible. At the same time, the discourses that constitute the *material* structures through which ideology works are shaped by the *material* relations which comprise economic and political practices," *Materialist Feminism and the Politics of Discourse* (New York: Routledge, 1993), 75. In short, the material is that which (re)produces what counts as reality, which for Hennessy includes ideology (and discourse, which she formulates as ideology), as well as economic and political forces (which are also shaped by ideology).

46. Jacqueline Rose, *The Haunting of Sylvia Plath* (Cambridge: Harvard University Press, 1992), 2.

47. In fact, given the trouble that Rose had with Ted Hughes and his sister, who wanted to edit or delete some of Rose's interpretations, one might say that Hughes has become a spirit who haunts *The Haunting of Sylvia Plath*.

48. William H. Epstein, *Recognizing Biography* (Philadelphia: University of Pennsylvania Press, 1987), 39.

49. Cheryl Walker, "Persona Criticism and the Death of the Author," in *Contesting the Subject: Essays in the Postmodern Theory and Practice of Biography and Biographical Criticism*, ed. William H. Epstein (West Lafayette, Ind.: Purdue University Press, 1991), 113.

50. Janet Wolff, *The Social Production of Art* (London: Macmillan, 1981), 129.

51. Richard Dyer, "Believing in Fairies: The Author and the Homosexual," in *Inside/Out: Lesbian Theories, Gay Theories*, ed. Diana Fuss (New York: Routledge, 1991), 188.

52. Hans Robert Jauss, *Question and Answer: Forms of Dialogic Understanding*, ed. and trans. Michael Hays (Minneapolis: University of Minnesota Press, 1989), 26.

53. Fredric Jameson, *The Political Unconscious: Narrative as a Socially Symbolic Act* (Ithaca, N.Y.: Cornell University Press, 1981), 35.

54. To quote Jameson again: "the affirmation of such nonhegemonic cultural voices [black, ethnic, women's, gay] remains ineffective if it is limited to the merely 'sociological' perspective of the pluralistic rediscovery of other isolated social groups: only an ultimate rewriting of these utterances in terms of their essentially polemic and subversive strategies restores them to their proper place in the dialogical system of the social classes," 86.

55. As Joan Copjec states, "One cannot argue that the subject is constructed by language and then overlook the essential fact of language's duplicity [an idea that Lacan elaborates in his work], that is, the fact that whatever it says can be denied. This duplicity insures that the subject will *not* come into being as language's determinate meaning," "Cutting Up," in *Between Feminism and Psychoanalysis*, ed. Teresa Brennan (New York: Routledge, 1989), 238.

56. Susan Lanser, "Sexing the Narrative: Propriety, Desire, and the Engendering of Narratology," *Narrative* 3.1 (1995): 93.

57. Marlon Riggs, "Unleash the Queen," in *Black Popular Culture*, ed. Gina Dent (Seattle: Bay Press, 1992), 105.

58. Others who have used the term "the desire to desire" or a similar term include Mary Ann Doane and Lacan. Doane has employed the term to refer to a psychoanalytic paradigm in which woman's relation to desire is, at best, mediated; that is, because woman is theorized as lack in her deprivation of the phallus, which is the signifier of desire, she can only yearn for the desire which the male possesses, *The Desire to Desire: The Woman's Film of the 1940s* (Bloomington: Indiana University Press, 1987), 12. This position of woman is elaborated by Lacan in his idea of the "envy of desire": "Far from its being the case that the passivity of the act corresponds to this desire, feminine sexuality appears as the effort of a *jouissance* wrapped in its own contiguity (for which all circumcision might represent the symbolic rupture) to be *realised in the envy* of desire, which castration releases in the male by giving him its signifier in the phallus," "Guiding Remarks for a Congress on Feminine Sexuality," in *Feminine Sexuality: Jacques Lacan and the École Freudienne*, ed. Juliet Mitchell and Jacqueline Rose (New York: Norton, 1982), 97. As should be clear from my description of the desire to desire as a conscious relation to one's desire, my use of "desire to desire" differs from both Doane's identical phrase and Lacan's similar term, "the envy of desire."

59. Jacques Lacan, *Écrits: A Selection*, trans. Alan Sheridan (New York: W. W. Norton, 1977), 167; original emphasis.

60. Alan Sheridan, "Translator's Note," in *Écrits: A Selection*, by Jacques Lacan, trans. Alan Sheridan (New York: W. W. Norton, 1977), viii.

61. Judith Butler's explanation of the creative power of discourse in relation to the body might be helpful here. She states, "To claim that discourse is formative is not to claim that it originates, causes, or exhaustively composes that which it concedes; rather, it is to claim that there is no reference to a pure body which is not at the same time a further formation of that body," *Bodies That Matter: On the Discursive Limits of "Sex"* (New York: Routledge, 1993), 10. If we substitute "desire" for "body," then we can also understand how the social constitution of desire need not be its origination. Compare also what Davina Cooper says on this subject: "Although we experience our desires as integral and true . . . at the same time, desires have constantly to be repeated and reproduced. Thus (borrowing from Butler), they are always open to the possibility of being constructed differently. This occurs 'naturally' as social relations change, as struggles in other areas of life impact upon the sexual domain. But it can also take a more intentional form through engaging with the multiple conditions—forms of power—through which sexual desires and practices are generated," *Power in Struggle: Feminism, Sexuality and the State* (Washington Square: New York University Press, 1995), 36.

62. Jonathan Dollimore, *Sexual Dissidence: Augustine to Wilde, Freud to Foucault* (Oxford: Clarendon Press, 1991), 325.

63. Analyzing why our own forms of racism remain intimately bound up with sexuality and desire, Robert Young notes that the etymology of "commerce" includes "the exchange both of merchandise and of bodies in sexual intercourse. It was therefore wholly appropriate that sexual exchange, and its miscegenated product, which captures the violent, antagonistic power relations of sexual and cultural diffusion, should become the dominant paradigm through which the passionate economic and political trafficking of colonialism was conceived," *Colonial Desire: Hybridity in Theory, Culture and Race* (London: Routledge, 1995), 182.

64. Sagri Dhairyam, "Racing the Lesbian, Dodging White Critics," in *The Lesbian Postmodern*, ed. Laura Doan (New York: Columbia University Press, 1994), 43.

65. Phillip Brian Harper, "Eloquence and Epitaph: Black Nationalism and the Homophobic Impulse in Responses to the Death of Max Robinson," in *Fear of a Queer Planet: Queer Politics and Social Theory*, ed. Michael Warner (Minneapolis: University of Minnesota Press, 1993), 262.

66. Teresa de Lauretis, *The Practice of Love: Lesbian Sexuality and Perverse Desire* (Bloomington: Indiana University Press, 1994), 234.

67. Michel Foucault, *The History of Sexuality, Volume 1: An Introduction*, trans. Robert Hurley (1978; New York: Vintage, 1980), 101.

68. In *The Practice of Love*, de Lauretis observes "how the dynamic structure of semiosis can usefully account—is a useful interpretant—for intrapsychic processes," 306. To help explain this interaction of the semiotic and the psychic, she refers to Jean Laplanche and Jean-Bertrand Pontalis's emphasis on the structuring action of fantasy in which "the phantasy structures seek to express themselves, to find a way out into consciousness and action, and they are constantly drawing in new material," quoted in de Lauretis, 307. Given the active life of these fantasy structures, de Lauretis proposes that although the subject's infantile fantasies are grounded in the parental fantasies, the subject's later interaction with the external world will modify these fantasies through "other representations and interpretants," 307. Consequently, Foucault's reverse discourse "actually suggests something of the process by which a representation in the external world is subjectively assumed, reworked through fantasy, in the internal world and then returned to the external world resignified, rearticulated discursively and/or performatively in the subject's self-representation—in speech, gesture, costume, body, stance, and so forth," 308.

69. David Halperin, *Saint Foucault: Towards a Gay Hagiography* (Oxford: Oxford University Press, 1995), 60–61.

70. Ann Landers, "Wife Raising Son as Girl Must Receive Counseling," *The Columbus Dispatch*, 28 September 1990, Accent section.

71. For examples of this kind of scholarly work, see George Chauncey, Jr., *Gay New York: Gender, Urban Culture, and the Making of the Gay Male World, 1890–1940* (New York: Basic, 1994) and Ann Laura Stoler, *Race and the Education of Desire: Foucault's History of Sexuality and the Colonial Order of Things* (Durham: Duke University Press, 1995).

72. Chauncey, *Gay New York*, 28, 65.

73. Quoted in Mellow, 312–13.

74. Quoted in Brian, 67.

75. Ernest Hemingway, "The dark young man stood looking into the window . . . ," Ernest Hemingway Collection, John F. Kennedy Library (Boston), Item 355a.

76. From James D. Brasch and Joseph Sigman, *Hemingway's Library: A Composite Record* (New York: Garland, 1981).

77. Gioia Diliberto, *Hadley* (New York: Ticknor & Fields, 1992), 54–55.

78. Havelock Ellis, "Sexual Inversion," vol. 1, *Studies in the Psychology of Sex* (New York: Random House, 1936), 88.

79. Mellow, 193.

80. Ernest Hemingway, *The Sun Also Rises* (1926; New York: Charles Scribner's Sons, 1970), 20.

81. Ernest Hemingway, *Death in the Afternoon* (New York: Scribner's, 1932), 205.

82. Comley and Scholes, 120–21.

83. Alan Sinfield, *Cultural Politics—Queer Reading* (Philadelphia: University of Pennsylvania Press, 1994), 64.

84. Ernest Hemingway, *A Moveable Feast* (New York: Scribner's, 1964), 117.

85. Michael Warner, Introduction, in *Fear of a Queer Planet: Queer Politics and Social Theory*, ed. Michael Warner (Minneapolis: University of Minnesota Press, 1993), xxv.

86. Ernest Hemingway, "The Garden of Eden" manuscripts, Hemingway Collection, 422.1–36, pp. 5–6. In quoting from "The Garden of Eden" manuscripts, I will use pointed parentheses < > to indicate text that Hemingway added and square brackets [ ] to identify text that he eliminated. For readability, I have inserted apostrophes that Hemingway often omitted, especially when forming contractions. References to the manuscripts denote series, folder numbers, and pages as they were classified at the John F. Kennedy Library in the summer of 1993.

87. Alfred C. Kinsey, Wardell B. Pomeroy, and Clyde E. Martin, *Sexual Behavior in the Human Male* (Philadelphia: W. B. Saunders, 1948), 639.

88. The "Garden of Eden" manuscripts, 422.1–8, 2nd part of Chapter 13, p. 7.

89. Ernest Hemingway, "The Sea Change," in *The Complete Short Stories of Ernest Hemingway* (New York: Charles Scribner's Sons, 1987), 304.

90. A. E. Hotchner, *Papa Hemingway: A Personal Memoir* (1966; New York: Bantam, 1967), 139–40.

Chapter 3: Casting Out Forbidden Desires from *The Garden of Eden*

1. E. L. Doctorow, "Braver Than We Thought," review of *The Garden of Eden*, by Ernest Hemingway, *The New York Times Book Review*, 18 May 1986, sec. 7, 44.

2. Tom Jenks, "An Interview with Tom Jenks," in *Dictionary of Literary Biography: Yearbook 1986*, ed. J. M. Brook (Detroit: Gale, 1987), 87.

3. Barbara Solomon, "Ernest Hemingway's Real *Garden of Eden*," in *Horse-Trading and Ecstasy* (San Francisco: North Point Press, 1989), 31.

4. According to Morrison, the "voluptuous illegality" of *The Garden of Eden* is "enforced by the associations constantly made between darkness and desire, darkness and irrationality, darkness and the thrill of evil," *Playing in the Dark: Whiteness and the Literary Imagination* (Cambridge: Harvard University Press, 1992), 87.

5. Carl Eby, "'Come Back to the Beach Ag'in, David Honey!': Hemingway's Fetishization of Race in *The Garden of Eden* Manuscripts," *The Hemingway Review* 14.2 (1995): 107. In his recent book, Eby enlarges the portrait of Hemingway set forth in this article by providing an argument that links racial others, homoeroticism, and gender identity to the fetish. This link is filtered through what Eby sees as Hemingway's "unified psychology," *Hemingway's Fetishism: Psychoanalysis and the Mirror of Manhood* (Albany: State University of New York Press, 1999), 162.

6. I'm following the feminist understanding here where sex refers to biological sex (anatomy, male and female), gender refers to social prescriptions of behavior/appearance (feminine and masculine), and sexual orientation refers to the categories we have constructed in the twentieth century for talking about our sexual identities (homosexual, heterosexual, bisexual). As I explain in this chapter, these concepts have strong historical and social connections so that Catherine's changing of her sex (her biological designation) has implications also for her gender identity and sexual orientation. I'm attempting, therefore, to be consistent in my use of sex to refer to biology and of gender to refer to social roles, although, as Judith Butler has recently shown in *Gender Trouble* and *Bodies That Matter*, these two categories are more mutually dependent than mutually exclusive.

7. K. J. Peters, "The Thematic Integrity of *The Garden of Eden*," *The Hemingway Review* 10.2 (1991): 28.

8. Tom Jenks, "Editing Hemingway: *The Garden of Eden*," *The Hemingway Review* 7.1 (1987): 33.

9. For brief overviews of Scribner's efforts to assemble a publishable text of *Garden*, see Matthew Bruccoli, "Packaging Papa: *The Garden of Eden*," in *Dictionary of Literary Biography: Yearbook 1986*, ed. J. M. Brook (Detroit: Gale, 1987), 79; Peters, 17; and "Interview with Tom Jenks," 82.

10. As a rule of thumb, whenever Hemingway's text is included in Jenks's version of the story, I will cite the published novel rather than the manuscript. Not only will this enable readers to check these quotes for themselves, it will also provide a visible reminder of which parts of the manuscript Jenks included and which parts he excised.

11. bell hooks, "Eating the Other: Desire and Resistance," in *Black Looks: Race and Representation* (Boston: South End Press, 1992), 27.

12. Although they do occasionally mention lesbianism and male homosexuality in *Hemingway's Genders*, Comley and Scholes's preferred terminology is "abnormal" or "transgressive" sexuality or eroticism. Eby does explore some of David's homosexual desire by

reading David's actions through a Freudian paradigm of fetishism and narcissism. Eby concludes that in endowing the old elephant in his story with enormous overstated tusks, David "denies and displaces his own attachment to a homoerotic male bonding," "Come Back to the Beach," 109. The major critics who invoke "androgyny" are Rose Marie Burwell, Mark Spilka, Gerald Kennedy, and Barbara Solomon.

13. For a discussion of the "companionate marriage" campaign, see Christina Simmons, "Companionate Marriage and the Lesbian Threat," *Frontiers* 4.3 (1979): 54–59.

14. Ernest Hemingway, *The Garden of Eden* (New York: Scribner's, 1986), 14–15.

15. Eby points out that Hemingway emphasizes the phallic associations of the name "Peter" in a fragment among the *Garden* manuscripts: "I'd never known anyone named Peter that wasn't a prick" ("Come Back to the Beach," 115).

16. The reference to the Rodin statue has been the source of critical speculation that might serve as a compact example of the way in which critics attempt to bypass or distort appearances of homosexuality in Hemingway's work. As is common in recent Hemingway criticism, androgyny rears its innocuous head. For example, Barbara Solomon argues on page 27 that the statue symbolizes a process of metamorphosis, including androgyny, which is the primary theme of the novel. Similarly, Gerald Kennedy states that the statue serves as a symbolic source "for the androgynous transformations which affect all the major characters," *Imagining Paris: Exile, Writing, and American Identity* (New Haven, Conn.: Yale University Press, 1993), 128. Both of these positions echo that of Mark Spilka, the most influential theorist of the androgyny theme. Correctly identifying the two figures as lesbians, Spilka then confuses that observation, claiming that "the more active" of the two women looks "like a naked man with a woman's breast plainly visible on his chest as he enfolds a naked woman, but . . . proves on closer inspection to be a naked woman with a short haircut like Catherine's," *Hemingway's Quarrel with Androgyny* (Lincoln: University of Nebraska Press, 1990), 286. Spilka's reasoning here is hard to follow unless one allows that any woman with short hair, especially one embracing another woman, looks masculine and always requires "closer inspection" to determine her sex. More likely, Spilka needs this hetero/sexist misidentification in order to support his general thesis that Hemingway understood that "androgyny, and not homosexuality per se," was his underlying problem (284).

K. J. Peters's interpretation of the Rodin statue mirrors these others in its attempt to naturalize the scene from a heterosexist perspective. Peters insists that Rodin's statue actually depicts the two lovers Daphnis and Chloe, but that Rodin confused Daphnis with Sithon, whose sex fluctuated from male to female, "The Thematic Integrity," 19, 28. Although Catherine, too, seems to suggest that one of the figures in the statue is changing or has changed from male to female, clearly both figures are women as one can determine simply by looking at the statue and by noting its sculpting history. That Peters refuses to consider the implications of this lesbianism is telling but, as my description of other critics' analyses illustrates, not unusual.

So far as I can determine, only Kenneth Lynn, and Comley and Scholes have attempted to address the lesbianism of the statue. Lynn argues that Catherine and David are interested in the Rodin statue because it "symbolizes the cross-sexual experimentalism that dominates their lives and haunts their thoughts," 540. But although Lynn acknowledges the importance of lesbianism as part of this experimentation, he does not consider the possibility that male homosexuality is also involved, an important omission given that Lynn believes that Catherine often speaks for Hemingway. Comley and Scholes almost avoid this omission when they assess the statue's function in Catherine and David's lovemaking: "What is at stake here for David Bourne is not just the breaking of a sexual taboo but the loss of his own identity as a heterosexual male," 94. However, they do not explore the full ramifications of that loss or, perhaps more aptly, of the potential gain of a homosexual identity.

17. For information about Rodin's models, see Jacques de Caso and Patricia B. Sanders,

Rodin's Sculpture: A Critical Study of the Spreckels Collection (Rutland: Charles E. Tuttle, 1977), 113. The information about the location and naming of Rodin's figures within his work comes from Albert E. Elsen, *In Rodin's Studio: A Photographic Record of Sculpture in the Making* (Ithaca, N.Y.: Cornell University Press, 1980), Item 77, and from Elsen, *"The Gates of Hell" by Auguste Rodin* (Stanford: Stanford University Press, 1985), 211. Significantly, the reclining figure of the statue has her arms thrown across her eyes, an ambiguous gesture that could suggest unconditional surrender to lesbian desire or an effort to ward off or close one's eyes to the desire that will damn both women within the value structure of *The Gates of Hell*. As I argue in this chapter, such ambiguity functions as well in Hemingway's manuscript where the expression, and even the existence, of desires forbidden by "tribal law" is in constant tension with that law itself.

18. For example, in the manuscript, while in Madrid, Catherine asks David to "let me make the magic we made the first time at Le Grau de (sic) Roi." Kissing him, she changes and then says, "Now you change. Please. Don't make me change you. Must I? All right. I will. You're changed now. You did it too. You did it too. I did it to you but you did it. Yes you did" (422.1–8, chap. 13, p. 13). Although the gap is not long, there is a period here where both Catherine and David are "boys." Later, after Catherine visits the Prado as a boy, she wakes David in the night, telling him that she loves him but she's a boy. "You don't feel like a boy," David says. Catherine replies: "That's where you're lucky for you. But you do and you are and I love you and I feel so happy. I don't care how wrong it is. It isn't wrong for me because I don't mean wrong" (422.1–9, p. 16).

19. Foucault's account of the creation of the homosexual has been challenged in recent years, with some critics arguing that such an identity existed before 1870 and others suggesting that sexologists were less instrumental in the creation of the homosexual than Foucault's analysis allows. See Lisa Duggan, "The Trials of Alice Mitchell: Sensationalism, Sexology, and the Lesbian Subject in Turn-of-the-Century America," *Signs* 18.4 (1993): 791–814, and George Chauncey, "Christian Brotherhood or Sexual Perversion? Homosexual Identities and the Construction of Sexual Boundaries in the World War One Era," *Journal of Social History* 19 (1985): 189–211. Whether the sexologists actually created the homosexual, they nonetheless played a crucial role in codifying and defining this identity.

20. George Chauncey, "From Sexual Inversion to Homosexuality: Medicine and the Changing Conceptualization of Female Deviance," *Salmagundi* 58–59 (1982–83): 124.

21. Officially, Ellis distinguished three types of invertedness, only one of them having to do with gender inversion. "Homosexuality," he writes, refers to "all sexual attractions between persons of the same sex, even when seemingly due to the accidental absence of the natural objects of sexual attraction." "Homosexuality" is thus a more general term than "sexual inversion," which means "sexual instinct turned by inborn constitutional abnormality toward persons of the same sex." Inversion that leads a person to feel and act like a person of the opposite sex is called "sexo-esthetic inversion" or "Eonism," Ellis, "Sexual Inversion," 1–2.

22. Sigmund Freud, "The Psychogenesis of a Case of Homosexuality in a Woman (1920)," in *The Standard Edition of the Complete Psychological Works of Sigmund Freud*, trans. James Strachey (London: Hogarth, 1955), 18: 170.

23. Lisa Duggan observes that the "feminine" partners in lesbian relationships were not perceived as lesbian until the mid-twentieth century and later, "Trials," 809. This inability, or refusal, to identify "feminine" lesbians *as* lesbian emphasizes just how closely gender identity and sexual orientation have been tied historically.

24. Judith Roof, *A Lure of Knowledge: Lesbian Sexuality and Theory* (New York: Columbia University Press, 1991), 211. In general, Freud believes that women are more likely to possess both masculine and feminine traits than men are. For instance, in "The Psychogenesis of a Case of Homosexuality in a Woman," he states that in both sexes physical hermaphroditism is largely independent of psychical hermaphroditism, but then modifies

this statement to claim that the independence is less evident in women "where bodily and mental traits belonging to the opposite sex are apt to coincide," 154.

25. Kaja Silverman, *Male Subjectivity at the Margins* (New York: Routledge, 1992), 342.

26. Havelock Ellis, "Sexual Inversion in Women," *Alienist and Neurologist* 16 (1895): 144–47.

27. Most medical professionals of the time and later, such as Sandor Rado and Irving Bieber in the 1940s adhered to this aberrational view by maintaining that homosexuality was a mental illness to be cured, a position not reversed officially in the United States until 1973, Ronald Bayer, *Homosexuality and American Psychiatry: The Politics of Diagnosis* (Princeton: Princeton University Press, 1987), 28–34. Indeed, models of homosexuality have seldom displaced each other, especially in the public realm, so that the biological and the psychological, the congenital and the acquired, are often grafted onto each other without regard for logic or consistency. As Judith Roof puts it, the disease model has simply joined the earlier sin model and added "the possibility of a genetic predisposition to a stubborn belief in the homosexual's voluntary choice," 239.

Although *Garden* takes place in the 1920s, it is important to extend our vision into the 1940s and 50s when Hemingway was working on it so as to document changing views about sexuality and gender that might have influenced his conception of his characters. These years, as John D'Emilio points out, were a time of increased hostility towards homosexuals, as the Cold War escalated and McCarthy searched for communists. The homosexual was equated with the enemy, and within the federal government, homosexuality "took on the form of a contagious disease that threatened the health of anyone who came near it," "The Homosexual Menace: The Politics of Sexuality in Cold War America," in *Passion and Power*, ed. Kathy Peiss and Christina Simmons (Philadelphia: Temple University Press, 1989), 228. Moreover, because the American Psychiatric Association did not officially remove homosexuality from its *Diagnostic and Statistical Manual of Psychiatric Disorders* until 1973, Hemingway was surely aware of the association of homosexuality and mental illness. In fact, he owned several books published in the 1950s—Gordon Westwood's *Society and the Homosexual* (1952) and George W. Henry's *All the Sexes: A Study of Masculinity and Femininity* (1955)—which, although attempting to generate sympathy and tolerance for homosexuals, still advanced the hard-line position that homosexuality was a mental disease and an abnormality. If nothing else, Hemingway's public attitudes toward male homosexuality suggest he accepted the association.

But Hemingway also owned the most famous study of male sexuality to emerge during the period, a study that challenged the view that persons with homosexual histories are invariably perverse: Alfred C. Kinsey, Wardell B. Pomeroy, and Clyde E. Martin's *Sexual Behavior in the Human Male* (Philadelphia: W. B. Saunders, 1948). Kinsey and his associates determined that "at least 37 per cent of the [white] male population has some homosexual experience between the beginning of adolescence and old age" and that "only 50 per cent of the population is exclusively heterosexual throughout its adult life," *Sexual Behavior in the Human Male*, 623, 656. One of the most important conclusions to come from this first Kinsey study was that only a few men can be classified as exclusively homosexual or exclusively heterosexual; hence, the conclusion that, "It would encourage clearer thinking on these matters if persons were not characterized as heterosexual or homosexual, but as individuals who have had certain amounts of heterosexual experience and certain amounts of homosexual experience. Instead of using these terms as substantives which stand for persons, or even as adjectives to describe persons, they may better be used to describe the nature of the overt sexual relations, or of the stimuli to which an individual erotically responds," 617. The argument against defining people as homosexual or heterosexual seems to be one that Hemingway is advancing in *The Garden of Eden*, although neither he nor his characters can finally dismiss the societal view that the Kinsey report was targeting.

Information about books that Hemingway owned comes from James D. Brasch and Joseph Sigman, *Hemingway's Library: A Composite Record* (New York: Garland, 1981).

28. Kenneth Lewes observes that "Freud proposed several theories to account for the etiology of homosexuality" and that these theories are not consistent among themselves, *The Psychoanalytic Theory of Male Homosexuality* (New York: New American Library, 1988), 35, 36. Lewes arranges Freud's scattered ideas into four separate theories, identifying their inconsistencies and pointing out that, for Freud, "the child's tendency toward narcissistic object choice in homosexuality seriously limits the possibility of his sexuality resulting in mature object relations," 44. According to Lewes, Freud's subscription to "cultural norms that defined healthy psychic and sexual functioning by the way it corresponded to historically contingent establishments and customs" is a position that most of Freud's followers would claim as "a cornerstone of their theory," 47.

Lewes is referring here to male homosexuality, which, as Michael Warner observes, Freud especially associated with narcissism, "Homo-Narcissism; or, Heterosexuality," in *Engendering Men: The Question of Male Feminist Criticism*, ed. Joseph A. Boone and Michael Cadden (New York: Routledge, 1990), 190–206. But Freud also connects narcissism with lesbianism. In "A Case of Paranoia Running Counter to the Psycho-analytical Theory of the Disease (1915)," Freud describes a thirty-year-old woman who, instead of choosing her mother as a love object, identifies with her to the point of becoming her. He concludes: "The possibility of this regression points to the narcissistic origin of her homosexual object-choice and thus to the paranoiac disposition in her," *The Standard Edition of the Complete Psychological Works of Sigmund Freud*, trans. James Strachey (London: Hogarth, 1957), 14: 269. For a more detailed discussion of Freud's relation of narcissism to lesbianism, see Judith Roof's chapter "Freud Reads Lesbians" in *A Lure of Knowledge*.

29. Juliet Mitchell, *Psychoanalysis and Feminism: Freud, Reich, Laing and Women* (1974; New York: Vintage, 1975), 34.

30. In "Homosexuality: Its Psychobiological and Psychopathological Significance" in *The Urologic and Cutaneous Review* 33 (1929), John F. W. Meagher claimed that "A homosexual woman often wants to possess the male and not to be possessed by him. . . . With them orgasm is often only possible in the superior position" (quoted in Simmons, 57; and Chauncey, "Sexual Inversion," 121–22).

31. For instance, James Nagel states, "It is clear from the beginning that [Catherine] is emotionally unstable and self-destructive and that it is only a matter of time until their marriage must end, despite the fact that they are still on their honeymoon," "The Hunting Story in *The Garden of Eden*," in *Hemingway's Neglected Short Fiction: New Perspectives*, ed. Susan F. Beegel (Ann Arbor: UMI Research Press, 1989), 332.

32. Besides the fact that he rarely denies Catherine's request to make the change, David also occasionally admits to himself that their Devil things give him pleasure. "This nonsense that we do is fun," he says at one point (*Garden*, 31), and he reminds himself that he participated, accepted the change, and lived it (*Garden*, 21). In addition, Catherine comes to understand that David's reluctance is often a pose. When David asks her not to change into a boy, Catherine asks, "What makes your voice be different when you say it?" (*Garden*, 55). As Catherine says, "You always do everything I want because you really want to do it too" (*Garden*, 196).

33. Marcel Proust, *Sodom and Gomorrah*, vol. 4 of *In Search of Lost Time*, trans. C. K. Scott Moncrieff and Terence Kilmartin, revised by D. J. Enright (New York: Modern Library, 1993), 30–31.

34. George W. Henry, *All the Sexes: A Study of Masculinity and Femininity* (1955; reprint, New York: Octagon, 1978), 291.

35. Ernest Hemingway, "There's One in Every Town," Ernest Hemingway Collection, John F. Kennedy Library, Boston, Item 743, p. 2.

36. Marita also mentions that she has read the story about David and his fiancée and knows how they both were (422.1–35, p. 31), suggesting that David has a history of transgressing sexual norms and writing about it.

37. Rose Marie Burwell argues that the variety Marita offers David "puts her in the subservient, impersonal, position of an Arab boy" (219). Given the associations Hemingway draws between Marita and Arab men—associations that stereotypically would make her the partner who is anally penetrated—and given that Marita tells David, "But you never had what I am. Not even in Madrid" (quoted in Comley and Scholes, 100), Burwell's proposal that Marita and David reverse positions seems plausible. However, Marita's discussions with David also make clear that she plans to replicate Catherine's actions but without the remorse (see 422.1–36, pp. 34–35).

38. Hemingway's sexual experimentations may have begun much earlier in his life. Several critics have pointed out that he and his first two wives, Hadley and Pauline, wore matching hairstyles or made plans to cut or grow their hair the same length. In addition, Gerald Kennedy notes an excised section from the manuscript of *A Moveable Feast* that Hemingway worked on simultaneously with *The Garden of Eden* in which he discusses his and Hadley's plans to achieve unisex hairstyles and announces that they lived like savages after their return to Paris in 1924, keeping their own standards, secrets, taboos, and delights (134–35). Of course, the fictionality of *A Moveable Feast* is legendary by now. See Jacqueline Tavernier-Courbin, *Ernest Hemingway's* A Moveable Feast: *The Making of Myth* (Boston: Northeastern University Press, 1991). In addition, Hemingway never explains the nature of these secrets and taboos, so one must be cautious of reading too much into this fragment. But Rose Marie Burwell claims that evidence suggests that among Hemingway's four wives, "it was only Martha Gellhorn who would not engage in the gender-bending antics that he found erotic," 212. Perhaps the most one can say is what Kennedy concludes, that other evidence in *A Moveable Feast* indicates that Paris exposed Hemingway to "the multiformity of desire and raised troubling questions about sexuality itself," *Imagining Paris*, 139.

39. Judith Butler, "Critically Queer," *GLQ: A Journal of Lesbian and Gay Studies* 1.1 (1993): 22.

40. This point is not original but accords with Butler's understanding of heterosexuality as offering "normative sexual positions that are intrinsically impossible to embody." Thus, "the persistent failure to identify fully and without incoherence with these positions reveals heterosexuality itself not only as a compulsory law, but as an inevitable comedy," a "constant parody of itself," *Gender Trouble*, 122.

41. Eve Sedgwick provides an extended discussion of the relations among homosociality, homosexuality, sexism, and homophobia in *Between Men* (New York: Columbia University Press, 1985) and *Epistemology of the Closet* (Berkeley: University of California Press, 1990).

42. Leo Bersani, "Is the Rectum a Grave?" *October* 43 (1987): 212.

43. Rosemary Hennessy, "Queer Theory, Left Politics," *Rethinking Marxism* 7.3 (1994): 88.

44. Donald Lowe, *The Body in Late-Capitalist USA* (Durham: Duke University Press, 1995), 135.

45. Charles Scribner, Jr., "The Secret of Being Ernest (and the Secret of Keeping Ernest)," in *In the Web of Ideas: The Education of a Publisher* (New York: Scribner's, 1993), 35.

46. For more on Scribner's involvement in the editing, promotion, and circulation of Hemingway's works, see Leonard Leff's *Hemingway and His Conspirators: Hollywood, Scribners, and the Making of American Celebrity Culture* (Lanham, Md: Rowman and Littlefield, 1997). Leff chronicles the ways in which Scribner's, the American media, and film companies helped to construct Hemingway's popular image during the 1920s. For some serious reservations about Leff's argument regarding Hemingway's relationship with Scribner's, see Robert W. Trogdon's review in *The Hemingway Review* 17.2 (1998): 124–27. In *American Authors and the Literary Marketplace since 1900* (Philadelphia: University of Pennsylvania Press, 1988), James L.W. West, III, deals in detail with the role that publishers and the media have played in the construction of American authors and the promotion of those images to the American public.

47. As of spring 1990, the Hemingway family rescinded its permission to photocopy manuscripts of published works. According to Stephen Plotkin, an archivist with the Hemingway Collection, "This restriction includes manuscripts of the posthumously published material," as well as manuscripts connected to a published work. Researchers are still allowed to photocopy manuscripts of unpublished works, letters, etc. Letter to the author, 8 Jan. 1993.

Chapter 4: Re-Embodying Hemingway's Fiction and Life

1. Susan F. Beegel, "Conclusion: The Critical Reputation of Ernest Hemingway," in *The Cambridge Companion to Hemingway*, ed. Scott Donaldson (Cambridge: Cambridge University Press, 1996), 290.
2. I should also note that Beegel predicts that by the end of the 1990s, "talk of 'androgyny' will be old hat," "Conclusion," 293.
3. Peter F. Cohen has recently presented an argument regarding the intense male bonds in *A Farewell to Arms* that coincides with the one I make in this chapter regarding *The Sun Also Rises*. Drawing upon Eve Sedgwick's contention that male homosocial behavior lies on the same continuum as male homosexual desire, Cohen proposes that "Rinaldi 'trafficks' Catherine between himself and Frederic as a means of eroticizing his relationship with his roommate," "'I Won't Kiss You . . . . I'll Send Your English Girl': Homoerotic Desire in *A Farewell to Arms*," *The Hemingway Review* 15.1 (1995), 45. Although my argument posits a more comprehensive circulation of desire among the characters, Cohen has recognized that a Hemingway heroine might serve as an erotic go-between for two Hemingway heroes.
4. Gayatri Spivak, "A Response to 'The Difference Within': Feminism and Critical Theory," in *The Difference Within: Feminism and Critical Theory*, ed. Elizabeth Meese and Alice Parker (Philadelphia: John Benjamin, 1989), 213.
5. Arnold Davidson and Cathy Davidson, "Decoding the Hemingway Hero in *The Sun Also Rises*," in *New Essays on* The Sun Also Rises, ed. Linda Wagner-Martin (Cambridge: Cambridge University Press, 1987), 89–92.
6. Wendy Martin, "Brett Ashley as New Woman in *The Sun Also Rises*," in *New Essays on* The Sun Also Rises, ed. Linda Wagner-Martin (Cambridge: Cambridge University Press, 1987), 71.
7. Susan Gubar, "Blessings in Disguise: Cross-Dress as Re-Dressing for Female Modernists," *Massachusetts Review* 22 (1981): 478.
8. George Chauncey observes that Havelock Ellis, like other contemporary sexologists, attempted to differentiate sexual object choice from sexual roles and gender characteristics, an attempt reflected in the distinguishing of the sexual invert from the homosexual. Chauncey also notes, however, that the sexologists were less willing to apply this distinction to women. Hence, whereas Ellis could claim that male homosexuals were not necessarily effeminate or transvestites, he was less capable of separating a woman's behavior in sexual relations from other aspects of her gender role. See Chauncey, "Sexual Inversion," 124–25. For example, although he maintained that transvestism was unrelated to homosexuality, in Ellis's own "Sexual Inversion," he still provided numerous examples of lesbian transvestites and insisted that even lesbians who dressed in "female" attire usually showed some "masculine" traits in their clothing. Ellis also believed that a keen observer could detect "psychic abnormality" in a woman by watching her behavior. "The brusque energetic movements, the attitude of the arms, the direct speech, the inflexions of the voice, the masculine straight-forwardness and sense of honor, and especially the attitude towards men, free from any suggestion either of shyness or audacity, will often suggest the underlying psychic abnormality," "Sexual Inversion in Women," *Alienist and Neurologist* 16 (1895): 153.

Ellis's observations reflect his entrenchment in a heterosexual norm, assuming, as Shari Benstock remarks of many critics, that "all lesbian behavior has in common its *reaction* to the norm of compulsory heterosexuality and that all lesbians act out their sexual orientation in the same way—here, through cross-dressing." Benstock points out that different behavior patterns existed among members of the Parisian lesbian community of the 1920s (as they do among lesbian communities today) and suggests that many lesbians of the Left Bank based their choices on the sexuality of their audience, *Women of the Left Bank: Paris, 1900–1940* (Austin: University of Texas Press, 1986), 179–80.

9. Apparently, Hemingway did not feel kindly toward Georgette Leblanc. In a letter to Ezra Pound (c. 2 May 1924), Hemingway noted that Margaret Anderson was in Paris with "Georgette Mangeuse [man-eater] le Blanc," *Ernest Hemingway: Selected Letters, 1917–1961*, ed. Carlos Baker (New York: Charles Scribner's Sons, 1981), 115. But whether he knew her personally is uncertain. According to Bertram Sarason, Margaret Anderson claimed that Leblanc had never met Hemingway and did not know her name had been mentioned in the novel. *Hemingway and* The Sun Set (Washington, D.C.: Microcard Editions, 1972), 81. Interestingly, Jake's identification of Georgette Hobin as Georgette Leblanc suggests a special kind of knowledge about prostitutes that circulated at the time. In "Sexual Inversion," Havelock Ellis remarks that the frequency of homosexuality among prostitutes is very high, especially in Paris, 210. He quotes a friend who states, "From my experience of the Parisian prostitute, I gather that Lesbianism in Paris is extremely prevalent; indeed, one might almost say normal. In particular, most of the chahut-dancers of the Moulin-Rouge, Casino de Paris, and the other public balls are notorious for going in couples, and, for the most part, they prefer not to be separated, even in their most professional moments with the other sex," 211.

10. Also compare Hemingway's description several years later during his interview with George Plimpton in which he states that Jake's testicles "were intact and not damaged. Thus he was capable of all normal feelings as a *man* but incapable of consummating them. The important distinction is that his wound was physical and not psychological and that he was not emasculated," Interview, in *Writers at Work: The* Paris Review *Interviews*, 2d ser., ed. George Plimpton (New York: Penguin, 1977), 230; original emphasis.

11. Although this kind of statement does not need verifying, given the phallocentrism of our society, a quote from Havelock Ellis will contextualize Jake's wound in its historical time: "It is easy to understand why the penis should occupy this special place in man's thoughts as the supreme sexual organ. It is the one conspicuous and prominent portion of the sexual apparatus, while its aptitude for swelling and erecting itself involuntarily, under the influence of sexual emotion, gives it a peculiar and almost unique position in the body. At the same time it is the point at which, in the male body, all voluptuous sensation is concentrated, the only normal masculine center of sex," "Erotic Symbolism," vol. 3, *Studies in the Psychology of Sex* (New York: Random, 1936), 123.

12. Peter Messent's essay on *The Sun Also Rises* suggested this play on words, *New Readings of the American Novel* (London: Macmillan Education, 1990), 92. Although he does not state the matter as I have, he also seems to have borrowed this idea from Sandra M. Gilbert, "Costumes of the Mind: Transvestism as Metaphor in Modern Literature," *Critical Inquiry* 7 (1980): 409.

13. Peter Messent has also recently explored gender fluidity in *The Sun Also Rises*, and his reading lends support to many of the suppositions I set forth here. Messent states, "In *The Sun Also Rises*, gender roles have lost all stability," 112. Among other things, he points to Georgette's sexual forwardness with Jake, Brett's pre-dawn visit to Jake's room after he retired there with a "headache," the count's bringing of roses to Jake, and Jake's crying, 114.

14. As support for this argument, consider Susan Gubar's suggestion that seductive cross-dressers "can function as sex symbols for men, reflecting masculine attitudes that range from an attempt to eroticize (and thereby possess) the independent woman to only slightly

submerged homosexual fantasies," 483. While I do not discount the first possibility (eroticism in the service of possession), here I am tracing the latter function.

15. In *Gay New York*, George Chauncey argues that only in the 1930s, 1940s, and 1950s "did the now-conventional division of men into 'homosexuals' and 'heterosexuals,' based on the sex of their sexual partners, replace the division of men into 'fairies' and 'normal men' on the basis of their imaginary gender status as the hegemonic way of understanding sexuality," 13. But Chauncey also notes that "exclusive heterosexuality became a precondition for a man's identification as 'normal' in middle-class culture at least two generations before it did so in much of Euro-American and African-American working class culture," 14. To outside observers of the homosexual subculture, "faggot," in the 1930s, would have been the equivalent of "queer" and "fairy." However, to insiders, "queer" was reserved for men who had a homosexual interest, whereas "fairy" and "faggot" referred only to those men "who dressed or behaved in what they considered to be a flamboyantly effeminate manner," *Gay New York*, 15–16. Bill's comment about how his words and feelings might be interpreted in New York seem to indicate an awareness that he would be seen as inverting norms of both gender and sexuality.

16. Toni Morrison in *Playing in the Dark* (Cambridge: Harvard University Press, 1992) and Carl Eby in "'Come Back to the Beach Ag'in, David Honey!': Hemingway's Fetishization of Race in *The Garden of Eden* Manuscripts," *The Hemingway Review* 14.2 (1995): 98–117 stand as important exceptions to this claim that critics have overlooked the intersections of race and desire in Hemingway and his fiction. Both focus on *The Garden of Eden*, with Eby suggesting that racial otherness—along with hair and phallic women—functioned as fetish for Hemingway. Besides his experiences with African women, discussed later in this section, Hemingway was fascinated by other women of color who had cultural associations with the primitive, for example, Josephine Baker (see Eby) and Trudie Boulton, a Native American girl whom he knew when he was a boy and whom he fictionalized as Nick Adams's first lover (e.g., "The Last Good Country," "Fathers and Sons").

17. So significant is Hemingway's globe-trotting that John Raeburn proposes "world traveler" as one of nine roles that form the foundation of Hemingway's public personality. Raeburn suggests that this aspect of Hemingway's personality is intimately tied to his role as arbiter of taste, and it also seems linked to his role of insider, the man who could write with authority about places and professionals (bullfighters, soldiers, white hunters) because he saw them with the eyes of a native or an insider, (41–2). Hemingway's world-traveling also plays a strong part in critical constructions of his life and identity. In fact, many of his biographers organize their chapters around places that he visited or lived. For instance, Carlos Baker includes the following chapters in his *Ernest Hemingway: A Life Story*: "Milano," "Black Forest, Black Sea," "Lausanne," "Rapallo and Cortina," "Iberia," "To the Eastern Kingdom," "Highlands of Africa," "Bimini Discovered," "The Slopes of Kilimanjaro," "The Spanish Earth," "The Banks of the Ebro," "Pursuit to London," "Return to Normandy," "The Road to Paris," and "Uganda and After."

18. Kate Davy, "Outing Whiteness: A Feminist/Lesbian Project," *Theatre Journal* 47.2 (1995): 197.

19. See Marianna Torgovnick's *Gone Primitive: Savage Intellects, Modern Lives* (Chicago: University of Chicago Press, 1990) for other examples of this phenomenon. For a discussion of "primitivism," including Torgovnick's analysis of it, see David Theo Goldberg, *Racist Culture: Philosophy and the Politics of Meaning* (Cambridge, Mass.: Blackwell, 1993), 155–63.

20. Rob Wilson, "Producing American Selves: The Form of American Biography," *Contesting the Subject: Essays in the Postmodern Theory and Practice of Biography and Biographical Criticism*, ed. William H. Epstein (West Lafayette: Purdue University Press, 1991), 171.

21. Robert Fleming, *The Face in the Mirror: Hemingway's Writers* (Tuscaloosa: University of Alabama Press, 1994), 81.

22. This pattern of comparing Harry and Hemingway shows up throughout the criticism. To quote two other sources: Scott Macdonald asserts that "the achievement represented by the writing of 'The Snows of Kilimanjaro' is itself the ultimate standard against which the reader can measure Harry's failure," "Hemingway's 'The Snows of Kilimanjaro': Three Critical Problems," *Studies in Short Fiction* 11.1 (1974): 72, and Gennaro Santangelo writes that the "ultimate irony" of "Snows" is that "the achieved story itself denies its possible premises," for in contrast to Harry's lack of discipline and fakery, Hemingway has dedicated himself to his craft and written "a great work," "The Dark Snows of Kilimanjaro," in *The Short Stories of Ernest Hemingway: Critical Essays*, ed. Jackson J. Benson (Durham: Duke University Press, 1975), 261. Hemingway actually encouraged such a comparison when he supposedly told A. E. Hotchner, "Never wrote so directly about myself as in ['Snows']," Hotchner, 176. Hemingway turned his directness into indirectness when he apparently stated that the portrait of the artist in "Snows" presents him as he might have been, Baker, 289.

23. Ernest Hemingway, "The Snows of Kilimanjaro," in *The Complete Short Stories of Ernest Hemingway* (New York: Charles Scribner's Sons, 1987), 44.

24. Imperialism, capitalism, and racism have a lengthy history of cooperation. Generally speaking, imperialism is "the practice, the theory, and the attitudes of a dominating metropolitan center ruling a distant territory," Edward Said, *Culture and Imperialism* (1993; New York: Vintage, 1994), 9. Given this definition, the reasons why imperialism links up with capitalism and racism are not hard to fathom. In fact, Marxist proponents such as Lenin propose that imperialism emerged "as the development and direct continuation of the fundamental attributes of capitalism in general," "Imperialism, the Highest Stage of Capitalism," in *Essential Works of Lenin*, ed. Henry M. Christman (New York: Dover, 1987), 236. As Lenin suggests here, the more capitalism takes hold in a nation, the more that nation needs raw materials, including natural resources and cheap labor, if it is to continue to increase production and, therefore, profits. This search for raw materials expands all over the world so that eventually the nation must annex colonies to provide both resources and labor, Lenin, 232. For a brief review of other theories of imperialism as it manifested itself in Africa (e.g. psychological, diplomatic, African-centered), see G. N. Uzoigwe, "European Partition and Conquest of Africa: An Overview," in *General History of Africa, Vol. 7: Africa Under Colonial Domination 1880–1935*, ed. A. Adu Boahen (London: Heinemann, 1985), 19–44. Although Uzoigwe notes that a number of theorists have attacked the Marxist economic imperialism theory as it relates to Africa, he argues that "more serious investigations of African history" in the period from 1880–1935 indicate that "those who persist in trivializing the economic dimension of the partition do so at their own peril," 21.

25. Toni Morrison has recently revealed the extent to which black male "nurses" people the pages of Hemingway's fiction, although she doesn't explicitly mention "Snows." She divides these men into two categories, the loyal and the resistant. Given their apparent willingness to care for Harry and Helen, the African men of "Snows" seem to fit the former category, but who knows what they might be saying when not in the presence of "Bwana" and "Memsahib"? Morrison, 82–84.

26. David Spurr, *The Rhetoric of Empire: Colonial Discourse in Journalism, Travel Writing, and Imperial Administration* (Durham: Duke University Press, 1993), 14.

27. M. H. Y. Kaniki, "The Colonial Economy: The Former British Zones," in *General History of Africa, Vol. 7: Africa Under Colonial Domination 1880–1935*, ed. A. Adu Boahen (London: Heinemann, 1985), 397. In Kenya, the labor of African workers was closely monitored, most obviously by the requirement that every African adult male carry a work pass (kipande) "on which the employer recorded, among other things, the kind of work performed, time worked and wages earned. Failure to carry, or loss of the kipande rendered Africans liable to a fine and/or imprisonment up to three months. . . . The kipande

greatly restricted the African's freedom of movement. A man could not leave his job of his own accord . . . ," Kaniki, 397.

28. Ernest Hemingway, "The Short Happy Life of Francis Macomber," in *The Complete Short Stories of Ernest Hemingway* (New York: Charles Scribner's Sons, 1987), 7.

29. For differing views about British imperialism in Africa, see E. A. Brett, *Colonialism and Underdevelopment in East Africa: The Politics of Economic Change, 1919–1939* (London: Heinemann, 1973). As Brett points out, not all Britons supported British involvement in Africa; for example, the British Labour party adopted a strong line of anti-imperialist thinking during the 1920s and 1930s.

30. To a great degree, our own special brand of imperialism has been masked by such concepts as "manifest destiny," "making the world safe for democracy," and "Communist containment." Significantly, almost all the expansion of U. S. territory in the eighteenth and nineteenth centuries involved the displacement or genocide of people of color (especially American Indians and Mexicans), actions that were justified by beliefs that Anglo-Saxon races were religiously, morally, politically, and intellectually superior. Thus from the beginning of U. S. history, "the task of distributing and systematizing capitalist ownership in land"—See Anders Stephanson, *Manifest Destiny: American Expansion and the Empire of Right* (New York: Hill and Wang, 1995), 14—and the racist acquisition of additional territory have been closely tied. The racist underpinnings of U. S. capitalist-imperialism have not died out in the twentieth century, as can be seen in the imperialistic relationships our government has forged with such places as the Phillippines, Vietnam, and Central America. Nor have the ties between imperialism and capitalism been broken in an age of "deterritorialized capitalism," that is, in an age when capitalism has moved from the realm of the national marketplace to global production concentrated in large transnational corporations. In short, the business of empire both inside and outside United States borders has been tied to capitalism, and this capitalist-imperialism has frequently been bound up with racism.

31. For a collection of some of these views, both literary and non-literary, see *The Anti-Imperialist Reader, A Documentary History of Anti-Imperialism in the United States, Vol. I: From the Mexican War to the Election of 1900*, ed. Philip S. Foner and Richard C. Winchester (New York: Holmes & Meier, 1984), and *The Anti-Imperialist Reader, A Documentary of Anti-Imperialism in the United States, Vol. 2: The Literary Anti-Imperialists*, ed. Philip S. Foner (New York: Holmes & Meier, 1986).

32. Ernest Hemingway, *Green Hills of Africa* (1935; New York: Macmillan, 1987), 285.

33. This identification has been picked up by critics as well, most notably in John Howell's collection, *Hemingway's African Stories: The Stories, Their Sources, Their Critics* (New York: Charles Scribner's Sons, 1969), which focuses on "Snows" and "Macomber."

34. Hemingway's letter to Max Perkins is included in *Ernest Hemingway, Selected Letters, 1917–1961*, ed. Carlos Baker (New York: Charles Scribner's Sons, 1981), 442. His review of *Batouala* is quoted in Donald E. Herdeck, Introduction, *Batouala*, by René Maran, trans. Barbara Beck and Alexandre Mboukou (London: Heinemann, 1972), 2.

35. Raeburn notes that in a review of *Green Hills*, Edmund Wilson remarked that the book doesn't tell us much about the natives. According to Wilson, "the principal impression we carry away is that the Africans were simple people who enormously admired Hemingway" (quoted in Raeburn, 74). As Raeburn puts it: "*Green Hills of Africa* is a book about Hemingway set in Africa, rather than a book about Africa with him in it," 74.

36. As of early 1999, only selected portions of this book have been published in *Sports Illustrated* and *Look*. For a description of the fuller manuscript, see Rose Marie Burwell, "The African Book: An Alternative Life," chapt. 5 in *Hemingway: The Postwar Years and the Posthumous Novels* (Cambridge: Cambridge University Press, 1996).

37. The publicity generated by Hemingway's safari was beyond anyone's wildest expectations, for his and Mary's stay ended with two plane crashes and the premature headlines

in papers around the world that Hemingway had died in the first one. See the essays and photos in *Look*, 20 April 1954 and 4 May 1954.

38. Ernest Hemingway, "Safari," *Look*, 26 January 1954, 24.

39. In analyzing the colonialist project of *National Geographic*, Lisa Bloom suggests that whiteness brings with it connotations of safety. "Constructing Whiteness: Popular Science and *National Geographic* in the Age of Multiculturalism," *Configurations* 1 (1994): 15–32. It would seem that the Mau Mau war of black Africans against white "settlers" had stirred up enough concern in the United States that *Look*'s predominantly white audience required an experienced white adventurer such as Hemingway to reassure them that the "dark" dangers of Africa were nothing to be overly frightened of.

40. Besides his references to the war in the 26 January 1954 issue of *Look*, Hemingway also mentions it briefly in his 20 April 1954 *Look* article, which is devoted to the story of his two plane crashes. The brief mention is significant, however. "In the emergency," he writes, "which is the name we apply in understatement to an actual state of war, it was possible for me as an honorary game warden of Kenya to aid by taking this position," 29. Although it is hard to tell whether Hemingway is being sarcastic about Great Britain's downplaying of the rebellion or whether he is simply recognizing the increasing escalation of British resistance to the Mau Mau rebels in 1954, he clearly understands the seriousness of the fighting taking place. For a description and political analysis of the Mau Mau uprising, see Wunyabari O. Maloba, *Mau Mau and Kenya: An Analysis of a Peasant Revolt* (Bloomington: Indiana University Press, 1993).

41. Burwell speculates that Hemingway's "Africanization" and his writing about it in the African book are signs that he was thinking of dropping out of the world of writers, "exploring alternatives to the life in which he was judged, and could judge himself, only as a writer," 136. That he chose to execute such a plan in Africa suggests that Hemingway might have been acting out the Western assumption that "the primitive" represents "a state before there arose troubling differences—of sexuality, of economic life, of religious beliefs, of humans from nature," Torgovnick, 186. In fact, the other way white Westerners might act out the assumptions of this myth is to present themselves as possessing a superior, civilized knowledge that the natives are in need of.

A subset of this myth of the primitive is the notion that African women are more sexually knowledgeable and fertile than white women. Hemingway's desire for Wakumba women, especially for Debba, undoubtedly draws upon this aspect of the myth. Although he wonders in "the African book" about the reasons for generational and cultural differences in sexual mores (Burwell, 140), Hemingway does not take this curiosity to the next stage of critiquing his own cultural assumptions about the sexual desirability of African women. In a letter to Harvey Breit, written while the safari party camped on the Kenya-Tanganyika border, Hemingway asserts that "African girls, Kamba and Masai anyway, are really wonderful and all that nonsense about that they can't love you is not true. It is just that they are more cheerful than girls at home. My girl is completely impudent, her face is impudent in repose, but absolutely loving and delicate rough. I better quit writing about it because I want to write it really and I mustn't spoil it. Anyway it gives me too bad a hardon," 3 January 1954, *Ernest Hemingway: Selected Letters*, 827. According to Burwell, in Hemingway's account of his behavior in "the African book," he repeatedly refers to Debba pressing "the carved leather pistol holster hard against her thigh and then plac[ing] her left hand where she wanted it to be." Moreover, when Debba and Hemingway finally make love, as described in "the African book," he is confident that they have conceived a child, a testimony to his own sexual prowess but also to the fertility of African women. See Burwell, 144.

42. Even though he eventually left Africa, Hemingway never completely abandoned the idea of altering his racial affiliation. In letters written after his trip to Africa, he states that he belongs to "the Wakamba [sic] tribe," *Ernest Hemingway: Selected Letters*, 837. He also expresses his wish "to get somewhere that they don't have white peoples," a wish acceler-

ated by all the publicity that followed his reception of the Nobel Prize but also one that ignores the fact of his own whiteness. *Ernest Hemingway: Selected Letters*, 841.

43. The idea of "arrogant perception" comes from María Lugones who borrows it from Marilyn Frye. It refers to "the failure to identify with persons that one views arrogantly or has come to see as the products of arrogant perception," "Playfulness, 'World'-Travelling, and Loving Perception," *Making Face, Making Soul/Haciendo Caras*, ed. Gloria Anzaldúa (San Francisco: Aunt Lute, 1990), 390–91. Lugones also writes of world-traveling, but in a very different way. For her, such traveling reflects a flexibility of perception that women of color have acquired due to their frequent shifting from mainstream constructions of life "to other constructions of life where [they] are more or less 'at home'" (390).

44. Of course, Hemingway visited and made his home in many other places besides Africa, and typically, he attempted to learn the ways of the native residents, to speak the language, and to become an expert on local customs and political affairs. It might seem, then, that Hemingway was approaching Africa in the same way that he approached most of the places he visited or in which he lived. Yet if this is true, then Hemingway's time in Africa emphasizes that whiteness and American ideology travel differently and that, as a result, actions that have favorable connotations in one country take on the appearance of arrogant, unethical, and even colonialist behavior in another. But, in fact, Hemingway's actions in Africa indicate that he knew this, for his attraction to Debba was bound up not simply in his heterosexual desire but in his desire for someone he constructed as the racialized, primitive other.

45. David Mura, *Where the Body Meets Memory: An Odyssey of Race, Sexuality, and Identity* (New York: Anchor, 1996), 233–34.

46. In his famous essay on the racism of Conrad's *Heart of Darkness*, Chinua Achebe states that he originally intended to conclude with some thoughts about the advantages the West might derive from Africa "once it rid its mind of old prejudices and began to look at Africa . . . as a continent of people," but he was persuaded against this conclusion when he realized "that no easy optimism was possible." The West, he determines, is pervaded by stereotypes and distortions regarding Africa, and eliminating these "unwholesome thoughts" seems a difficult task. Indeed, Achebe claims, "it may well be that what is happening at this stage is more akin to reflex action than calculated malice. Which does not make the situation more but less hopeful," "An Image of Racism in Conrad's *Heart of Darkness*," in *Hopes and Impediments: Selected Essays, 1965–1987* (Oxford: Heinemann, 1988), 12–13. Although Achebe's piece was written twenty years ago, the situation he describes has not improved much. But a primary point of my argument in this section is that such improvement rests partly on white Western readers learning how to read our own racism and, as a consequence, learning different ways of being in the world. These obviously will not be easy tasks, but they seem infinitely preferable to the kind of easy liberalism in which white people deny that race matters. As Toni Morrison writes, "the habit of ignoring race is understood to be a graceful, even generous liberal gesture. To notice is to recognize an already discredited difference. To enforce its invisibility through silence is to allow the black body a shadowless participation in the dominant cultural body. According to this logic, every well-bred instinct argues against noticing and forecloses adult discourse," *Playing in the Dark*, 9–10.

47. The facts of Hemingway's rescue of an Italian soldier during a shelling in World War I are widely disputed. Many critics and biographers argue that Hemingway could not possibly have performed such a feat given the seriousness of his own injuries. Nonetheless, the story persists, as can be seen most recently in the depiction of this rescue in the Hollywood film *In Love and War* (1997).

48. The term "body in pain" is borrowed from Elaine Scarry, whose work is quoted later in this section.

49. Lennard Davis, *Enforcing Normalcy: Disability, Deafness, and the Body* (London: Verso, 1995), 45.

50. Rosemarie Garland Thomson, *Extraordinary Bodies: Figuring Physical Disability in American Culture and Literature* (New York: Columbia University Press, 1997), 9.

51. Young's theory can be found in *Ernest Hemingway* (1952, 1965; revised reprint, London: Routledge, 1995). In brief, he argues that the Hemingway hero will be repeatedly barraged with physical and mental troubles but will never be able to recover completely from his wounds. Young is more interested in the psychic wound, whereas my argument dwells on the need for and function of the physical mark itself.

52. Peter Lehman, *Running Scared: Masculinity and the Representation of the Male Body* (Philadelphia: Temple University Press, 1993), 63.

53. Ernest Hemingway, *A Farewell to Arms* (New York: Charles Scribner's Sons, 1929), 59, 142, 299.

54. Ernest Hemingway, *Across the River and Into the Trees* (1950; reprint, New York: Collier Books, 1987), 10, 180.

55. Ernest Hemingway, *The Old Man and the Sea* (New York: Charles Scribner's Sons, 1953), 9–10, 114–15.

56. For reference to David Bourne's wound, see J. Gerald Kennedy, "Life as Fiction: The Lure of Hemingway's *Garden*," *The Southern Review* 24.2 (1988): 456.

57. Ernest Hemingway, *Islands in the Stream* (New York: Charles Scribner's Sons, 1970), 131.

58. Ernest Hemingway, *To Have and Have Not* (New York: Charles Scribner's Sons, 1937; Collier, 1987), 97.

59. Elaine Scarry, *The Body in Pain: The Making and Unmaking of the World* (New York: Oxford University Press, 1985), 118.

60. The risk of the hero's body being reclassified racially is minimal since the few identifying features that we do receive about Hemingway's heroes identify those heroes as white.

61. For instance, in *A Farewell to Arms*, Catherine determines that if Frederic will let his hair grow longer while she cuts hers, "we'd be just alike only one of us blonde and one of us dark. . . . Oh, darling, I want you so much I want to be you too." Frederic replies, "We're the same one," to which Catherine states, "I know it. At night we are," 299. Maria expresses a similar urge to Robert Jordan, "I would have us exactly the same. . . . if thou should ever wish to change I would be glad to change. I would be thee because I love thee so," *For Whom the Bell Tolls*, 284. In *Across the River and Into the Trees*, the male hero seems even more receptive to this request for change and/or merger. When Renata tells the Colonel that she wants to be him, he replies, "That's awfully complicated. We could try of course," 156. Finally, in *Islands in the Stream*, Thomas Hudson has a dream in which his first wife asks, "Should I be you or you be me?" He says that she has first choice, so she decides that she'll be him. Thomas claims that he can't be her, but he'll try. Following her advice to "Try to lose everything and take everything too," he says he is doing it, and "It's wonderful," 344.

62. Michael S. Kimmel, "Masculinity as Homophobia: Fear, Shame, and Silence in the Construction of Gender Identity," in *Theorizing Masculinities*, ed. Harry Brod and Michael Kaufman (Thousand Oaks: Sage, 1994), 127.

63. Michael S. Kimmel states that "men prove their manhood in the eyes of other men," that masculinity is therefore a homosocial enactment, 129. Although Hemingway's masculinity surely fits this assessment, here I am asserting more than just a need for male approval; rather, I am focusing on Hemingway's desire for the male gaze, a homoerotic enactment.

Chapter 5: Critical Multiculturalism, Canonized Authors, and Desire

1. Here it seems critical to observe that some of these categories—such as class and sexuality—are not studied at *all* levels of education. In fact, in the case of sexuality, many

schools at all levels refuse to engage it in any extended manner, and even mandate that teachers and curricula not mention homosexuality. The most likely place for sexuality to be included in multicultural pedagogy is at the college level, but this is only a likelihood, not a certainty. In fact, *Writing in Multicultural Settings*, a recent book published by the Modern Language Association, the organization that supposedly represents and speaks for college and university English and Foreign Language teachers throughout the U.S. and elsewhere, does not include any essays devoted to sexuality. The book's four sections are "Cultural and Linguistic Diversity," "The Roles of Teachers and Texts," "ESL Issues," and "Sociocultural and Pedagogical Tensions." Although one can find examples of multicultural texts that do include discussions of sexuality, the example of *Writing in Multicultural Settings* is not unusual and indicates the uncertain place that sexuality has within many educators' understanding and practice of multiculturalism.

2. Chicago Cultural Studies Group, "Critical Multiculturalism," *Critical Inquiry* 18 (1992): 550.

3. As Amy Kaplan writes in her introduction to *Cultures of United States Imperialism*, American nationality will continue to be seen as monolithic and self-contained "if it remains implicitly defined by its internal social relations, and not in political struggles for power with other cultures and nations, struggles which make America's conceptual and geographic borders fluid, contested, and historically changing," "'Left Alone with America': The Absence of Empire in the Study of American Culture," in *Cultures of United States Imperialism*, ed. Amy Kaplan and Donald E. Pease (Durham: Duke University Press, 1993), 15.

4. So far as I know no one has addressed the relation of critical multiculturalism to what is being called the New American Studies. In reading the work of critics who self-identify as one or the other, I find considerable confusion about whether critical multiculturalism is a subset of, a contrast to, or identical with the New American Studies. Some of this confusion has to be attributed to the instability of both terms, the proliferation of meanings they have inspired. For instance, in his introduction to "The New American Studies," Philip Fisher labels multiculturalism a new "regionalism" and conceives all national conflicts as "civil wars" over representation that inevitably help to cement the center. See Kaplan, 15. Fisher seems to understand multiculturalism simply as cultural pluralism, an understanding that critical multiculturalism contests. In contrast, Donald E. Pease seems to view critical multiculturalism as directly aligned with the New American Studies in understanding the connection between disciplinary practices and oppositional political movements, "New Americanists: Revisionist Interventions into the Canon," *boundary 2* 17.1 (1990): 19; see also Donald Pease, "New Perspectives on U.S. Culture and Imperialism," in *Cultures of United States Imperialism*, ed. Amy Kaplan and Donald E. Pease (Durham: Duke University Press, 1993), esp. 25–26. It is still too soon to predict how these debates will turn out, which term will prevail (if either does). My work in this chapter, however, is intended to participate in this conversation over what U.S. literary studies might look like given the multiple pressures urging its transformation.

5. Ellen Rooney, *Seductive Reasoning: Pluralism as the Problematic of Contemporary Literary History* (Ithaca, N.Y.: Cornell University Press, 1989), 8.

6. Biddy Martin, "Introduction: Teaching Literature, Changing Cultures," *PMLA* 112 (1997): 15.

7. Charles Taylor, *Multiculturalism and "The Politics of Recognition"* (Princeton: Princeton University Press, 1992), 36.

8. John Guillory, *Cultural Capital: The Problem of Literary Canon Formation* (Chicago: University of Chicago Press, 1993), 21.

9. Wahneema Lubiano, "Multiculturalism: Negotiating Politics and Knowledge," *Concerns* 22.3 (1992): 19.

10. Deborah P. Britzman, Kelvin Santiago-Válles, Gladys Jiménez-Múñoz, and Laura M. Lamash, "Slips That Show and Tell: Fashioning Multiculture as a Problem of Repre-

sentation," in *Race, Identity, and Representation in Education*, ed. Cameron McCarthy and Warren Crichlow (New York: Routledge, 1993), 189.

11. Desire affects other choices we make as educators, teachers, political subjects, but these pursuits of desire would require another book. In fact, a number of books attempt to address this matter in one way or another. For two examples, see *Professions of Desire*, ed. George E. Haggerty and Bonnie Zimmerman (New York: MLA, 1995); and bell hooks, *Teaching to Transgress: Education as the Practice of Freedom* (New York: Routledge, 1994).

12. This is not to say that all U.S. canonized writers are white and male (for instance, Emily Dickinson and even Toni Morrison might fit this category), nor is it to assert that all canonized writers are heterosexual, middle-class, or able-bodied. I am referring to reader assumptions about the identities of these authors and about which identities have traditionally counted as meaningful. Again, homosexuality, as Eve Sedgwick and others have shown would be among those identities that critics have presumed were unimportant.

13. Gregory Jay, *American Literature and the Culture Wars* (Ithaca, N.Y.: Cornell University Press, 1997), 115.

14. Lisa Kahaleole Chang Hall, "Compromising Positions," in *Beyond a Dream Deferred: Multicultural Education and the Politics of Excellence*, ed. Becky W. Thompson and Sangeeta Tyagi (Minneapolis: University of Minnesota Press, 1993), 164; original emphasis.

15. AnnLouise Keating, "Interrogating 'Whiteness,' (De)Constructing 'Race,'" *College English* 57.8 (1995): 904.

16. Peggy McIntosh, "White Privilege and Male Privilege: A Personal Account of Coming to See Correspondences Through Work in Women's Studies" (Wellesley: Publications Department, Center for Research on Women, 1988).

17. Christine E. Sleeter, "How White Teachers Construct Race," in *Race, Identity and Representation in Education*, ed. Cameron McCarthy and Warren Crichlow (New York: Routledge, 1993), 162.

18. Lisa Duggan, "Queering the State," *Social Text* 39 (1994): 9.

19. Linda Singer, *Erotic Welfare: Sexual Theory and Politics in the Age of Epidemic* (New York: Routledge, 1993), 173.

20. Leslie G. Roman, "Denying (White) Racial Privilege: Redemption Discourses and the Uses of Fantasy," in *Off White: Readings on Race, Power, and Society*, ed. Michelle Fine, Lois Weis, Linda C. Powell, and L. Mun Wong (New York: Routledge, 1997), 272.

21. According to Paul Lauter, "Behind the Scenes at the Canon Melodrama," *Newsletter for the Heath Anthology of American Literature* 16 (1997): 1.

22. W. H. Auden, "Law Like Love," in *W. H. Auden: Collected Poems*, ed. Edward Mendelson (New York: Random House, 1976), 209. According to Richard Davenport-Hines, Auden wrote "Law Like Love" while in his early raptures over his love affair with Chester Kallman. See Richard Davenport-Hines, *Auden* (New York: Pantheon, 1995), 192. I am aware that Auden is a British poet and therefore does not fit in an American literature curriculum. I use his work in my critical writing (introduction to literature) classes, but certainly the assignment I am describing here could be replicated in the American literature classroom, with an appropriate substitute for Auden.

23. Eve Sedgwick, "White Glasses," in *Tendencies* (Durham: Duke University Press, 1993), 253.

WORKS CITED

Achebe, Chinua. "An Image of Racism in Conrad's *Heart of Darkness*." In *Hopes and Impediments: Selected Essays, 1965–1987*. Oxford: Heinemann, 1988: 1–13.

Althusser, Louis. "Ideology and Ideological State Apparatuses (Notes towards an Investigation)." In *Lenin and Philosophy and Other Essays*, translated by Ben Brewster. New York: Monthly Review Press, 1971: 127–86.

Auden, W. H. "Law Like Love." In *W. H. Auden: Collected Poems*, edited by Edward Mendelson. New York: Random House, 1976: 208–9.

August, Jo. "A Note on the Hemingway Collection." *College Literature* 7.3 (1980): introductory note.

Baker, Carlos. *Ernest Hemingway: A Life Story*. New York: Charles Scribner's Sons, 1969.

Barthes, Roland. "The Death of the Author." In *Image-Music-Text*, translated by Stephen Heath. New York: Noonday, 1977: 142–48.

———. "The Discourse of History," translated by Stephen Bann. In *Comparative Criticism: A Yearbook*, edited by E. S. Shaffer. Cambridge: Cambridge University Press, 1981: 3–20.

———. *The Pleasure of the Text*, translated by Richard Miller. New York: Hill and Wang, 1975.

———. *Sade, Fourier, Loyola*, translated by Richard Miller. Berkeley: University of California Press, 1976.

Bayer, Ronald. *Homosexuality and American Psychiatry: The Politics of Diagnosis*. Princeton: Princeton University Press, 1987.

Beegel, Susan F. "Conclusion: The Critical Reputation of Ernest Hemingway." In *The Cambridge Companion to Hemingway*, edited by Scott Donaldson. Cambridge: Cambridge University Press, 1996: 260–99.

———. Introduction. *Hemingway's Neglected Short Fiction: New Perspectives*, edited by Susan F. Beegel. Ann Arbor: UMI Research Press, 1989: 1–18.

Bem, Sandra Lipsitz. *The Lenses of Gender: Transforming the Debate on Sexual Inequality.* New Haven: Yale University Press, 1993.

Benson, Jackson J. "Ernest Hemingway: The Life as Fiction and the Fiction as Life." In *Hemingway: Essays of Reassessment,* edited by Frank Scafella. New York: Oxford University Press, 1991: 155–68.

———. "Hemingway Criticism: Getting at the Hard Questions." In *Hemingway: A Revaluation,* edited by Donald R. Noble. Troy, N.Y.: Whitston, 1983: 17–47.

Benstock, Shari. *Women of the Left Bank: Paris, 1900–1940.* Austin: University of Texas Press, 1986.

Bersani, Leo. "Is the Rectum a Grave?" *October* 43 (1987): 197–222.

Biriotti, Maurice. "Introduction: Authorship, Authority, Authorisation." In *What Is an Author?* edited by Maurice Biriotti and Nicola Miller. Manchester: Manchester University Press, 1993: 1–16.

Bloom, Lisa. "Constructing Whiteness: Popular Science and *National Geographic* in the Age of Multiculturalism." *Configurations* 1 (1994): 15–32.

Brady, James. "In Step With Mariel Hemingway." *Parade Magazine* 18 January 1998: 17.

Brasch, James D., and Joseph Sigman. *Hemingway's Library: A Composite Record.* New York: Garland, 1981.

Brenner, Gerry. *Concealments in Hemingway's Works.* Columbus: Ohio State University Press, 1983.

Brett, E. A. *Colonialism and Underdevelopment in East Africa: The Politics of Economic Change, 1919–1939.* London: Heinemann, 1973.

Brian, Denis. *The True Gen: An Intimate Portrait of Hemingway by Those Who Knew Him.* New York: Grove, 1988.

Britzman, Deborah P., Kelvin Santiago-Válles, Gladys Jiménez-Múñoz, and Laura M. Lamash. "Slips That Show and Tell: Fashioning Multiculture as a Problem of Representation." In *Race, Identity, and Representation in Education,* edited by Cameron McCarthy and Warren Crichlow. New York: Routledge, 1993: 188–200.

Brown, Wendy. *States of Injury: Power and Freedom in Late Modernity.* Princeton: Princeton University Press, 1995.

Bruccoli, Matthew J. "Packaging Papa: *The Garden of Eden.*" In *Dictionary of Literary Biography: Yearbook 1986,* edited by J. M. Brook. Detroit: Gale, 1987: 79–82.

Burke, Seán. *The Death and Return of the Author: Criticism and Subjectivity in Barthes, Foucault and Derrida.* Edinburgh: Edinburgh University Press, 1992.

Burrill, William. *Hemingway: The Toronto Years.* Toronto: Doubleday Canada, 1994.

Burwell, Rose Marie. *Hemingway: The Postwar Years and the Posthumous Novels.* Cambridge: Cambridge University Press, 1996.

Butler, Judith. *Bodies That Matter: On the Discursive Limits of "Sex."* New York: Routledge, 1993.

———. "Critically Queer." *GLQ: A Journal of Lesbian and Gay Studies* 1.1 (1993): 17–32.

———. *Gender Trouble: Feminism and the Subversion of Identity.* New York: Routledge, 1990.

Chauncey, George, Jr. "Christian Brotherhood or Sexual Perversion? Homosexual Identities and the Construction of Sexual Boundaries in the World War One Era." *Journal of Social History* 19 (1985): 189–211.

———. "From Sexual Inversion to Homosexuality: Medicine and the Changing Conceptualization of Female Deviance." *Salmagundi* 58–59 (1982–83): 114–46.

———. *Gay New York: Gender, Urban Culture, and the Making of the Gay Male World, 1890–1940.* New York: Basic, 1994.

Chicago Cultural Studies Group. "Critical Multiculturalism." *Critical Inquiry* 18 (1992): 530–55.

Cohen, Peter F. "'I Won't Kiss You . . . . I'll Send Your English Girl': Homoerotic Desire in *A Farewell to Arms.*" *The Hemingway Review* 15.1 (1995): 42–53.

Comley, Nancy, and Robert Scholes. *Hemingway's Genders: Rereading the Hemingway Text*. New Haven: Yale University Press, 1994.

Connolly, William. *Identity/Difference: Democratic Negotiations of Political Paradox*. Ithaca: Cornell University Press, 1991.

Cooper, Davina. *Power in Struggle: Feminism, Sexuality and the State*. Washington Square: New York University Press, 1995.

Copjec, Joan. "Cutting Up." In *Between Feminism and Psychoanalysis*, edited by Teresa Brennan. New York: Routledge, 1989: 227–46.

———. *Read My Desire: Lacan Against the Historicists*. Cambridge: MIT Press, 1994.

Crozier, Robert D. "The Mask of Death, The Face of Life: Hemingway's Feminique." *The Hemingway Review* 8.1 (1984): 2–13.

Davenport-Hines, Richard. *Auden*. New York: Pantheon, 1995.

Davidson, Arnold, and Cathy Davidson. "Decoding the Hemingway Hero in *The Sun Also Rises*." In *New Essays on* The Sun Also Rises, edited by Linda Wagner-Martin. Cambridge: Cambridge University Press, 1987: 83–107.

Davis, Lennard. *Enforcing Normalcy: Disability, Deafness, and the Body*. London: Verso, 1995.

Davy, Kate. "Outing Whiteness: A Feminist/Lesbian Project." *Theatre Journal* 47.2 (1995): 189–205.

de Caso, Jacques, and Patricia B. Sanders. *Rodin's Sculpture: A Critical Study of the Spreckels Collection*. Rutland, Vt.: Charles E. Tuttle, 1977.

De Certeau, Michel. *The Writing of History*, translated by Tom Conley. 1975. New York: Columbia University Press, 1988.

De Lauretis, Teresa. *The Practice of Love: Lesbian Sexuality and Perverse Desire*. Bloomington: Indiana University Press, 1994.

———. *Technologies of Gender: Essays on Theory, Film, and Fiction*. Bloomington: Indiana University Press, 1987.

D'Emilio, John. "The Homosexual Menace: The Politics of Sexuality in Cold War America." In *Passion and Power*, edited by Kathy Peiss and Christina Simmons. Philadelphia: Temple University Press, 1989: 226–40.

Derrida, Jacques. "Signature, Event, Context." *Glyph* 1 (1977): 172–97.

Dhairyam, Sagri. "Racing the Lesbian, Dodging White Critics." In *The Lesbian Postmodern*, edited by Laura Doan. New York: Columbia University Press, 1994: 25–46.

Diliberto, Gioia. *Hadley*. New York: Ticknor & Fields, 1992.

Doane, Mary Ann. *The Desire to Desire: The Woman's Film of the 1940s*. Bloomington: Indiana University Press, 1987.

Doctorow, E. L. "Braver Than We Thought." Review of *The Garden of Eden*, by Ernest Hemingway. *The New York Times Book Review* 18 May 1986, sec. 7, p. 1.

Dollimore, Jonathan. *Sexual Dissidence: Augustine to Wilde, Freud to Foucault*. Oxford: Clarendon Press, 1991.

Donaldson, Scott. *By Force of Will: The Life and Art of Ernest Hemingway*. New York: Viking, 1977.

Drinnon, Richard. "In the American Heartland: Hemingway and Death." *The Psychoanalytic Review* 52.2 (1965): 5–31.

Duggan, Lisa. "Queering the State." *Social Text* 39 (1994): 1–14.

———. "The Trials of Alice Mitchell: Sensationalism, Sexology, and the Lesbian Subject in Turn-of-the-Century America." *Signs* 18.4 (1993): 791–814.

Dyer, Richard. "Believing in Fairies: The Author and the Homosexual." In *Inside/Out: Lesbian Theories, Gay Theories*, edited by Diana Fuss. New York: Routledge, 1991: 185–201.

Eby, Carl. "'Come Back to the Beach Ag'in, David Honey!': Hemingway's Fetishization of Race in *The Garden of Eden* Manuscripts." *The Hemingway Review* 14.2 (1995): 98–117.

———. *Hemingway's Fetishism: Psychoanalysis and the Mirror of Manhood*. Albany: State University of New York Press, 1999.

Ellis, Havelock. "Erotic Symbolism." *Studies in the Psychology of Sex.* Vol. 3. New York: Random, 1936.

———. "Sexual Inversion." *Studies in the Psychology of Sex.* Vol. 1. New York: Random House, 1936.

———. "Sexual Inversion in Women." *Alienist and Neurologist* 16 (1895): 141–58.

Elsen, Albert E. The Gates of Hell *by Auguste Rodin.* Stanford: Stanford University Press, 1985.

———. *In Rodin's Studio: A Photographic Record of Sculpture in the Making.* Ithaca: Cornell University Press, 1980.

Epstein, William H. "(Post) Modern Lives: Abducting the Biographical Subject." In *Contesting the Subject: Essays in the Postmodern Theory and Practice of Biography and Biographical Criticism,* edited by William H. Epstein. West Lafayette: Purdue University Press, 1991: 217–36.

———. *Recognizing Biography.* Philadelphia: University of Pennsylvania Press, 1987.

Fleming, Robert. *The Face in the Mirror: Hemingway's Writers.* Tuscaloosa: University of Alabama Press, 1994.

Foner, Philip S., ed. *The Anti-Imperialist Reader, A Documentary History of Anti-Imperialism in the United States: The Literary Anti-Imperialists.* Vol. 2. New York: Holmes & Meier, 1986.

Foner, Philip S., and Richard C. Winchester, ed. *The Anti-Imperialist Reader, A Documentary History of Anti-Imperialism in the United States: From the Mexican War to the Election of 1900.* Vol. 1. New York: Holmes & Meier, 1984.

Fontana, Ernest. "Hemingway's 'A Pursuit Race.'" *Explicator* 42.4 (1984): 42–45.

Foucault, Michel. *The History of Sexuality: An Introduction,* translated by Robert Hurley. New York: Vintage, 1980.

———. "Polemics, Politics, and Problemizations: An Interview with Michel Foucault," translated by Lydia Davis. In *The Foucault Reader,* edited by Paul Rabinow. New York: Pantheon, 1984: 381–90.

———. "What Is an Author?" translated by Josué V. Harari. In *The Foucault Reader,* edited by Paul Rabinow. New York: Pantheon, 1984: 101–20.

Freud, Sigmund. "A Case of Paranoia Running Counter to the Psycho-analytical Theory of the Disease (1915)." *The Standard Edition of the Complete Psychological Works of Sigmund Freud,* translated by James Strachey. Vol. 14. London: Hogarth, 1957: 261–72.

———. "The Psychogenesis of a Case of Homosexuality in a Woman (1920)." *The Standard Edition of the Complete Psychological Works of Sigmund Freud,* translated by James Strachey. Vol. 18. London: Hogarth, 1955: 145–72.

Fuss, Diana. *Identification Papers.* New York: Routledge, 1995.

Gaggin, John. *Hemingway and Nineteenth-Century Aestheticism.* Ann Arbor: UMI Research Press, 1988.

Gajdusek, Robert. "Elephant Hunt in Eden: A Study of New and Old Myths and Other Strange Beasts in Hemingway's Garden." *The Hemingway Review* 7.1 (1987): 14–19.

Gilbert, Sandra M. "Costumes of the Mind: Transvestism as Metaphor in Modern Literature." *Critical Inquiry* 7 (1980): 391–417.

Goldberg, David Theo. *Racist Culture: Philosophy and the Politics of Meaning.* Cambridge, Mass.: Blackwell, 1993.

Gubar, Susan. "Blessings in Disguise: Cross-Dressing as Re-Dressing for Female Modernists." *Massachusetts Review* 22 (1981): 477–598.

Guillory, John. *Cultural Capital: The Problem of Literary Canon Formation.* Chicago: University of Chicago Press, 1993.

Hall, Lisa Kahaleole Chang. "Compromising Positions." In *Beyond a Dream Deferred: Multicultural Education and the Politics of Excellence,* edited by Becky W. Thompson and Sangeeta Tyagi. Minneapolis: University of Minnesota Press, 1993: 162–73.

Halperin, David M. *Saint Foucault: Towards a Gay Hagiography*. Oxford: Oxford University Press, 1995.

Harper, Phillip Brian. "Eloquence and Epitaph: Black Nationalism and the Homophobic Impulse in Responses to the Death of Max Robinson." In *Fear of a Queer Planet: Queer Politics and Social Theory*, edited by Michael Warner. Minneapolis: University of Minnesota Press, 1993: 239–63.

Harris, Daniel. "Androgyny: The Sexist Myth in Disguise." *Women's Studies: An Interdisciplinary Journal* 2 (1974): 171–84.

Heilbrun, Carolyn G. "Androgyny and the Psychology of Sex Differences." In *The Future of Difference*, edited by Hester Eisenstein and Alice Jardine. New Brunswick: Rutgers University Press, 1985: 258–66.

Hemingway, Ernest. *Across the River and Into the Trees*. 1950. New York: Collier, 1987.

———. "The dark young man stood looking into the window. . . ." Ernest Hemingway Collection. John F. Kennedy Library, Boston: Item 355a.

———. *Death in the Afternoon*. New York: Charles Scribner's Sons, 1932.

———. *Ernest Hemingway: Selected Letters, 1917–1961*, edited by Carlos Baker. New York: Charles Scribner's Sons, 1981.

———. *A Farewell to Arms*. New York: Charles Scribner's Sons, 1929.

———. *For Whom the Bell Tolls*. New York: Charles Scribner's Sons, 1940.

———. *The Garden of Eden*. New York: Charles Scribner's Sons, 1986.

———. "The Garden of Eden" manuscripts. Ernest Hemingway Collection. John F. Kennedy Library, Boston.

———. *Green Hills of Africa*. 1935. New York: Macmillan, 1987.

———. Interview. *Writers at Work: The Paris Review Interviews*. 2nd ser., edited by George Plimpton. New York: Penguin, 1977: 215–39.

———. *Islands in the Stream*. New York: Charles Scribner's Sons, 1970.

———. *A Moveable Feast*. New York: Charles Scribner's Sons, 1964.

———. *The Old Man and the Sea*. New York: Charles Scribner's Sons, 1953.

———. "Preface to 'The First Forty-nine.'" In *The Complete Short Stories of Ernest Hemingway*. New York: Charles Scribner's Sons, 1987: 3–4.

———. "Safari." *Look* 26 January 1954: 19–34.

———. "The Sea Change." In *The Complete Short Stories of Ernest Hemingway*. New York: Charles Scribner's Sons, 1987: 302–05.

———. "The Short Happy Life of Francis Macomber." In *The Complete Short Stories of Ernest Hemingway*. New York: Charles Scribner's Sons, 1987: 5–28.

———. "The Snows of Kilimanjaro." In *The Complete Short Stories of Ernest Hemingway*. New York: Charles Scribner's Sons, 1987: 39–56.

———. *The Sun Also Rises*. 1926. New York: Charles Scribner's Sons, 1970.

———. "There's One in Every Town." Ernest Hemingway Collection. John F. Kennedy Library, Boston: Item 743.

———. *To Have and Have Not*. 1937. New York: Collier, 1987.

Hemingway, Mary. *How It Was*. New York: Knopf, 1976.

Hennessy, Rosemary. *Materialist Feminism and the Politics of Discourse*. New York: Routledge, 1993.

———. "Queer Theory, Left Politics." *Rethinking Marxism* 7.3 (1994): 85–111.

Henry, George W. *All the Sexes: A Study of Masculinity and Femininity*. New York: Holt, Rinehart and Winston, 1955. New York: Octagon, 1978.

Herdeck, Donald E. Introduction. *Batouala*, by René Maran, translated by Barbara Beck and Alexandre Mboukou. London: Heinemann, 1972: 1–6.

Herzog, Alfred W. Introduction to *The Autobiography of an Androgyne*, by Ralph Werther (1919), edited by Alfred W. Herzog. New York: Arno, 1975: i–xiii.

Hollway, Wendy. "Gender Difference and the Production of Subjectivity." In *Changing the Subject: Psychology, Social Regulation and Subjectivity*, edited by Julian Henriques et al. London: Methuen, 1984: 227–63.

hooks, bell. "Eating the Other: Desire and Resistance." In *Black Looks: Race and Representation*. Boston: South End Press, 1992: 21–39.

———. *Teaching to Transgress: Education as the Practice of Freedom*. New York: Routledge, 1994.

Hotchner, A. E. *Papa Hemingway: A Personal Memoir*. 1966. New York: Bantam, 1967.

Howell, John. *Hemingway's African Stories: The Stories, Their Sources, Their Critics*. New York: Charles Scribner's Sons, 1969.

Jameson, Fredric. *The Political Unconscious: Narrative as a Socially Symbolic Act*. Ithaca: Cornell University Press, 1981.

Jauss, Hans Robert. *Question and Answer: Forms of Dialogic Understanding*, edited and translated by Michael Hays. Minneapolis: University of Minnesota Press, 1989.

Jay, Gregory. *American Literature and the Culture Wars*. Ithaca: Cornell University Press, 1997.

Jenks, Tom. "Editing Hemingway: *The Garden of Eden*." *The Hemingway Review* 7.1 (1987): 30–33.

———. "An Interview with Tom Jenks." In *Dictionary of Literary Biography: Yearbook 1986*, edited by J. M. Brook. Detroit: Gale, 1987: 79–87.

Kaniki, M. H. Y. "The Colonial Economy: The Former British Zones." In *General History of Africa: Africa Under Colonial Domination 1880–1935*, edited by A. Adu Boahen. Vol. 7. London: Heinemann, 1985: 382–419.

Kaplan, Amy. "'Left Alone with America': The Absence of Empire in the Study of American Culture." In *Cultures of United States Imperialism*, edited by Amy Kaplan and Donald E. Pease. Durham: Duke University Press, 1993: 3–21.

Keating, AnnLouise. "Interrogating 'Whiteness,' (De)Constructing 'Race.'" *College English* 57.8 (1995): 901–18.

Kennedy, J. Gerald. "Hemingway's Gender Trouble." *American Literature* 63 (1991): 187–207.

———. *Imagining Paris: Exile, Writing, and American Identity*. New Haven: Yale University Press, 1993.

———. "Life as Fiction: The Lure of Hemingway's *Garden*." *The Southern Review* 24.2 (1988): 451–61.

Kimmel, Michael S. "Masculinity as Homophobia: Fear, Shame, and Silence in the Construction of Gender Identity." In *Theorizing Masculinities*, edited by Harry Brod and Michael Kaufman. Thousand Oaks, Calif.: Sage, 1994: 119–41.

Kinsey, Alfred C., Wardell B. Pomeroy, and Clyde E. Martin. *Sexual Behavior in the Human Male*. Philadelphia: W. B. Saunders, 1948.

Kriegel, Leonard. *On Men and Manhood*. New York: Hawthorn, 1979.

Kumar, Sukrita Paul. *Man, Woman and Androgyny: A Study of the Novels of Theodore Dreiser, Scott Fitzgerald and Ernest Hemingway*. New Delhi: Indus Publishing, 1989.

Lacan, Jacques. *Écrits: A Selection*, translated by Alan Sheridan. New York: W. W. Norton, 1977.

———. "Guiding Remarks for a Congress on Feminine Sexuality." In *Jacques Lacan and the École Freudienne*, edited by Juliet Mitchell and Jacqueline Rose. New York: Norton, 1982.

Landers, Ann. "Wife Raising Son as Girl Must Receive Counseling." *The Columbus Dispatch*, 28 September 1990, Accent Section.

Lanser, Susan S. "Sexing the Narrative: Propriety, Desire, and the Engendering of Narratology." *Narrative* 3.1 (1995): 85–94.

Larson, Kelli A. "Introduction." *Ernest Hemingway: A Reference Guide, 1974–1989*. Boston: G. K. Hall, 1991: vii–xix.

Latham, Aaron. "A Farewell to Machismo." *The New York Times Magazine*, 16 October 1977: 52 ff.

Lauter, Paul. "Behind the Scenes at the Canon Melodrama." *Newsletter for The Heath Anthology of American Literature* 16 (1997): 1, 10–11.

Lehman, Peter. *Running Scared: Masculinity and the Representation of the Male Body*. Philadelphia: Temple University Press, 1993.

Leff, Leonard J. *Hemingway and His Conspirators: Hollywood, Scribners, and the Making of American Celebrity Culture*. Lanham, Md.: Rowman and Littlefield, 1997.

Lenin, V. I. "Imperialism, the Highest Stage of Capitalism." In *Essential Works of Lenin*, edited by Henry M. Christman. New York: Dover, 1987: 177–270.

Lewes, Kenneth. *The Psychoanalytic Theory of Male Homosexuality*. New York: New American Library, 1988.

Lowe, Donald M. *The Body in Late-Capitalist USA*. Durham: Duke University Press, 1995.

Lubiano, Wahneema. "Multiculturalism: Negotiating Politics and Knowledge." *Concerns* 22.3 (1992): 11–21.

Lugones, María. "Playfulness, 'World'-Travelling, and Loving Perception." In *Making Face, Making Soul/Haciendo Caras*, edited by Gloria Anzaldúa. San Francisco: Aunt Lute, 1990: 390–402.

Lynn, Kenneth. *Hemingway*. New York: Simon and Schuster, 1987.

Macdonald, Scott. "Hemingway's 'The Snows of Kilimanjaro': Three Critical Problems." *Studies in Short Fiction* 11.1 (1974): 67–74.

Maloba, Wunyabari O. *Mau Mau and Kenya: An Analysis of a Peasant Revolt*. Bloomington: Indiana University Press, 1993.

Martin, Biddy. "Introduction: Teaching Literature, Changing Cultures." *PMLA* 112 (1997): 7–25.

Martin, Wendy. "Brett Ashley as New Woman in *The Sun Also Rises*." In *New Essays on The Sun Also Rises*, edited by Linda Wagner-Martin. Cambridge: Cambridge University Press, 1987: 65–82.

McIntosh, Peggy. "White Privilege and Male Privilege: A Personal Account of Coming to See Correspondences Through Work in Women's Studies." Wellesley, Mass.: Publications Department, Center for Research on Women, 1988.

Mellow, James. *Hemingway: A Life Without Consequences*. Boston: Houghton Mifflin, 1992.

Messent, Peter. *New Readings of the American Novel*. London: Macmillan Education, 1990.

Meyers, Jeffrey. *Hemingway: A Biography*. New York: Perennial, 1985.

———. "Hemingway: Wanted by the FBI." In *The Spirit of Biography*. Ann Arbor: UMI Research Press, 1989: 215–22.

Miller, Madelaine Hemingway. *Ernie: Hemingway's Sister "Sunny" Remembers*. New York: Crown, 1975.

Miller, Nancy. "Changing the Subject: Authorship, Writing, and the Reader." In *Feminist Studies/Critical Studies*, edited by Teresa de Lauretis. Bloomington: Indiana University Press, 1986: 102–20.

Mitchell, Juliet. *Psychoanalysis and Feminism: Freud, Reich, Laing and Women*. New York: Vintage, 1975.

Morrison, Toni. *Playing in the Dark: Whiteness and the Literary Imagination*. Cambridge: Harvard University Press, 1992.

Mura, David. *Where the Body Meets Memory: An Odyssey of Race, Sexuality, and Identity*. New York: Anchor, 1996.

Nagel, James. "The Hunting Story in *The Garden of Eden*." In *Hemingway's Neglected Short Fiction: New Perspectives*, edited by Susan F. Beegel. Ann Arbor: UMI Research Press, 1989: 329–38.

Ní Fhlathúin, Máire. "Postcolonialism and the Author: The Case of Salman Rushdie." In *Authorship: From Plato to the Postmodern*, edited by Seán Burke. Edinburgh: Edinburgh University Press, 1995: 277–84.

Pease, Donald E. "New Americanists: Revisionist Interventions into the Canon." *boundary 2* 17.1 (1990): 1–37.

———. "New Perspectives on U.S. Culture and Imperialism." In *Cultures of United States Imperialism*, edited by Amy Kaplan and Donald E. Pease. Durham: Duke University Press, 1993: 22–37.

Peters, K. J. "The Thematic Integrity of *The Garden of Eden*." *The Hemingway Review* 10.2 (1991): 17–29.

Plotkin, Stephen. Letter to the author. 8 January 1993.

Proust, Marcel. *Sodom and Gomorrah*. Vol. 4 of *In Search of Lost Time*, translated by C. K. Scott Moncrieff and Terence Kilmartin. Revised translation by D. J. Enright. New York: Modern Library, 1993.

Raeburn, John. *Fame Became of Him: Hemingway as Public Writer*. Bloomington: Indiana University Press, 1984.

Ray, Nina M. "The Endorsement Potential Also Rises: The Merchandising of Ernest Hemingway." *The Hemingway Review* 13.2 (1994): 74–86.

Reynolds, Michael. *Hemingway: The American Homecoming*. Oxford: Blackwell, 1992.

———. *Hemingway: The 1930s*. New York: Norton, 1997.

———. *Hemingway: The Paris Years*. Oxford: Blackwell, 1989.

———. "Up Against the Crannied Wall: The Limits of Biography." In *Hemingway: Essays of Reassessment*, edited by Frank Scafella. New York: Oxford University Press, 1991: 170–78.

———. *The Young Hemingway*. Oxford: Blackwell, 1986.

Rich, Adrienne. *Blood, Bread, and Poetry: Selected Prose, 1979–1985*. New York: Norton, 1986.

———. *Of Woman Born: Motherhood as Experience and Institution*. New York: Norton, 1976.

Riggs, Marlon. "Unleash the Queen." In *Black Popular Culture*, edited by Gina Dent. Seattle: Bay Press, 1992: 99–105.

Roman, Leslie G. "Denying (White) Racial Privilege: Redemption Discourses and the Uses of Fantasy." In *Off White: Readings on Race, Power, and Society*, edited by Michelle Fine, Lois Weis, Linda C. Powell, and L. Mun Wong. New York: Routledge, 1997: 270–82.

Roof, Judith. *A Lure of Knowledge: Lesbian Sexuality and Theory*. New York: Columbia University Press, 1991.

Rooney, Ellen. *Seductive Reasoning: Pluralism as the Problematic of Contemporary Literary History*. Ithaca: Cornell University Press, 1989.

Rose, Jacqueline. *The Haunting of Sylvia Plath*. Cambridge: Harvard University Press, 1992.

Ross, Valerie. "Too Close to Home: Repressing Biography, Instituting Authority." In *Contesting the Subject: Essays in the Postmodern Theory and Practice of Biography and Biographical Criticism*, edited by William H. Epstein. West Lafayette: Purdue University Press, 1991: 135–65.

Rovit, Earl, and Gerry Brenner. *Ernest Hemingway*. Revised edition. Boston: Twayne, 1986.

Said, Edward. *Culture and Imperialism*. New York: Vintage, 1994.

Sanford, Marcelline Hemingway. *At the Hemingways*. Boston: Little, Brown, 1962.

Santangelo, Gennaro. "The Dark Snows of Kilimanjaro." In *The Short Stories of Ernest Hemingway: Critical Essays*, edited by Jackson J. Benson. Durham: Duke University Press, 1975: 251–61.

Sarason, Bertram. *Hemingway and* The Sun Set. Washington, D.C.: Microcard Editions, 1972.

Sarotte, Georges-Michel. "Ernest Hemingway: The (Almost) Total Sublimation of the Homosexual Instinct." In *Like a Brother, Like a Lover: Male Homosexuality in the American Novel and Theater from Herman Melville to James Baldwin*, translated by Richard Miller. Garden City: Anchor, 1978: 262–78.

Saunders, David, and Ian Hunter. "Lessons from the 'Literatory': How to Historicise Authorship." *Critical Inquiry* 17 (1991): 479–509.

Scarry, Elaine. *The Body in Pain: The Making and Unmaking of the World.* New York: Oxford University Press, 1985.

Scott, Joan W. "The Evidence of Experience." *Critical Inquiry* 17.4 (1991): 773–95.

Scribner, Charles, Jr. "The Secret of Being Ernest (and the Secret of Keeping Ernest)." In *In the Web of Ideas: The Education of a Publisher.* New York: Scribner's, 1993: 13–62.

Sedgwick, Eve Kosofsky. *Between Men: English Literature and Male Homosocial Desire.* New York: Columbia University Press, 1985.

———. *Epistemology of the Closet.* Berkeley: University of California Press, 1990.

———. "White Glasses." In *Tendencies.* Durham: Duke University Press, 1993: 252–66.

Sheridan, Alan. Translator's Note to *Écrits: A Selection,* by Jacques Lacan. New York: Norton, 1977: vii–xii.

Silverman, Kaja. *Male Subjectivity at the Margins.* New York: Routledge, 1992.

Simmons, Christina. "Companionate Marriage and the Lesbian Threat." *Frontiers* 4.3 (1979): 54–59.

Sinfield, Alan. *Cultural Politics—Queer Reading.* Philadelphia: University of Pennsylvania Press, 1994.

Singer, Linda. *Erotic Welfare: Sexual Theory and Politics in the Age of Epidemic.* New York: Routledge, 1993.

Sleeter, Christine E. "How White Teachers Construct Race." In *Race, Identity, and Representation in Education,* edited by Cameron McCarthy and Warren Crichlow. New York: Routledge, 1993: 157–71.

Solomon, Barbara. "Ernest Hemingway's Real *Garden of Eden.*" In *Horse-Trading and Ecstasy.* San Francisco: North Point Press, 1989: 22–31.

Spilka, Mark. "Hemingway and Fauntleroy: An Androgynous Pursuit." In *American Novelists Revisited: Essays in Feminist Criticism,* edited by Fritz Fleischmann. Boston: G. K. Hall, 1982: 339–70.

———. *Hemingway's Quarrel with Androgyny.* Lincoln: University of Nebraska Press, 1990.

Spivak, Gayatri. "A Response to 'The Difference Within': Feminism and Critical Theory." In *The Difference Within: Feminism and Critical Theory,* edited by Elizabeth Meese and Alice Parker. Philadelphia: John Benjamin, 1989: 207–20.

Spurr, David. *The Rhetoric of Empire: Colonial Discourse in Journalism, Travel Writing, and Imperial Administration.* Durham: Duke University Press, 1993.

Stein, Gertrude. *The Autobiography of Alice B. Toklas.* In *Selected Writings of Gertrude Stein,* edited by Carl Van Vechten. New York: Vintage, 1972: 3–237.

Stephanson, Anders. *Manifest Destiny: American Expansion and the Empire of Right.* New York: Hill and Wang, 1995.

Stetler, Charles, and Gerald Locklin. "Beneath the Tip of the Iceberg in Hemingway's 'The Mother of a Queen.'" *The Hemingway Review* 1.1 (1981): 27–32.

Stimpson, Catharine. "The Androgyne and the Homosexual." *Women's Studies: An Interdisciplinary Journal* 2 (1974): 237–48.

Stoler, Ann Laura. *Race and the Education of Desire: Foucault's* History of Sexuality *and the Colonial Order of Things.* Durham: Duke University Press, 1995.

Tavernier-Courbin, Jacqueline. *Ernest Hemingway's* A Moveable Feast: *The Making of Myth.* Boston: Northeastern University Press, 1991.

Taylor, Charles. *Multiculturalism and "The Politics of Recognition."* Princeton: Princeton University Press, 1992.

Thomson, Rosemarie Garland. *Extraordinary Bodies: Figuring Physical Disability in American Culture and Literature.* New York: Columbia University Press, 1997.

Trogdon, Robert W. Review of *Hemingway and His Conspirators: Hollywood, Scribners, and the Making of American Celebrity Culture,* by Leonard Leff. *The Hemingway Review* 17.2 (1998): 124–27.

Uzoigwe, G. N. "European Partition and Conquest of Africa: An Overview." In *General*

History of Africa: Africa Under Colonial Domination 1880–1935, edited by A. Adu Boahen. Vol. 7. London: Heinemann, 1985: 19–44.

Villard, Henry, and James Nagel. *Hemingway in Love and War: The Lost Diary of Agnes von Kurowsky, Her Letters, and Correspondence of Ernest Hemingway*. Boston: Northeastern University Press, 1989.

Walker, Cheryl. "Feminist Literary Criticism and the Author." *Critical Inquiry* 16 (1990): 551–71.

———. "Persona Criticism and the Death of the Author." In *Contesting the Subject: Essays in the Postmodern Theory and Practice of Biography and Biographical Criticism*. West Lafayette: Purdue University Press, 1991: 109–21.

Warner, Michael. "Homo-Narcissism; or, Heterosexuality." In *Engendering Men: The Question of Male Feminist Criticism*, edited by Joseph A. Boone and Michael Cadden. New York: Routledge, 1990: 190–206.

———. Introduction to *Fear of a Queer Planet: Queer Politics and Social Theory*, edited by Michael Warner. Minneapolis: University of Minnesota Press, 1993: vii–xxxi.

Weil, Kari. *Androgyny and the Denial of Difference*. Charlottesville: University of Virginia Press, 1992.

Werther, Ralph. *Autobiography of an Androgyne*. 1919. Reprint, New York: Arno, 1975.

———. *The Female-Impersonators*. 1922. Reprint, New York: Arno, 1975.

West, James L. W., III. *American Authors and the Literary Marketplace since 1900*. Philadelphia: University of Pennsylvania Press, 1988.

Westwood, Gordon. *Society and the Homosexual*. 1952. Reprint, Westport: Greenwood, 1985.

White, Hayden. *Tropics of Discourse: Essays in Cultural Criticism*. Baltimore: Johns Hopkins University Press, 1978.

Whiting, Charles. *Papa Goes to War: Ernest Hemingway in Europe, 1944–45*. Warminster, Wiltshire: Crowood Press, 1990.

Wilson, Emma. *Sexuality and the Reading Encounter: Identity and Desire in Proust, Duras, Tournier, and Cixous*. Oxford: Clarendon Press, 1996.

Wilson, Rob. "Producing American Selves: The Form of American Biography." In *Contesting the Subject: Essays in the Postmodern Theory and Practice of Biography and Biographical Criticism*, edited by William H. Epstein. West Lafayette: Purdue University Press, 1991: 167–92.

Wolff, Janet. *The Social Production of Art*. London: Macmillan, 1981.

Woolf, Virginia. "An Essay in Criticism." In *Ernest Hemingway: The Critical Reception*, edited by Robert O. Stephens. N.p.: Burt Franklin, 1977: 53–54.

Young, Philip. *Ernest Hemingway*. New York: Rinehart, 1952.

———. *Ernest Hemingway*. Revised edition. 1965. London: Routledge, 1995.

Young, Robert J. C. *Colonial Desire: Hybridity in Theory, Culture and Race*. London: Routledge, 1995.

INDEX

Capitalism, 61, 63–64, 89, 104, 138; connections to imperialism, 102, 106–12, 117, 168, 169

Chauncey, George, 51, 70–71, 72, 73, 80, 158, 161, 165, 167

Chicago Cultural Studies Group, 132, 173

Christian, Barbara, 13

Class, 85, 131–33, 137, 139–40, 146. See also Identity: structures of

Cohen, Peter F., 165

Comley, Nancy, 3, 4, 28, 32, 34–35, 54, 59–60, 65, 66, 147, 158, 159, 160

Companionate marriage, 67–68, 160

Connolly, William, 16, 136, 149

Cooper, Davina, 48, 157

Copjec, Joan, 156

Crozier, Robert, 31, 154

Davenport-Hines, Richard, 174

Davidson, Arnold, 28, 35, 93, 96, 165

Davidson, Cathy, 28, 35, 93, 96, 165

Davis, Lennard, 120, 171

Davy, Kate, 101, 167

Debba, 116, 170–71

De Certeau, Michel, 153

De Lauretis, Teresa, 44, 157, 158

D'Emilio, John, 162

Derrida, Jacques, 12, 13–14, 150

Desire: compared to identification, 140–41, 147; compared to sexuality and sexual behavior, 5; definition of, 44–45, 131; interracial and intraracial, 44, 47, 117; reader's relation to (the desire to desire), 6, 7, 43, 46–47, 56, 92, 157; relation to (dis)ability, 5, 47, 57, 92; relation to nationality, 5; relation to racial structuring, 5, 57, 92. See also Homosexual desire

Dhairyam, Sagri, 44, 157

(Dis)ability, 5, 8, 47, 92, 100, 119–30, 131–33, 137, 138, 139–40, 146. See also Identity: structures of; Desire: relation to (dis)ability

Doane, Mary Ann, 157

Doctorow, E. L., 59, 159

Dollimore, Jonathan, 44, 47, 83, 157

Donaldson, Scott, 152–53

Drinnon, Richard, 152

Duggan, Lisa, 138, 161, 174

Dyer, Richard, 39, 156

Eby, Carl, 35, 59–60, 91, 147–48, 155, 159–60, 167

Ellis, Havelock, 52, 70–71, 72, 95, 158, 161, 162, 165–66

Epstein, William, 27, 38, 153, 156

Feminism, 2, 7, 13, 20, 31, 37, 51, 135, 159; black, 135

Fisher, Philip, 173

Fitzgerald, F. Scott, 105

Fitzgerald, Zelda, 24

Fleming, Robert, 104, 167

Fontana, Ernest, 152

Foucault, Michel, 7, 12, 14, 46, 50, 155, 158, 161; History of Sexuality, 45, 60–61, 70, 158; "Polemics, Politics, Problemizations," 131; "What Is an Author?," 14, 17, 19–21, 149, 151

Freud, Sigmund, 43, 70–71, 72, 83, 147, 148, 151, 160, 161–62, 163

Fuss, Diana, 147

Gaggin, John, 30, 153–54

Gajdusek, Robert, 30, 153–54

Gates, Henry Louis, 13

Gay: literature, 4, 140; men, 3, 45–46, 48, 51, 55, 70–74, 133, 137, 154; studies, 13, 42, 50; See also Homosexual

Gender, 8, 18, 60, 71, 84–85, 92, 131, 133, 134, 137, 139–40, 159. See also Identity: structures of

Gilbert, Sandra, 166

Goldberg, David Theo, 101, 167

Gubar, Susan, 94, 165, 166–67

Guillory, John, 134, 139, 173

Hall, Lisa Kahaleole Chang, 137, 174

Hall, Radclyffe, 71

Halperin, David, 45–46, 158

Harper, Phillip Brian, 44, 157

Harris, Daniel, 31, 154

Heilbrun, Carolyn, 31, 154

Hemingway, Clarence Edmonds, 32, 49

Hemingway, Ernest: as biographical subject, 10, 15, 23, 28, 42, 84, 102–4; childhood twinning experience of, 24–27, 49, 152–53; endorsement potential of, 10, 148–49; heterosexual identity of, 4, 6, 22, 27–29, 33, 35, 42, 43, 48, 50, 56, 61, 64, 89, 92, 100, 136, 142; homosexual desire of, 3, 24, 32, 35, 42, 56, 83–86, 91, 117, 143, 155; as queer, 4–5, 35, 42–43, 148; racial identity of, 57, 92, 100, 102, 116–19, 136, 170–71; racism of, 67, 116; relationship to Africa, 111–19, 170–71; relationship to (dis)ability, 57, 92, 119–20, 130; on safari, 7, 111, 113–18, 169–71; sexual identity of, 3, 7, 35, 61, 92, 164; as world traveler, 100, 111, 113, 167. See